# TRANSITIONS IN BIBLICAL SCHOLARSHIP

# ESSAYS IN DIVINITY

JERALD C. BRAUER, GENERAL EDITOR

# Transitions in Biblical Scholarship

BY G. W. AHLSTRÖM, WILLIAM A. BEARDSLEE,

KENNETH W. CLARK, ERNEST C. COLWELL,

DONALD E. GOWAN, ROBERT M. GRANT, NORMAN PERRIN,

FREDERICK C. PRUSSNER, MARTIN RIST,

J. COERT RYLAARSDAM, WILLIAM R. SCHOEDEL,

PAUL SCHUBERT, JAY A. WILCOXEN,

WALTER G. WILLIAMS

*Edited by* J. COERT RYLAARSDAM

THE UNIVERSITY OF CHICAGO PRESS

CHICAGO AND LONDON

THE UNIVERSITY OF CHICAGO PRESS
CHICAGO 60637
*The University of Chicago Press, Ltd., London W.C.1*

© 1968 by The University of Chicago
All rights reserved. Published 1968

*Library of Congress Catalog Card Number: 68–9135*

Printed in the United States of America

## General Editor's Preface

The present volume is the sixth in a series of eight books being published under the general title "Essays in Divinity." This does not appear, at first glance, as a particularly auspicious moment for such a formidable enterprise. At the very moment the so-called radical theologians announce that "God is dead," an eight-volume series investigating various dimensions of the study of religion or of theology is published. Is this not an ill-timed venture?

In point of fact, however, in America the discipline of theology was never in a healthier state. To be sure, there are no giants such as Tillich or Niebuhr on the scene, but there are many new and exciting factors in the picture. The very presence of the "God is dead" movement is evidence of a new vitality and ferment among the younger theologians. In no sense does such a movement herald the end of systematic theology or the impossibility of using God-language. It is but one of many significant attempts being made now at basic reconstruction and reinterpretation of Christian theology.

One primary fact marks this new age — the pre-eminence of dialogue in all aspects of divinity. Basic conversation between Roman Catholicism, Protestantism, and Judaism is just beginning, and its full effect on theological construction lies ahead. At the time systematic theology entered the preliminary phase of dialogue, Paul Tillich's last lecture pointed to the future of this discipline in relation to the world's religions. Dialogue is not to be understood as the "in" movement in religion today; it is to be viewed as providing a new base that will profoundly affect not only the systematic study of doctrines and beliefs but every dimension of religious studies.

Another mark of the vitality of religious studies today is its dialogic relationship to other disciplines. Studies in divinity have never been carried on in complete isolation from other areas of human knowledge, but in some periods the relationship has been more fully explored than in others. The contemporary scene is marked by the increasing tempo of creative interchange and mutual stimulation between divinity and other disciplines. Several new theological disciplines have emerged recently to demonstrate this fact. The interplay between theology and literature, between theology and the psychological sciences, and between theology and the social sciences promises to reshape the traditional study of religion, as our major theological faculties are beginning rapidly to realize.

The emergence and increasing role of the History of Religions is a case in point. Until recently it has been a stepchild in the theological curriculum. Today it is developing a methodological study. History of Religions also appears to be the way that most state universities will introduce the serious and disciplined study of religion into strictly secular curriculums.

These are but a few of the factors that demonstrate the present vitality of the study of religion today. It makes both possible and necessary a series of books such as this. The particular occasion for the publication of "Essays in Divinity" is supplied by the one hundredth anniversary of the Divinity School of The University of Chicago and by the University's seventy-fifth anniversary.

The editor of this series proposed that this event be celebrated by the Divinity School faculty and alumni by holding seven conferences, each of which was focused on the works of one of the seven academic fields of the School. Out of these conferences have come eight volumes which will, it is hoped, mark the progress in the various disciplines of theological study and point to the ongoing tradition of scholarship in the University's Divinity School.

Though something may have been lost in thus limiting the

roster of contributors to these books, this very limitation may have the effect of marking the distinctive genius of one theological center long noted for its production of scholar-teachers in American theology. Also, it will enable an observer to determine the extent to which several generations have been shaped by, and have shaped, a particular institution. It will be possible to note the variations of approach and concern that mark respective generations of that institution. Furthermore, it will help to assess the particular genius, if any, that a given institution possesses. It will demonstrate to what extent its graduates and professors are in the midst of contemporary theological scholarship. It is to be hoped that the series will provide both a bench mark for today's scholarly discussions and research in religion and a record from which future generations can assess the contributions of an institution at the turn of its first century.

None of these volumes pretends to be definitive in its area; it is hoped, however, that each will make a useful contribution to its area of specialization and that the entire series will suggestively illuminate the basic tendencies of religious scholarship at the present moment. The intent has been to devote each volume to a particular issue or area of inquiry that is of special significance for scholarly religious research today, and thus to keep each volume from being simply a disconnected series of essays. It is hoped that these books will be found to have, each in its own terms, a genuine unity and that the reader will note a cumulative effect, as he moves from essay to essay in each volume.

The history of the Biblical Field in the Divinity School is unusual and most interesting. Two of the first three presidents of the University of Chicago, William Rainey Harper and Ernest DeWitt Burton, were biblical scholars and members of the divinity faculty, and during the latter period of the chancellorship of Robert Maynard Hutchins, E. C. Colwell, professor of New Testament in the Divinity School, served as president of the University. During the early years of the University, the professors in the Biblical Field served in the Humanities Field in order not to be placed under any ecclesiastical pressure as members of a divinity faculty. It was not until 1942 that all of the work in the biblical disciplines was to be located again in the Divinity School.

Meanwhile, biblical scholars at Chicago developed a distinguished and remarkable record of scholarship and contribution to the religious community both in America and abroad. This is fully sketched out in Professor Rylaarsdam's introduction. The present volume is a demonstration of the fact that the work begun by Harper, Burton, and Goodspeed continues. In the best Chicago tradition this does not continue through slavish repetition but in an effort to find the new ways and methods through which the biblical materials can be interpreted and appropriated today. This is no easy task. Present biblical scholarship makes clear that the discipline is now passing through the concluding stages of one phase and is entering a new phase, the exact direction of which is not yet certain. This transition is in itself promising for the future of biblical studies.

JERALD C. BRAUER, *General Editor*

# CONTENTS

# CONTENTS

# Introduction: *The Chicago School—And After*

## J. COERT RYLAARSDAM

This centennial volume in honor of biblical studies at Chicago is in many respects simply an exemplification of the general story of modern critical research. But there are also overtones and examples that illustrate the distinctive role Chicago has played in this enterprise. The essays dealing with the issues, problems, aims, and methods of textual history serve as explicit examples of one concern that has flourished here. More inadvertently, most of the others reflect features of an empirical, descriptive, or historical sort that mark them with the influence of the Chicago School, even though in both concern and method they have combined these with many other perspectives. The masterful essay by Professor Schubert is a good illustration of this.

In the curriculum of the Baptist Union Theological Seminary of Morgan Park, biblical studies occupied a large sector. The biblical scholars who worked there and then continued their careers in the Divinity School provided some of the firmest ties in the continuity of ethos and work that bound the two institutions together. William Rainey Harper joined the faculty in Morgan Park in 1876, as instructor in Hebrew. Eventually, after a detour at Yale, he came back to Chicago, as professor of Old Testament and president of the University. Ira M. Price had taken Harper's place at Morgan Park. In 1892 he also came to the Divinity School as a part of the original nucleus of the faculty in Bible. All the evidence indicates that Morgan Park had been an intrepid pioneer in the matter of critical and historical methods of study.

Professor Harper was a philological and historical exegete of the first rank who was productive on many fronts. But he devoted his gifts for originality to the development of methods for teaching Hebrew and in this produced results that were both revolutionary and enduring. His classic, *Elements of Hebrew, by an Inductive Method,* had already reached its sixth edition by 1885. Professor J. M. P. Smith did a revised edition in 1921. There was another new edition in 1958, with a preface by Professor Raymond A. Bowman, which went through its third impression in 1966. Ninety years after he began as an instructor, the influence of Harper's principles and methods continues to grow.

Professor Price also wrote a classic. *The Ancestry of Our English Bible* appeared first in 1906. The author himself did a "first revised edition" in 1934. Professors William A. Irwin and Allen P. Wikgren brought out a second revised edition in 1949 which incorporated a mass of new information about textual history and the history of translation. Price, the historian of the Bible, along with Harper, gave biblical studies at Chicago many of their more persistent directions. Research in the biblical languages, in textual history, and in the history of the canon has always flourished here. This was to bear great fruit in the science and art of translation itself.

Professor Edgar J. Goodspeed was a linguist and textual historian who knew how to put his scientific knowledge to creative use in a unique way. The publication of his *The New Testament, an American Translation* in 1923 marked the beginning of an era in American religious history. This modern-speech version appeared when the fundamentalist-liberal controversy was raging. Inevitably, the issues and partisanships relating to that conflict played a role in the evaluation of this translation, which had broken with so many hallowed traditions, both cultural and theological. There was a flood of criticism. But, as Mr. Goodspeed stated twenty-five years later, this provided him with an opportunity to make the literary and linguistic argument for modern-speech translations.[1] His utilization of that opportunity brought fame to him and to his work. For two decades "the

[1] E. G. Goodspeed, "Preface to the Twenty-fifth Anniversary Edition," *The New Testament, an American Translation* (Chicago: University of Chicago Press, 1948), p. vii.

Goodspeed translation" of the New Testament, as it was popularly known, was fashionable in English departments and college chapels. Besides, it won massive acceptance with the common reader.

A comparable modern-speech version of the Old Testament and the Goodspeed translation of the New were combined and published as *The Bible, an American Translation*, in 1931. This came to be known as "the Chicago Bible." Later Goodspeed's work, *The Apocrypha, an American Translation*, was added, and the project was brought to a close in 1939 with the publication of *The Complete Bible, an American Translation*.

The subtitle remained constant throughout. There was nothing casual about that. Goodspeed felt that for too long American readers had had to depend on British versions. He was determined to provide the Bible in an American idiom. A sturdy and realistic cultural nationalism guided him. In asking for "a New Testament free from expressions . . . strange to American ears"[2] he may have been reacting somewhat to James Moffatt's modern-speech version, published a decade earlier. But his concern was more general and lay deeper. He was making his specific and personal witness to an attitude and point of view which, as we shall note again, has characterized the life and work of the Biblical Field at Chicago, and, indeed, of the entire Divinity School, rather persistently. Set in the American Midwest, there has been an independent quality of spirit about this left-wing Puritan foundation. To a greater degree than any other faculty of its kind in America it has insisted on dealing with universally acknowledged issues and tasks in an American way.

It is quite impossible to make full reference to all the projects that have issued from the directions set by the historians of the Bible and the linguists. But we must mention the International Greek New Testament project. This Anglo-American enterprise, which promises now to include continental Europe as well, was launched at Chicago by Dean

[2] *Ibid.*, "Preface," *The New Testament, an American Translation* (Chicago: University of Chicago Press, 1923).

Ernest C. Colwell. Under the executive direction of Professor Merrill M. Parvis, the project was located in the Divinity School for many years. It traveled with him when he left to join the theological faculty at Emory University. Now it is being relocated at Claremont and is assured of the full-time attention of Dean Colwell and Professor Kenneth W. Clark. Since its inception, Professor Wikgren has served as the American committee's specialist on lectionary texts. Two essays in this book reflect the issues and problems of the project. Mr. Colwell's is equally revealing as a cue to the story of biblical studies at Chicago.

Colwell clearly feels that textual criticism has been wandering in the wilderness. He thinks it has lost its way and lost sight of its goal because it has listened to contemporary theologians for whom "historical probability has lost its relevance." [3] He chides those who despair of (R. M. Grant) or are indifferent to (K. Aland, B. M. Metzger) the restoration of the original wording of the New Testament text through a reconstruction of "the history of the manuscript tradition." Colwell wants to bring Hort back to life and restore *Historismus*. But how can this be done effectively, given the vagaries of theology and the shift in the style of perspectives of interpretation? Dean Colwell is very probably correct that a chronological and genetic reconstruction of the history of the text, to establish the original, is an indispensable goal for textual critics. It may be noted, however, that the significance of this reconstruction as such can probably not be stated in the same way in which it once was and carry the weight it then did. *Historismus* represented a faith as well as a method. The faith no longer lives. It was a part of that faith that the very process of historical reconstruction was an enterprise simultaneously historical and theological. The relevance of historical probability can no longer be defined in terms of that congruence. It will have to be stated in a new way; for Colwell is right: chronological reconstruction is an abiding goal of the textual criticism.

[3] E. C. Colwell, "Hort Redivivus," this volume.

4

Mr. Colwell writes as one would expect an heir of Goodspeed and Case to do. With great perspicacity and feeling, he expresses many of the loyalties and anxieties present in the biblical faculty at Chicago in recent decades. Without necessarily sharing it in an unqualified manner, he alludes to an assumption sometimes taken for granted in the Field; namely, that empirical, analytic and synthetic research, whether philological and textual or sociohistorical and cultic, is the starting point for all legitimate theology; and that the road that leads on to it should, ideally, be limited to one-way traffic.

Historicism did flourish in biblical studies at Chicago; and it served its time exceedingly well. The focus was on the data; not on the data in the light of some tradition of faith or interpretive perspective, but on the data as such. This was not only true of text historians, of whom one might always expect this; it was true of all the Bible's interpreters. Assuming that the Bible was a temporally and culturally conditioned book, they sought to reconstruct the world that had produced it — intellectually, politically, economically, religiously, socially, psychologically — to discover what it said and meant. Dean Shailer Mathews, who had come to Chicago as professor of New Testament History in 1894, and his successor, Dean Case, developed the distinctive style of the sociohistorical method in biblical studies that will always be associated with Chicago. They, perhaps more than any others, were the founders of the Chicago School of Theology.

Mathews was concerned with the problem of authority, because he was convinced that all inherited forms of religious authority — confessional, cultic-traditional, and even biblical — had lost their validity in the modern world. They had become pernicious to the health of true religion. The social sciences were useful not simply in reconstructing the biblical world but in laying new foundations for truth. For a religious leader who spent a large part of his career in combat with fundamentalism, the finality implied by this double role is understandable, though it may have facili-

5

tated the introduction of an element of inflexibility into his own position.

Since Mathews did most of his work in the history of Christian thought, Shirley Jackson Case is the decisive figure to illustrate the use of the sociohistorical method in biblical studies. It is interesting to note, in passing, that in this period New Testament scholars set the pace; work in the Old Testament simply followed the general pattern of method and meaning, though a distinctive emphasis is sometimes discernible, as in the work of W. C. Graham and M. G. May, with its mythological and cultic emphases.

Case was interested in the figure of Jesus. His first book, *The Historicity of Jesus*, published in 1912, refuted those who questioned that he had lived. His most epoch-making and controversial book, *Jesus: A New Biography*, appeared in 1927. It is reported that at his death, in 1947, he left an unfinished manuscript on "the personal religion of Jesus."[4] Whether he was dealing with the experience and development of the early church or with the personal life of Jesus, the "environmental factors" provided the key for his understanding. His characteristic empiricism expressed itself in his attempt to reconstruct the social, political, and religious world in which both Jesus and the church were set. His aims seem not to have differed greatly from those of early form critics such as Martin Dibelius and C. H. Dodd, who also wanted to describe Jesus and the Christian movement. But instead of their intense preoccupation with the text of the Gospels, in which they analyzed literary forms in relation to the context in which they had been used, Case relied more emphatically on his reconstructions of the extrabiblical environment. From these he made the inferences that enabled him to write his biography of Jesus and his history of early Christianity.

Case rejected Schweitzer. He had no doubts about the attainability of a reliable life of Jesus. Nor was he hospitable to the notion that Jesus was an apocalypticist. His Jesus was

[4] Harvey Arnold, *Near the Edge of Battle* (Chicago: The Divinity School Association, 1967), p. 47.

a rather normal Jew, an urgent preacher of the Kingdom of God. He was neither Essene nor Zealot; nor did he think of himself as the expected Messiah. His messiahship and the apocalyptic character of his message represent the revisionism of the early church. Professor Norman Perrin's vivid book, *Rediscovering the Teaching of Jesus*, implies a historical figure who corresponds closely in many ways to the Jesus of Case. It must be remembered, none the less, that the two men assign a radically different theological function to this Jesus of history.

It seems a bit ironic that a Baptist school should have nurtured a movement which located the center of action and meaning in social process and tradition rather than in individual personality. For Case both the New Testament and Christian theology were products of the experience of the early church. His presidential address before the Society of Biblical Literature, "The Alleged Messianic Consciousness of Jesus," was a decisive statement that has been debated ever since.[5] Written forty years ago, it forms an appropriate setting for the first sentence in Rudolf Bultmann's *Theology of the New Testament*: "The message of Jesus is a presupposition for the theology of the New Testament, rather than a part of that theology itself."[6] However, in contrast to Bultmann, Case continued to define the Christian message in terms of his understanding of the historical figure of Jesus. He remained a Baptist!

It appears that what was unique about the Chicago School in its pioneer work under Case was neither its technical method nor its scientific conclusions. Others used the methods; and the Chicago results have been confirmed in many ways. The difference was in the theological outlook. Case was apparently prepared, if need be, to ignore both Christian dogmatic tradition and the New Testament to redefine Christian faith on the basis of his understanding of the person and message of Jesus, seen in the context of the

[5] In *Journal of Biblical Literature*, 46 (1927): 1–19
[6] Rudolf Bultmann, *Theology of the New Testament*, trans. Kendrick Grobel (New York: Charles Scribner's Sons, 1951), 1:3.

world of the first century. The tag "radical," if applied to Case, should properly refer to that theological position.

This daring theological independence has roots that are simultaneously American and left-wing Puritan. The degree to which it has dominated the scene at Chicago has distinguished the Divinity School from other American theological centers. Anglicans, Lutherans, and Reformed constitute the Protestant traditions in the American scene that have a legacy of theological and cultural colonialism. They also think in terms of traditions. But until after World War II they played no role of a constructive sort in Chicago's academic and theological work. Moreover, left-wing Puritans are indigenously American in a special way, and until recently their ethos dominated the culture. The distinctly American quality of the Chicago School is thus rooted in its total heritage.

For Mathews and Case, scientific method — epitomized by the sociohistorical method — served as a surrogate for dethroned authorities. The road to religious understanding was open to one-way traffic; it ran from fact to faith. Given the perspective and the method, the reality of God was to be located in the social process. Professional theology at Chicago, represented by men such as G. B. Foster and G. B. Smith, had supported this viewpoint. But, with the rise here of a theological outlook and methods that questioned the adequacy of the sociohistorical perspective to fully identify the object of the quest, the movement in biblical studies displayed rigidity and defensiveness as well as adaptability. Nor did it find it easy to respond to the challenge of radically different theological perspectives from abroad which announced that it was looking in the wrong place altogether.

We have used the title, the Chicago School, for the movement in biblical studies dominated by Dean Case. Today the term is more commonly applied to the school of process theology founded by Professors Wieman and Hartshorne. The Librarian of the Divinity School, Mr. Harvey Arnold, has produced an intellectual history of the theological faculty in which he applies the title to both, treating the two

movements as parts of a single, organically related whole.[7]
At first glance this seems incongruous, for, initially, the
meeting of the movements produced more clash than agreement. Most of the heirs of Case in the Biblical Field experienced process theology as a threat. The theologians were,
indeed, as empirically oriented as the historians. But they
began with nature rather than history, and they included
both in their more comprehensive circle. Moreover, their
methods and norms were epistemological and philosophical
rather than philological and sociological. Their philosophical theology was candidly metaphysical in character, not
simply an extrapolation from the results of historical research.

The theologians as well as the historians equated method
with meaning and truth. They too insisted on one-way
traffic! Perhaps more than anything else, that fact makes the
single title, the Chicago School, appropriate for both. But
this bond of continuity also became the greatest source of
tension. The theologians insisted that their perspective could
provide the integrating criteria by which the results of sociohistorical research could be made culturally and theologically communicable. The historians sometimes interpreted
this as a denial of the self-evident truth of their work that
threatened to compromise their academic freedom. The
theologians, for their part, often intimated that an amplifica-
tion of the descriptive enterprise was essentially superfluous
in view of their conviction that the basic definition of its
meaning was already established. It was too often true, unfortunately, that the philologians and historians had little
knowledge of or taste for theology and philosophy in a
technical sense; and also that the theologians misunderstood
and undervalued historical studies because they had been
bored by the manuals crammed full of the data that were
the results of research in the literary and cultural history of
the Bible but failed to explicate its relevance, either theologically or culturally.

Very probably such anxiety as biblical scholarship expe-

[7] Arnold, *Near the Edge of Battle.*

rienced at Chicago in the forties was stirred up as much by the impact of neoorthodox theology from abroad as by the rise of process theology here. It certainly added to the confusion and the impatience, so that, for some, theology almost became a dirty word. Neoorthodoxy broke up the organic and programmatic relationship between scientific research and biblical truth; it not only qualified but actually canceled the theological significance of what the heirs of Case were doing. Besides, psychologically speaking, neoorthodoxy, especially as utilized by Reinhold Niebuhr, demolished, even more effectively than neonaturalism, the remnants of ethical idealism of which the members of the sociohistorical movement were often the emotional and ecclesiastical heirs.

While the initial meeting of the two expressions of the Chicago School often took the form of a clash that was of no help to either, there was some basic communication from the very first. Wherever this occurred it soon became apparent that the affinities of the two perspectives for each other were close and were capable of producing results that were rich, original, and important. The work and career of Professor John Knox provided early and ample evidence for that.

Over the years, the two movements have shown a growing appreciation for each other. Younger process theologians, including such leaders as Schubert Ogden and John Cobb, exhibit a deep involvement with the biblical ethos. Their recognition of its distinctiveness might, in some respects, have disturbed both Case and Weiman! On the other side, in this volume Professor William A. Beardslee develops the view that the perspectives of process theology can carry and communicate both this biblical ethos and the critical concerns of sociohistorical and religiohistorical research. He expresses the reasonable hope that further communication may promote a new interpretive idiom, suited to the current cultural climate in America. He pleads for an affirmation of the meaningfulness of continuities in time. Implicit in this, it seems, is a contrast between the empiricist and the existentialist, or the Puritan and the Lutheran.

The transition of biblical studies in the Divinity School into the current period actually began before the clash between the historical and theological movements, cited above, had become acute. Its starting point coincides with the beginning of Dean Colwell's administration, 1939.

Mr. Colwell took note of the fact that students no longer experienced the relevance of the historical work in Bible, which had apparently been so self-evident to the heirs of Case and Smith that they had neglected to communicate it in a clear and contagious fashion. Students found that the manuals about literary and social history did not mark a road that led from past to present — not even a one-way road! Mr. Colwell also took note of the fact that the Divinity School had ceased to be a center where parish clergy were trained in great numbers, as it had been in the Mathews era. He was resolved to revitalize biblical studies and to reactivate the training of ministers. He initiated a series of practical administrative moves designed to deal with both concerns. He created and organized the Biblical Field as an integral facet of the faculty of theology. This incorporation of largely the entire staff of biblical scholars into the Divinity School challenged them to define the meaning of their work in the light of the entire theological enterprise. Dean Colwell was also the prime mover in the establishment of the Federated Theological Faculty. The practical result of this was that the biblical scholars in the Divinity School once more became responsible for a share in the preparation of large numbers of students for the parish ministry and were faced with the challenge to articulate the relevance of their work in that context. Finally, in making new appointments, Mr. Colwell looked for scholars, younger and older, who grasped his diagnosis of the problem and were sympathetic with his aims. His concern, in the first instance, was to articulate the theological relevance or function of the Bible in some way, rather than to develop biblical theology in a more technical sense.

The transition, initiated as a quest for relevance over twenty-five years ago, has continued to unfold. It takes many directions and constantly presents itself in new forms. The techniques and disciplines used in scientific interpretation continue to grow; they can be combined for use in an almost endless variety of ways. For example, documentary history, whether in the Pentateuch or the Synoptics, has made way for form criticism; and form criticism is crowded by tradition history. Nevertheless, all three continue to play a role. To cite another example, by combining literary analysis with history of religion, the Scandinavians have taught us much about the cult and faith of the people who wrote the Old Testament that we had never seen before. The subjects and areas that present themselves for investigation multiply, partly because the results of earlier work raise new questions and partly because entirely new data are discovered. In our period the Dead Sea Scrolls and the Gnostic literature dramatically illustrate this. Finally, and perhaps most of all, the gifts, the imagination, and the personal concerns and interests of the scholars in the field insure the importance and multiplication of variety.

In comparing the scene in the Biblical Field today with the Chicago School of the past, one must note both continuities and discontinuities. The latter are usually the more subtle. The historical character of biblical scholarship is stressed as much as ever; but the historicism of the past is gone. The meaning of the term "historical" has itself been amplified and its role extends far beyond the establishment of genetic and chronological connections. Indeed, it seems that precisely because the ideological function of historical method has been relativized, its role for descriptive purposes has become much more supple and adaptable. It is used in a wide range of interpretive perspectives without being equated with any one of them. There is more caution, perhaps, in treating the results of descriptive analysis as documentation for normative perspectives.

The essays in this volume, including those by lineal heirs of the Chicago School, reflect this tentativeness and this uneasiness about claiming too wide or definitive a range of application for the results of research. Thus, most probably not even Colwell is pleading for a return to historicism in the ideological sense; all he really asks for is a reaffirmation of the effective utility of historical method as the tool for the reconstruction of the story of the text of the Greek New Testament in chronological sequence. He does not imply that such a reconstruction can validate his faith; he just thinks that it might illumine it. In any case he does not wish to be deprived of his definition of his descriptive task by the a priori claims or decisions of some normative perspective following in the wake of historicism that may today be tempted to play the game of cultural imperialism. Since biblical studies preoccupy themselves mainly with the relativities of history, normative claims and schemes are usually largely strange to those concentrating in them, and therefore by turn frightening and seductive! At Chicago today neither the fear nor the attraction is overpowering.

Hermeneutically, the openness of our current situation produces a wide range of attitudes and responses; but, for the most part, being tentative and limited in scope and objective, they seldom threaten one another. Everyone has his own views about how, in interpreting the Bible, one moves from a descriptive account of its contents to a normative utilization of them; and there is some disposition to feel that rigid prescriptive formulations of method would involve losses equal to the gains. This is understandable. Hermeneutics is a rationalization of what has been going on. It contains a call for conformity that qualifies the openness of a situation. There is agreement that there are normative as well as descriptive dimensions to the full task of interpretation and that this involves both a movement from the past into the present and from the interpreter into the past. Biblical scholarship at Chicago no longer holds to the notion that its work should be done in a situation limited to one-way traffic. But there is great diversity of view both about how one should deal with the oncoming traffic and whether it is proper for a biblical scholar in his professional function to travel in both directions.

Three examples will serve to illustrate this variety. Professor G. W. Ahlström, who specializes in the history of religion in the Old Testament and in its setting in the ancient Near East, feels that the biblical scholar should limit himself to the descriptive side of the interpretive enterprise. All his work, including his essay in this volume, reflects this. To introduce normative considerations of meaning and value into the professional's scientific scene, or simply to tolerate their unbidden presence, inevitably confuses it and mars the clarity and meaning of the results. The biblical scholar, he feels, should ignore the traffic on the other side of the road and, if need be, build a wall to make that possible. In no case should he presume to travel on it; it is reserved for the dogmatic theologians and philosophers of culture who are responsible for the normative utilization of the results of the work of the biblical scholar, and also for the hermeneutical principles that make this possible.

Professor Norman Perrin, in New Testament, illustrates a second emphasis. His published work as an interpreter also falls mainly into the descriptive category. Indeed, what is most notable about his impressive work, *Rediscovering the Teaching of Jesus*, is both its sophisticated refinement of the methods of scientific analysis in the service of descriptive reconstruction and the quality of finality associated with the results. Despite all this, Perrin is not an historicist. On the contrary, he would most vehemently disavow any theologically normative significance for his historical work as such. Moreover, he does feel that the biblical scholar, in his professional capacity, should travel on both sides of the road of interpretation. Indeed, he would probably consider the descriptive side of the road as relatively preliminary and minor. Much more than any other member of the biblical faculty, he is committed to the construction of a hermeneutics which shall stipulate and organize the factors governing the character of the relationship between historical and theological interpretation, so that it may serve as a recipe, especially for beginners. He is not apprehensive about the close integration of the descriptive and normative facets of the process of interpretation in the context of a single, all-inclusive ideological perspective.

The third point of view cannot be associated so easily with a single name. It covers an area that can be said to lie between the two already cited. The hermeneutical essay in Robert M. Grant's *A Historical Introduction to the New Testament* reflects much of its mood and outlook. Biblical scholarship is basically a scientific, descriptive enterprise. Those who engage in it are not necessarily disinterested, however; nor would it always be better if they were, either for them or for their work. The normative interests of the interpreter, whether confessional or cultural, are not always explicit. Moreover, the facets of these interests that come into the focus of concern may expand and change as the scientific work proceeds and yields results. There is an organic relationship between the descriptive work and the normative concern. Professor Grant's essay in this volume, "Church History in the Early Church," illustrates this very well. The results of the historical work often suggest the shape of what is normatively important. The relationship between description and theology is not a formal one, controlled by an a priori inclusive hermeneutical program. It is personal, occasional, informal, and usually eclectic. The perspectives of meaning are somewhat kaleidoscopic and often overlap, being conditioned by the personal experience and situation of the interpreter. The relation between the normative and the descriptive remains an open and dialectical one, with each constantly playing upon the other. The interpreter is, in effect, driving on both sides of the road throughout, meeting himself over and over, showing signal flags, now green, now red! Interpretation is an inductive and never-ending dialogue between descriptive reconstructions of the past and normative traditions of faith or perspectives of meaning in the present. And when the interpreter is moved to reconsider his understanding of the meaning of the received tradition in synagogue or church in the light of the results of his scientific work, he will be doing biblical theology.

# 1

*The Covenant of David and the Problem of Unity*
*in Old Testament Theology*

## FREDERICK C. PRUSSNER

From the dual perspective of the occasion which has brought
us together and of the problem which is now to be before
us, it is a significant coincidence that at this time we are
observing not only the centennial of the Divinity School but
also the centennial of a work which has come to be recognized as one of the milestones in the history of Old Testament scholarship. For a century has now also passed since
the publication of Karl Heinrich Graf's study, *The Historical
Books of the Old Testament*,[1] in which he came to the important conclusion that the priestly legislation constituted
the latest literary stratum in the Pentateuch and that it was
to be dated in the time of Ezra. Graf's findings were, to be
sure, not completely novel — he had been anticipated, for
example, by Reuss and Vatke — but his own distinct contribution lay in providing the critical justification for them on
the basis of solid literary analysis. In the years which followed, others, especially Wellhausen, were to move to the
forefront of the examination of the Pentateuchal sources,
but it is a tribute to the recognition which was accorded
to Graf's crucial place in this enterprise that the critical
view which eventually gained the assent of the majority of
scholars in the late nineteenth century came to be named
the "Graf-Wellhausen theory."

Our present interest in the centennial of Graf's work is,
however, not so much literary as theological. We need to

[1] K. H. Graf, *Die geschichtlichen Bücher des Alten Testaments*
(Leipzig: T. O. Weigl, 1866).

remember that the early and middle decades of the nineteenth century had witnessed a flowering of the theological
treatment of the Old Testament at the hands of conservative and moderate scholars alike. Despite their many differences in major as well as minor questions, there existed
among them a general agreement that the religion of the
Old Testament was grounded in a revelation to Moses of
divine truth which had found its literary expression in the
Pentateuch or, at least, in the major part of the Pentateuch.
Starting from this initial revelation, the religion had been
grown and developed and had finally achieved its highest
expression in the New Testament. Despite such change and
growth, it was thought, nevertheless, to have remained
fundamentally the same religion. It is perhaps an indication
of the zeitgeist of the period, which saw, among other
things, the rise of the biological sciences, that the favorite
form of stating the progressive movement of biblical religion
was the analogy of the growth which occurs from seed to
full-grown plant or from bud to ripened fruit. The words
most frequently used to characterize this view of the unity
of biblical religion were "organic" and "genetic." Gustav
Oehler may be taken as more or less typical of his generation of Old Testament theologians when he describes his
viewpoint and methodological procedure in the following
words:

> But now *Biblical Theology*, which proposes to set forth
> revelation in its whole course and in the totality of its
> phenomena, must comprehend these forms as *members
> of an organic process of development* . . . . The *genetic*
> method seeks to reproduce the living process of the
> thing itself. This method refuses, however, to find ripe
> fruit where only the bud exists; it aims to show how
> the fruit grew from the bud; it sketches the earlier
> stages in a way that makes it clear how the higher stages
> could, and necessarily did, spring from the former.[2]

[2] G. F. Oehler, *Old Testament Theology*, rev. ed., trans. G. A. Day
(New York: Funk & Wagnalls, 1883), pp. 41–42.

Not unexpectedly, theory here too did not always coincide with practice. In Oehler's treatment, for example, the Mosaic revelation occupied almost three-fifths of the discussion and what was supposed to be the bud turned out to be very nearly the whole fruit.

Against this background, the impact of Graf's work on the Pentateuch, together with the refinements his successors introduced later, takes on a clearer focus. For the effort to solve the problem of the theological unity of the Old Testament along organic and genetic lines under the assumption of an original, reasonably complete revelation was bound to suffer from the demonstration that none of the major documentary sections of the Pentateuch went back to the time of Moses and that, in fact, the levitical legislation was chronologically late. It is scarcely a coincidence that the years of the ever-widening acceptance of the Graf-Wellhausen theory were also the very years in which occurred the late nineteenth-century demise of Old Testament theology. Of course, the success of the theory was not the only reason for this demise. Other factors played their part, for example, (1) a declining interest in theological circles generally in the concept of revelation, (2) the increasing interest, under the influence of the social sciences, in treating religion as an expression of human culture, and (3) the growing conviction among Old Testament scholars that early Israelite religion had actully been quite primitive and not significantly different from primitive religion elsewhere. Even so, one must not fail to see that Graf's epoch-making conclusions regarding the composition of the Pentateuch helped to destroy the hitherto prevailing sense of the essential theological unity of the Old Testament and so set the stage for developments in the area of Old Testament theology which continue to have an important bearing in our day.

When the eclipse of the theological study of the Old Testament ended during the thirties of our own century, the problem of the inner unity of its theology immediately became again one of the thorniest issues confronting those who were attracted to the discipline. The preceding century's legacy of literary and historical criticism still remained basically intact, although, under the influence of form-criticism and archeology, new data and new viewpoints had brought about numerous changes in the picture then beginning to emerge of the early periods in the history of Israel's religion. Furthermore, no fundamental modification had taken place in the long-held conviction that both the extended chronological scope of the literature in the Old Testament and the inescapable evidence of theological variety within that literature made some form of historical treatment unavoidable. Without ignoring the difficulties thus posed to a distinctively theological study of Israel's faith, the new generation of Old Testament theologians has continued to seek the solution to the problem of unity and, in doing so, has frequently moved in hitherto untraveled directions. To this task they brought genuine creativity and a masterful insight into the character of Israel's faith. However, I believe it must be said that a final solution is still awaited and that the absence of a commonly accepted answer to this problem is one of the more important explanations for the often noted lack of unanimity concerning what Old Testament theology actually is.

Without endeavoring to provide a complete review of all the Old Testament theologies which have been published since the revitalization of the discipline in our century, it is necessary to take a quick account of the distinctive ways in which representative scholars have dealt with the problem of unity. Walther Eichrodt's celebrated three-volume *Theologie des Alten Testaments*, which began to appear in 1933, assumed that it was possible "to present the religion recorded in the writings of the Old Testament as an integrated quantity which, despite its chequered historical career, remained fundamentally of one tendency and type."[3] That which gave to the Old Testament its inherent unity — and also, from the point of view of a "biblical" theology, tied the Old Testament inextricably to the New — was the

[3] W. Eichrodt, *Theologie des Alten Testaments* (Leipzig: J. C. Hinrichs, 1933–39), 1:v.

"entry (*Einbruch*) and expansion (*Durchsetzung*) of God's
kingly rule in this world." [4] By employing categories which
he derived directly from the Old Testament's own thought
and idiom rather than from extraneous dogmatic structures,
he envisaged this "kingly rule" of God as taking place in
three realms (*Hauptkreise*), namely (1)God and People, (2)
God and World, and (3) God and Man. Within this structure he saw the *covenant idea* as providing the centralizing
and unifying concept of the Old Testament "world of belief" and emphasized in defense of its use in this role that
"the concept of the covenant . . . establishes from the first
the peculiarity of Israel's understanding of God." [5] It is, however, also at this very point that Eichrodt has been most
severely criticized. For although the impressiveness of his
theological treatment of the covenant idea in all its con-
ceptual and institutional ramifications is widely acknowledged, there is also general agreement that he makes his
case only for the first of the three relationships just mentioned, that of "God and People." In the other dimensions
of Israel's faith, those concerned with "God and World" and
"God and Man," the covenant idea, even in his hands, can
scarcely be said to play a real role as organizing principle.

Published in the same year as Eichrodt's first volume,
Ernst Sellin's *Alttestamentliche Theologie auf religionsgeschichtlicher Grundlage* took a very different approach. Its
first volume contained a "History of the Israelite-Jewish
Religion" and thus carried on the widely prevailing practice
of treating Israel's religion along historical lines. The purpose of this part of the work was to picture the development and growth of the religion from the standpoint of
both "the natural-human influences" which played upon it
and "the divine revelation which pulsated and found expression here." [6] To this historical "overview" Sellin then added,
in a second volume, a treatment of the theology of the Old

[4] *Ibid.*, 1:1.
[5] *Ibid.*, p. 6.
[6] E. Sellin, *Alttestamentliche Theologie auf religionsgeschichtlicher
Grundlage* (Leipzig: Quelle & Meyer, 1933), 1:1.

Testament and identified its particular objective as that of
setting forth

> systematically the religious teachings and the faith
> which were fashioned in the Jewish community on the
> basis of the sacred writings during the fifth to the sec-
> ond pre-Christian centuries, but only in so far as they
> were recognized by Jesus Christ and his apostles as
> the presupposition and the foundation of their gospel,
> in so far as they, therefore, to use Luther's phrase in
> its widest sense, "deal with Christ." [7]

Sellin's solution to the problem of unity was, therefore,
grounded on a Christian-theological eclecticism, but also on
what one might call the element of "canonical coherence"
which had resulted from the selection of suitable Scriptures
by the postexilic Jewish community. In general, his critics
have especially questioned the restrictiveness which is present in his program to confine Old Testament theology to
"the long line which found its fulfillment in the Gospel" [8]
and which led him, for example, to emphasize the "harsh
contrast" [9] between *prophetic* and *cultic-priestly-legalistic*
religion.

Ludwig Koehler's *Theologie des Alten Testaments*, published in 1936, produced one of the simplest plans to be
found in our day for the treatment of Old Testament theology. Its purpose, we are told, was to offer a "synthesis, in
their correct relationship, of those views, ideas, and concepts of the Old Testament which are or can be theologically
important.[10] The clearly pragmatic character of Koehler's
definition permitted him to eschew all elaboration upon
what he meant by such phrases as "synthesis" or "theologically important." It is also quite in keeping with this avoid-
ance of methodological theory that he omitted all general
discussion of the theological unity of the Old Testament

[7] *Ibid.*
[8] *Ibid.*, 2:1.
[9] *Ibid.*, p. 111.
[10] L. Koehler, *Theologie des Alten Testaments*. (Tübingen: Mohr,
1936), p. v.

except to observe that the central idea underlying all of the Old Testament is God's *Lordship.*

> The one and fundamental statement of the theology of the Old Testament is that God is the governing Lord. . . . Herefrom all else flows. All else leans on it. In its light and only in its light everything can be understood. All else is subordinate to it.[11]

During the decades following World War II the flowering of Old Testament theology has continued to such a degree that R. C. Dentan has identified the period as "a golden age."[12] The number of major studies devoted to the discipline is now approaching the dozen mark. Somewhat arbitrarily, however, any comment here will be restricted to only three, those by Vriezen (1949, 2d ed. 1954, Engl. trans. 1958), Jacob (1955, Engl. trans. 1958), and von Rad (1957–60, Engl. trans. 1962–65).

Vriezen's reflections upon the problem of the theological unity of the Old Testament can perhaps be best approached through his description of Old Testament theology as a branch of scholarship which has the threefold task of defining "the characteristic features of *the message of the Old Testament,*" of seeking "*particularly the element of revelation in the message of the Old Testament,*" and of giving "*its own evaluation of the Old Testament message on the ground of its Christian theological starting-point.*"[13] In a different context he specifies that the "essential internal unity of the Old Testament" is the result of the presence in it of "not only great unanimity among the different authors but especially a fundamental spiritual agreement, springing from the certainty of being received into living communion with the same living God."[14] Such unanimity and agreement, for their part, result from the "domination" over the

[11] *Ibid.,* p. 12.

[12] R. C. Dentan, *Preface to Old Testament Theology,* rev. ed. (New York: Seabury Press, 1963), p. 72.

[13] T. C. Vriezen, *An Outline of Old Testament Theology,* trans., S. Neuijen (Oxford: B. Blackwell, 1958), p. 122 (italics in the original).

[14] *Ibid.,* p. 40.

entire Old Testament of the "prophetic testimony" which the great crises of Israel's history had authenticated and marked for permanent preservation.

> The Old Testament contains that part of the Israelite religious writings which could be salvaged from the ruins left by the catastrophe of 586, in terms of the prophetical criticism, and further it contains this prophetical criticism itself and the writings that were written afterwards from the point of view of this prophetical criticism.[15]

Vriezen's emphasis on the importance of maintaining a perspective in terms of the revelation in Christ and the central role he accords to the "prophetic testimony" at once remind one of Sellin's views and, of course, lead one also to question, as in Sellin's case, whether his position is not too restrictive in relation to the total theological content of the Old Testament.

Edmond Jacob's conception of Old Testament theology, which he defines as "the systematic account of the specific religious ideas which can be found throughout the Old Testament and which form its profound unity,"[16] also regards a satisfactory solution of the problem of unity as necessary to the discipline. What he means in the foregoing definition by the "profound unity" of the Old Testament is partially apparent in his insistence that a true theology of the Old Testament "can only be a Christology."[17] Such a christological orientation is valid, he maintains, not only because "what was revealed under the old covenant . . . is gathered together and brought to perfection in Christ,"[18] but also because the Old and New Testaments are one in that they proclaim the same message about the same God.

[15] *Ibid.*
[16] E. Jacob, *Theology of the Old Testament*, trans., A. W. Heathcote and P. J. Allcock. (London: Hodder & Stoughton and New York: Harper & Row, 1958), p. 11.
[17] *Ibid.*, p. 12.
[18] *Ibid.*

. . . a perfectly objective study makes us discern already in the Old Testament the same message of the God who is present, of the God who saves and of the God who comes, which characterizes the Gospel. Unless it is based upon the principle of the unity of the two Testaments, and a fortiori on the internal unity of the Old Testament itself, it is not possible to speak of a theology of the Old Testament.[19]

The emphasis he places in this citation upon the concept of God explains one other element in his view of Old Testament theology. For it is in keeping with this emphasis that he — following somewhat in the footsteps of Koehler — locates the central idea of Israel's faith in the idea of the "sovereignty of God."

What gives the Old Testament its force and its unity is the affirmation of the sovereignty of God. God is the basis of all things and all that exists only exists by his will.[20]

The theologies we have examined up to this point all characterize the discipline as concerned in one way or another with a "system of religious ideas." They have looked for the structure of thought or for the thought world of the Old Testament. They have sought to see this structure, more often than not, in terms of unifying ideas. They seek to be objective or descriptive statements of ancient Israel's faith in terms of itself, though not without recourse to the results of the comparative study of religion. For the most part, however, they are also conceived in a normative sense in that they demand that the Old Testament theologian view his subject from the standpoint of the New Testament as well, and even, in the case of Vriezen, from the standpoint of dogmatic theology. If they have any weakness, apart from the questionable insistence on some peculiarly Christian orientation as inhering in the very method of the discipline,

[19] *Ibid.*, pp. 12–13.
[20] *Ibid.*, p. 37.

it is that they are preoccupied with the need for system. Since Israel's Scriptures do not come to us, after all, in the form of a system of religious ideas, any kind of systematization is, therefore, bound in some fashion to involve an element of artificiality. The last of the works to pass before us, von Rad's now justly renowned *Old Testament Theology* (two volumes) has sought not only to avoid some of the pitfalls of theological systematization but also to open up new paths.

Von Rad's theological method is rooted in his thoroughgoing acceptance of form criticism. The well-known insistence of form critics that a literary form is intimately related to content as well as to the specific life situation (*Sitz im Leben*) in which it has its origins is everywhere apparent in his work. It needs to be recalled at the outset that one of von Rad's major critical contributions has been his demonstration that the Hexateuch in its present form is an expansion upon or enlargement of Israel's earliest confessions and recitals of her "salvation history," among which the most important is the so-called Little Credo in Deut. 26:5–9.[21] From this standpoint we may grasp why von Rad in the end comes to view not only the Hexateuch but the entire Old Testament as made up of Israel's testimonies to Yahweh's saving activities in her history — and these, he believes, are properly the subject matter of Old Testament theology.

> In the Old Testament it is thus this world made up of testimonies that is above all the subject of a theology of the Old Testament. The subject cannot be a systematically ordered "world of the faith" of Israel or of the really overwhelming vitality and creative productivity of Jahwism, for the world of faith is not the subject of these testimonies which Israel raised to Jahweh's action in history. . . . Religious thought cannot be separated out from these traditions and represented

[21] G. von Rad, *Das formgeschichtliche Problem des Hexateuch,* BWANT, vol. 26 (Stuttgart, 1938). Engl. trans. by E. W. T. Dicken in *The Problem of the Hexateuch and Other Essays* (Edinburgh: Oliver & Boyd, 1966).

thus in abstract. If we divorced Israel's confessional utterances from the divine acts in history which they so passionately embrace, what a bloodless ghost we would be left with! If, however, we put Israel's picture of her history in the fore-front of our theological consideration, we encounter what appropriately is the most essential subject of a theology of the Old Testament, the living word of Jahweh coming on and on to Israel for ever, and this in the message uttered by his mighty acts. It was a message so living and actual for each moment that it accompanied her on her journey through time, interpreting itself afresh to every generation, and informing every generation what it had to do.[22]

His fundamental orientation is thus his concern with Israel's *Heilsgeschichte* and with what Israel believed because of what she had experienced in this "salvation history." However, what Israel believed about the meaning of Yahweh's saving acts changed with the centuries. Each generation interpreted this meaning afresh as it sought to "make the divine acts of salvation relevant for every new age and day" — [23] and, because this was so, the overall picture of Israel's faith necessarily was not one of static identicalness but of dynamic adaptability. Von Rad's work is, for this reason, really a series of theologies, identified by the connection they have with the various literary sections of the Old Testament. While the major portion of the first volume is devoted to the theology of the Hexateuch, the same volume also deals — though in much less elaborate form — with the theologies of the Deuteronomist, of the Chronicler, of the Psalms and, finally, of the wisdom writings. The element of disunity is especially apparent in the distinction which he draws between these theologies and the theology of the prophets, to whom the second volume is chiefly devoted. The basis for this distinction is that

[22] G. von Rad, *Old Testament Theology*, trans. D. M. G. Stalker (Edinburgh: Oliver & Boyd and New York: Harper & Row, 1962–65), 1:111–12.
[23] *Ibid.*, p. vi.

within the scope of a theology of the historical traditions there can be no mention of the prophets, as the
characteristic thing about their proclamation is that
they deny the efficacy of the old divine actions for their
contemporaries, and they perceive God's rising up to
completely new acts in history in their time.[24]

Whether von Rad's conception of Old Testament theology
results in a more adequate discussion of the subject than that
found in the other studies which we have examined may be
disputed. R. C. Dentan has questioned whether the work
can actually be identified as a "theology" and has, instead,
preferred to characterize it as "a study in the history of traditions."[25] Certainly the issue of the inner unity of Israel's
faith is not always solved very well. A particular case in
point may be seen in his treatment of the wisdom literature
from the perspective of "salvation history." On the one side,
the wisdom literature contains, as does also the Psalter, Israel's "response" to the saving events of her history in the
form of praise, but also of inquiry and even of complaint.
Moreover, later (i.e. postexilic) wisdom came to interrelate
world history and saving history in "a tremendous scheme."
Indeed, it might be said that the aim of the wise men of that
era in their "theological reflexions upon history . . . was
nothing less than an aetiology of Israel and Israel's special
place among the nations."[26] It is, therefore, all the more
startling when, on the other side, one is told that the theology of the wisdom literature was not greatly interested in
the phenomenon of history and that, as a matter of fact:

> . . . in the circles of wisdom teaching, interest in the
> traditions of the saving history had grown weak. It was
> all the more turned towards the miracle of Creation,
> its systematic arrangement, its technical riddles and its
> rules. . . . It is here that the Wisdom literature be-
> comes enthusiastic, here is the field where it knew itself

[24] *Ibid.*, p. vii.
[25] Dentan, *Preface*, p. 79.
[26] Von Rad, *Old Testament Theology*, 1:445.

theologically challenged and where indeed it became productive.[27]

In such ways his work illustrates the validity of the observation of G. Ernest Wright — who was himself under admitted indebtedness to von Rad — that "in any attempt to outline a discussion of Biblical faith it is the Wisdom literature which offers the chief difficulty because it does not fit into the type of faith exhibited in the historical and prophetic literatures." [28]

Von Rad has also been completely opposed, quite in keeping with his conception of the nature of Old Testament theology, to any methodology which seeks to unify it around a *central idea.* "The road back," he tells us, "to an all-inclusive fundamental idea, to a 'fundamental structure,' or to some 'basic tendency' cannot be found so easily in our day." And he proceeds then to ask:

> What validity can we attach to this question, which is raised almost with one voice, concerning the "unity," the "center" of the Old Testament? . . . Or does such a postulate not imply less an interest in historical or theological understanding than in a speculative-philosophical principle which then goes into operation as a subconscious premise? [29]

The question of identifying the theological unity of the Old Testament remains one of the controversial issues in biblical interpretation today. It is, of course, possible that the religious content of Israel's scriptures is so diversified that we should not expect to find the common denominator which holds everything together in an all-embracing harmony. On the other hand, it may also be that not all possible directions have been adequately explored. As a suggestion that such an area for further examination does exist, it is

[27] *Ibid.*, p. 449–50.

[28] G. E. Wright, *God Who Acts*, Studies in Biblical Theology no. 2 (Chicago: H. Regnery, 1950), p. 103.

[29] G. von Rad, "Offene Fragen im Umkreis einer Theologie des Alten Testaments," *Theologische Literarzeitung* 88 (1963): 405.

here proposed that a look be taken at the theological meaning and effect of the "Covenant with David."

The reason for the undeniable attraction which Eichrodt's *Theology of the Old Testament* has always enjoyed is the extraordinary use he has made of the idea of the covenant. Even with his inability to include every realm of Israel's faith under it, he was certainly able to show its fundamental importance in any effort to get to the heart of that faith. As he conceived of it, however, it was tied almost entirely to the Sinai covenant and to its understanding of Israel's relationship to God as that of the obedient People of God who had been brought out of Egypt and had therewith experienced the grace of divine election. For him, no other of the various Old Testament covenants could approach the Sinai covenant in theological meaning. Characteristically, he devoted only a single paragraph to the Davidic covenant, and in fact went to some pains to stress its insignificance.

In more recent times, on the other hand, the Davidic covenant has been moved to a place of higher importance in Old Testament theology. G. E. Wright some years ago referred to the "problem of theological accommodation to the covenant faith" which arose when Israel adopted the institution of the monarchy and was then confronted with the rise of a distinct and, for her, novel religious form — a "royal theology which we know must have been fostered in the royal court of the Davidic dynasty in Jerusalem." [30] The significance which von Rad attaches to the Davidic covenant can be measured by the fact that he devotes an entire chapter to it and to its theological impact upon the Psalms, the Deuteronomic history work, and the Chronicler's history. Especially relevant is his observation that two events in Israel's history were unusually productive in a theological sense: the saving history which culminated in the conquest of Canaan, and the covenant with David. His words are so pertinent that they deserve to be quoted in extenso.

> If we reduce the comprehensive accounts of her history which Israel wrote to what is basic theologically, that

[30] Wright, *God Who Acts*, p. 79.

is, to those actions of Jahweh which were constitutive for Israel, the result is as follows: Jahweh twice intervened in Israel's history in a special way, to lay a basis of salvation for his people. The first was in the complex of acts which are gathered together in the avowal made by the canonical saving history (that is, from Abraham to Joshua), the other was in the confirmation of David and his throne for all time. . . . On these two saving data rested the whole of Israel's existence before Jahweh. Even the prophets in their proclamation of the new creation of Israel cannot hark back to any other than them, the covenant at Sinai and the covenant with David.[31]

The inner history of Israel's faith appears here as the history of *two* covenants, their rise individually and their relationship to one another. The two together are looked upon as constituting the foundation upon which the *whole of Israel's existence before Jahweh* rested. This is a far cry from Eichrodt's reduction of the Davidic covenant to the point of theological indifference.

How then shall we view the impact which the Davidic covenant had on Israel's theology? A sense for historical continuity requires that we begin with a quick delineation of the order of faith and life for which the Sinai covenant was the focus and which came to be embodied in what is now commonly — although not without dissent — called the amphictyonic league of the period of the Judges.[32] Early Israelite confessions such as Deut. 26:5–9 indicate that the faith of this amphictyony was grounded on Israel's experience of acts by which her God, Yahweh, had saved her, notably in a deliverance from Egyptian bondage and in the gift of Canaan as her homeland. In the context of these events Israel had become Yahweh's people, had bound herself to him, and he to her, in a covenant of loyalty, and had so

[31] Von Rad, *Old Testament Theology*, 1:355.
[32] On the character of the amphictyonic league see especially M. Noth, *The History of Israel*, 2d ed., rev., trans. P. R. Ackroyd (New York: Harper & Row, 1960), pp. 85–108.

31

come to know him as her gracious and victorious lord. More-over, her divine lord had communicated to her the nature of the obligations under the covenant by giving her a "law of God" consisting of "statutes and ordinances" (note here the especially revealing account in Josh. 24:25–27).

The amphictyonic order of life derived uniquely from this faith. Its central structure was not political — politically speaking, the organization of the twelve tribes always re-mained weak — but religious, and had its tangible expression in a central shrine containing as its most significant feature the ark of the covenant. The earliest location of this shrine was very likely the city of Shechem, but later on it was moved elsewhere and for a while, at least, it stood in the city of Shiloh. Regular pilgrimages to this shrine from all over Israel served to promote a sense of cohesiveness, but they especially provided the occasions for a recital of Israel's salvation history and for instruction in Israel's covenant obligations. It has been suggested that the liturgical material in Deut. 27:11–26 may presuppose some ceremony of cove-nant renewal in which essential elements of the covenant requirements were reaffirmed at either annual or seven-year intervals. Other characteristics of the amphictyony were (1) a number of permanent offices such as those of tribal repre-sentatives, judges, and a hereditary priesthood which served at the central shrine; (2) a charismatic type of leadership in the persons of prophets and of military commanders whose major qualification was that "the Spirit of the Lord came upon" them; (3) the reliance on the institutions of the *Holy War* in the defense of the people against invaders; and (4) a repudiation of any kind of political leadership which de-rived from some form of dynastic succession (cf. especially Gideon's refusal to become a king, Judg. 8:22–23).

The story of the league's collapse and of its replacement by a monarchical government is the theme of the familiar accounts about Israel's first kings, Saul, David, and Solomon. In the face of irresistible Philistine attacks on their territory, the Israelites turned to a stronger form of leadership which could give a more centralized direction in the struggle. Ultimately they succeeded — although not until the first king had himself died on the battlefield — in not only gaining the upper hand over the Philistines but also in establishing an empire which included most of the neighboring nations from the Red Sea to central Syria. What is even more important is that the adoption of the monarchical form of government also effected a change in Israel's religious affairs and that this change had consequences which were far more lasting than the shift in political structure. It is true that under the first two kings a number of the essential characteristics of Israel's life which were associated with the amphictyony continued to be observed. Both Saul and David possessed the necessary charismatic qualifications, and David made it a point to bring the ark to Jerusalem, his new capital. On the other hand, however, it was also David who began the process of basing royal authority, at least in part, on the fighting strength of a professional soldiery made up quite often of foreign mercenaries. In so doing he went far to dilute the importance of the military structure which had fought the holy wars of the amphictyony, the so-called host consisting of every able-bodied Israelite.

This, now, brings us to the crucial innovation. We are told in II Samuel that when "the Lord had given him (David) rest from all his enemies round about" (vs. 1) the prophet Nathan conveyed to him Yahweh's promise that "your house and your kingdom shall be made sure for ever before me; your throne shall be established for ever" (vs. 16).[33] This divine pledge has its significant echo in the ancient poem known as "the Last Words of David" (II Sam. 23:1-7),[34] especially in verse 5, which declares,

[33] In the following examination of 2 Sam. 7 the historical analysis which L. Rost has made of the chapter is assumed to be substantially correct. See his *Die Ueberlieferung von der Thronnachfolge Davids*, BWANT 3d series, no. 6 (Stuttgart: W. Kohlhammer, 1926), pp. 47–74. Consult also G. von Rad, *Old Testament Theology*, 1:310–11.

[34] On the antiquity of the poem see H. W. Hertzberg, *I & II Samuel* (London: SCM Press, 1964), p. 400: "Today an increasing body of opinion, in accordance with tradition, regards David as the author of the poem from at least v. 3b onwards; there are hardly any decisive arguments to be brought against this position."

Yea, does not my house stand so with God?
For he has made with me an everlasting covenant,
 ordered in all things and secure.
For will he not cause to prosper
 all my help and my desire?

The assurance here given to David and his "house" that the Davidic kingdom would be "sure for ever" thus came to be formulated as an *everlasting covenant* and continued to be so regarded by later generations (Pss. 89:3; 132:14) who, on occasion, applied to it the slightly varied but equally covenantal rubric of Yahweh's "steadfast, sure love for David" (Isa. 55:3; Pss. 21:7; 89:24, 28, 33).

The original tradition regarding the "covenant with David" at some later time — possibly even as early as Solomon's reign [35] — was enlarged to include a startlingly novel line of thought whereby the peculiar association between Yahweh and the Davidic dynasty was designated as a father-son relationship and the ruling Davidic king was identified as Yahweh's "son" (II Sam. 7:14, "I will be his father, and he shall be my son"). Here we suddenly enter a whole new world of thought, unrelated to anything Israel had hitherto known but not very different from the practice common in the countries around Israel of looking upon a king, in some manner or another, as a "son of god."

The new directions in Israel's faith, represented in the Davidic covenant, achieved full-grown expression in Solomon's reign and came to their clearest focus in the temple, which was to become his most famous accomplishment. Although it served as a "resting place" of the ark and thus perpetuated the traditional central shrine of the amphictyony, its real character was that of a "royal" shrine which incorporated in its style and furnishings a profusion of Canaanite religious motifs. Its dominant theme may be described as *kingship* — first of all, Yahweh's kingship, but at

---

[35] So G. von Rad, *Old Testament Theology*, 1:310 against L. Rost, *Die Ueberlieferung*, p. 67, who ties the introduction of this "father-son" theme to the period after Jerusalem's miraculous deliverance from Sennacherib's siege.

the same time it also stood for the authority of the human king ruling in Jerusalem.

It symbolized divine kingship in its designation as a *hekhal*, a word which means temple, but also palace. Many of the psalms which came out of the context of its worship emphasize that Yahweh is "King." In a related vein, we remember that S. Mowinckel has theorized rather cogently about an "enthronement festival" which he considered to be the *Sitz im Leben* of the so-called enthronement psalms. The one prophet whose call took place at this temple, namely, Isaiah, reports that he saw "the King." What is known as the "molten sea" in I Kings 7:23 is probably to be understood in the same light. The Babylonian creation myth and the Ugaritic texts, to name but two examples, both describe how the gods Marduk (Babylonia) and Baal (Ugarit) achieved their kingship over the other gods and hence over all of life by defeating an adversary who was identified with the sea. That such a victory leading to Yahweh's kingship also figured in the thought forms associated with the Jerusalem temple is made more than likely by the words of an ancient hymnic fragment now incorporated into Psalm 74:

Yet God my King is from of old,
    working salvation in the midst of the earth.
Thou didst divide the sea by thy might;
    thou didst break the heads of the dragons on the waters.
Thou didst crush the heads of Leviathan.

This same "molten sea" very probably also played another symbolic role, just as important theologically as the connection with the kingship theme. In Babylonia, Marduk's victory, so crucial to his kingship, led directly to various acts which resulted in the creation of the world and of life. The Ugaritic materials lack any such a clear correlation between kingship and creation, but the reason for the omission may simply be the fragmentary character of these texts. In terms of Israel's thought, this important interconnection is again most evident. A case in point is provided by the

psalm fragment just quoted which, having coupled Yahweh's kingship with his defeat of Leviathan, goes on to
describe his acts as creator:

> Thou didst cleave open springs and brooks;
>> thou didst dry up ever-flowing streams.
> Thine is the day, thine also the night;
>> thou hast established the luminaries and the sun.
> Thou hast fixed all the bounds of the earth;
>> thou hast made summer and winter.

Without going into details, one finds the same association
of kingship and cosmic creation in most of the psalms which
glorify Yahweh as "King" (e.g. Pss. 93; 95:1–5; 96:5, 10;
98:7–9).

Though centering on Yahweh's kingship, Solomon's temple served an additional purpose as well, namely that of
giving expression to the legitimacy and the divine appointment of the Davidic kings ruling in Jerusalem. In its most
tangible form, this role was probably attached to the two
pillars standing at its front. R. B. Y. Scott's explanation of
the names by which they came to be known (Jachin and
Boaz) as the first words of dynastic formulas which were
inscribed on them is a most attractive one and goes far to
account for the custom of the kings of Judah to stand by
"the pillar" when undertaking highly important actions
(II Kings 11:14 and 23:3).[36] Our most instructive information in this regard, however, comes from the several so-
called royal psalms, for these psalms shed considerable
light on the distinctively sacral role assigned to the Davidic
kings. Such a king was Yahweh's son and begotten by Yahweh (Ps. 2:7; some form of adoptive sonship is apparently
intended). His authority issues from a decree given by
Yahweh himself. He sits at Yahweh's right hand and receives divine help in making his enemies "his footstool."
Indeed he is a "priest for ever" (Ps. 110:1, 4). It is, in fact,

[36] R. B. Y. Scott, "The Pillars Jachin and Boaz," *Journal of Biblical
Literature*, 68 (1939): 143 ff.

just possible — our uncertainty is due to the ambiguity of the phrase employed — that he might even be addressed as "God" (Elohim; Ps. 45:6). If we are to take our cue from Psalm 89, the function of the human king was that of the guardian and mediator of the order of life which the divine King had brought into being. The assurance that this would ever remain so is what gives to the "covenant with David" its theological content.

Important though this "royal theology" might be for an understanding of the character and worship of the Solomonic temple, its significance becomes even greater for the total picture of Israel's faith. In the first place, it probably did bring about — though not everywhere in Israel — an eclipse of the amphictyonic traditions and with them of the Sinai covenant. Whether this involved a complete replacement of the faith and order which that covenant expressed in favor of the royal theology is something which is hard to judge. It is worth noting, for example, that the royal psalms and not a few of the enthronement psalms speak only of Yahweh's role as creator and as the one who established the Davidic kingdom for all time. Of his role as the one who delivered Israel out of Egypt and who gave her the long-promised land of Canaan they say little or nothing at all. The extent of the eclipse may indeed be reflected in the comment in II Kings 23:21–23 that Josiah reinstituted the passover festival in Jerusalem after it had gone unobserved since the days of the judges. At the same time, however, there is reason to think that the amphictyonic traditions remained very much alive in certain circles, especially of the Northern Kingdom. They may have been part of the forces which led to the disruption of the monarchy after Solomon's death. The dynastic instabilities of the Northern Kingdom during its entire history may again in part be the result of the antidynastic stance in these traditions. We should also recall that von Rad has located the origins of Deuteronomy — which is so strongly affected by the outlook of the amphictyony — among the Levites of the Northern

Kingdom.[37] Similarly, the northern prophetic groups, represented by such men as Ahijah, Elijah, Elisha, and particularly Hosea, appear to have been especially active bearers of the amphictyonic legacy.

The impact of the "royal theology" on the totality of Israel's faith made itself felt in yet another respect: the encounter with paganism. Since it represented an adaptation to Israel's circumstances of ideas and customs which were indigenous to the ancient Oriental culture world, there was always the real danger not only of a thoroughgoing paganization of the Yahweh faith (cf. Ahaz' use of an Assyrian altar for the worship of Yahweh, II Kings 16:1–16) but of the introduction of pagan gods and cults as well. The clearest examples of such subversion and modification for which Israelite kings bore responsibility come from the reigns of Manasseh in Judah (II Kings 21:3–6) and of Ahab in the Northern Kingdom, where the royal cult had apparently also been established (I Kings 16:32–33).[38] Several kings of Judah (Asa and Hezekiah) and at least one in the Northern Kingdom (Jehu) are said to have taken measures to eliminate pagan accretions, but their efforts were not crowned with permanent success. It was only in the Reform of Josiah of 621 B.C. that something like a lasting solution of the problem posed by this openness of the royal cult to paganism was achieved.

Josiah's reform, in its essential character, was nothing less than a conjoining of the amphictyonic traditions with the official Davidic cult, that is to say, of the Sinaitic covenant and the Davidic covenant. Nowhere is this union of Israel's two major covenantal spheres of faith and life seen more dramatically than in the famous temple scene of II Kings 23:1–3 in which Josiah, the scion of David, leads his people

[37] G. von Rad, *Studies in Deuteronomy*, trans. David Stalker, Studies in Biblical Theology, no. 9 (Chicago: H. Regnery Co., 1953), pp. 60–69. More recently also in his *Das fünfte Buch Mose*, vol. 8 of *Das Alte Testament Deutsch*, ed. V. Herntrich and A. Weiser (Göttingen: Vandenhoeck & Ruprecht, 1964), pp. 16–21.

[38] This seems to be implied, for example, in the words of the priest Amaziah to Amos, referring to the shrine at Bethel as "the king's Santuary" and "a temple of the kingdom" (Amos 7:13).

in a solemn covenant of commitment to the newly discovered book of law which was believed to contain "the law
of Moses" (II Kings 23:25). The Deuteronomic history,
representing the most important literary outgrowth of the
reform movement, envisages the same confluence of the two
covenants. It begins at the point of the establishment of
the covenant of Sinai, reaches a second climax in the events
surrounding the Davidic covenant, and ends with the Josianic
reform. Particularly expressive are the judgments it passes
on the two focal personalities who appear at its two ex-
tremes: essentially the same evaluation in quite similar language is applied to both Moses and Josiah, possibly suggesting that, while Moses was the unique and incomparable
prophet, Josiah was the unique and incomparable king
(compare Deut. 34:10 with II Kings 23:25).

In the exilic and postexilic Jewish community the conjunction of the two covenants and the spheres of faith and
life which they represented continued, although, because of
the disappearance of the monarchy and also because of the
political subservience of the community to foreign powers,
the ideas surrounding the covenant with David necessarily
underwent important transformation. Inevitably also attention came to be increasingly focused on the figure of Moses
as the unique mediator of Yahweh's order of life for his
covenant people. The Mosaic Law, now greatly enlarged
over what it had contained even in the Deuteronomic law-
code, became the entire basis of the community's existence.
To this degree, therefore, the Exodus and Sinai events constituted again the primary realm of the saving acts of Yahweh. David's role, by contrast, as seen in the Chronicler's
history, was largely reduced to that of "a second Moses"
whose function was one of implementing the prescriptions
for Israel's worship which the original Moses was thought
to have promulgated (so II Chron. 23:18).[39]

Theologically speaking, however, the influence of the
Davidic covenant and of the royal theology suffered no important decline in at least two dimensions, those of the crea-

[39] See G. von Rad, *Old Testament Theology*, 1:351.

tion doctrine and of kingship. While it may be true that the faith surrounding the Sinai covenant included some form of creation doctrine from the start,[40] the texts associated with the amphictyony, for example, do not allow us to recognize it as a fundamental element of Israel's earliest faith. How different in this respect are Second Isaiah or the P document, where the recognition given to Yahweh as Lord of creation almost equals that accorded him as the Lord of Israel's life and history. The second area, in which the ideas first brought to prominence through the medium of the Davidic covenant maintained a continuing hold, was that connected with the belief in the permanence of the "throne of David." Although one can detect signs of the hope for an ideal future king in preexilic times (as in the prophecies of Isaiah), it was not until after the Exile that the expectation of a coming Messiah became widespread and central to the hope in the "consolation of Israel" (Luke 2:25). Thus both the promise to David that his throne would be "for ever" and the conceptions which in the time of the monarchy had come to be attached to the person of the king now were transferred from the present to the future and provided the foundation upon which Judaism's messianic hope was erected.

This brings us to a final point. The difficulty of incorporating the wisdom literature into the general theology of the Old Testament has always resulted ultimately from the effort to identify the essential character of Israel's faith with her salvation history and election in the context of the Exodus. For the fact remains inescapable that the wisdom writings of the Old Testament show a total unconcern for this facet of Israel's experience. On the other hand, it is also clear that they show a most active interest in such areas as creation and the eternal order of life which the universe embodies. The book of Proverbs, moreover, concerns itself extensively with kings and kingship, the lessons of statecraft, and even such trivialities as court etiquette. The inference is

[40] See J. Priest, "Where Is Wisdom To Be Placed?" *Journal of Biblical Literature*, 31 (1963): 280.

obvious: the theological home of this literature is the complex of ideas and manner of life which we have come to associate broadly with the covenant of David. If one is justified in viewing the total picture of Israel's faith as the history of two covenants which, though potentially separate and distinct, came to be seen as necessary complements to one another, then the wisdom literature ceases to be the grave problem it has been for Old Testament theology.[41]

The conclusions toward which we have been moving might now be summarized in the following triadic sequence. First, the Davidic covenant has a theological importance commensurate with that of the Sinaitic covenant. Furthermore, by keeping in mind that the faith of the Old Testament is the result of the conjunction of these two covenants, we may find here the center from which that faith derives its essential unity. Finally, it permits us to recover, in the study of Old Testament theology, a sense for the basic wholeness of belief which Israel achieved, particularly in the postexilic period, and of which her sacred scriptures are our most impressive monument.

[41] From the standpoint of the wisdom literature and its relationship to Israel's faith, it is important to keep in mind that during the intertestamental period Law and Wisdom became virtually identical (see Ecclus. 24:1–29).

# 2

## Narrative Structure and Cult Legend: A Study of Joshua 1–6

### JAY A. WILCOXEN

There exists in recent Old Testament scholarship a difference in judgment about the degree to which the narrative literature of the Old Testament was shaped and produced within the cultus in ancient Israel. The difference exists within a framework of agreement. On one hand, there is general agreement that many smaller units of Old Testament literature must have received their original forms in cultic contexts and for the sake of cultic functions.[1] On the other hand, the large narrative works now found in the Old Testament are agreed to be the result of literary activity, of men arranging and depositing in writing older traditional materials adapted or edited to form such comprehensive works as the "Tetrateuch," the "Deuteronomic History," or the Chronicler's work.[2] The area of disagreement concerns

This paper is based upon the third chapter of the writer's unpublished Ph.D. dissertation, "The Israelite Passover: Its Context and Function in the Later Old Testament Period" (Divinity School, University of Chicago, 1967).

[1] Aage Bentzen, *Introduction to the Old Testament*, 3d ed. (Copenhagen: G. E. C. Gad, 1957) 1:141–44, 232–43; Otto Eissfeldt, *The Old Testament: An Introduction*, trans. P. R. Ackroyd (New York: Harper and Row, 1965), pp. 17–18, 31–32, 42–47, 70–76; E. Sellin, *Einleitung in das Alte Testament*, 10th ed. fully revised by Georg Fohrer (Heidelberg: Quelle & Meyer, 1965), pp. 83–104. The study of the life settings of the small narrative units was given its impetus by Hermann Gunkel's introduction to his Genesis commentary, *Genesis*, 2d ed., Handkommentar zum Alten Testament (Göttingen: Vandenhoeck und Ruprecht, 1902).

[2] On recent criticism of the Pentateuch (or Hexateuch or Tetrateuch), C. R. North, "Pentateuchal Criticism," in *The Old Testament and Mod-*

the intermediate stages of literary composition and the intermediate-sized narrative units. These intermediate-sized units are narrative complexes that themselves consist of smaller narrative episodes, but that also form relatively self-contained and complete developments of separate narrative topics.

The narrative of the exodus, in Exod. 1–15:21,[3] is an example of such a narrative complex, and the different views of its formation held on one hand by Johannes Pedersen[4] and on the other hand by Martin Noth[5] illustrate the difference in judgment about the relation of the literature to the cultus. Pedersen understands the exodus narrative to have been "the Paschal legend," a narrative recitation that served at all detectable stages of its history (except the very last) to interpret and dramatize the Passover observance for those taking part in it.[6] The total narrative thus has the parts and structure that it has because these were the actions and

---

*ern Study*, ed. H. H. Rowley (Oxford: At the Clarendon Press, 1951), pp. 48–83; John Bright, "Modern Study of Old Testament Literature," in *The Bible and the Ancient Near East*, Albright Festschrift, ed. G. Ernest Wright (Garden City, N.Y.: Doubleday, 1961), pp. 14–25; Sellin-Fohrer, *Einleitung*, pp. 115–31; Sigmund Mowinckel, *Tetrateuch-Pentateuch-Hexateuch*, BZAW, no. 90; (Berlin: Töpelmann, 1964). On the other historical works, Martin Noth, *Ueberlieferungsgeschichtliche Studien*, 2d unchanged ed. (Tübingen: Niemeyer Verlag, 1957); Eissfeldt, *Old Testament*, pp. 241–48.

[3] This is the extent usually assigned to the exodus narrative, by the scholars, for example, to be discussed here. Good reasons can be given, however, for confining the exodus narrative proper to Exod. 1–13:16. The question cannot be discussed here, but cf. Ulrich Mauser, *Christ in the Wilderness*, Studies in Biblical Theology no. 39 (Naperville, Ill.: Allenson, 1963), p. 21.

[4] "Passahfest und Passahlegende," ZAW, 52 (1934): 161–75; and *Israel: Its Life and Culture*, III–IV (London: Oxford University Press, 1940), 384–415, 728–37.

[5] *Ueberlieferungsgeschichte des Pentateuch* (Stuttgart: Kohlhammer, 1948), pp. 50–54, 70–77; *Das zweite Buch Mose, Exodus*, Das Alte Testament Deutsch, no. 5 (Göttingen: Vandenhoeck und Ruprecht, 1959), pp. 4–100.

[6] Pedersen recognizes that written forms of the legend materials may have existed in relatively early times but that these did not determine the development of the culticly oriented complexes of legends and laws, *Israel*, III–IV: 727.

motifs actually present in the cultic celebration of the exodus at the time of the Passover observance. The narrative was filled in and amplified continuously over a long period of time, but these changes reflected and were the result of shifts in the way the primeval exodus events were represented at the Passover observances. What episodes were included and what was the dramatic structure of the whole story were determined by the character of the cultic observance and not simply by writers or redactors working with views and purposes quite independent of the cultus.

Martin Noth, who knew Pedersen's view when he made his own study of the tradition history of the exodus narrative, grants that Pedersen's argument is cogent in the case of one part of the exodus narrative: the story of the plagues, Noth thinks, probably did develop as a cult legend for the Passover observance, the last in the series of plagues serving always as the occasion for the Passover ritual.[7] In other respects, however, Noth follows the more customary analysis of the exodus narrative into older documents, the Yahwist, the Elohist, and the Priestly document. The total narrative resulted only from the combination, editing, and supplementing of these documents, and the later stages of this process of formation went on apart from possible cultic functions of the materials. The narrative structure now presented in Exodus 1–15, therefore, was never the structure or plot of a cultic recitation for the Passover observance in Israelite times.[8]

[7] *Ueberlieferungsgeschichte des Pentateuch*, pp. 71–72.

[8] S. Mowinckel sought to separate the question of documentary analysis of the exodus narrative from the question of the cultic function of different versions of the narrative. He thus identified two documents with different conceptions and portrayals of the exodus events but recognized that the story itself was a festival myth, "Die vermeintliche 'Passahlegende' Ex. 1–15 in Bezug auf die Frage: Literarkritik und Traditionskritik," *Studia Theologica*, 5 (1952): 66–88. The issue that seems to remain between Mowinckel and Pedersen is whether the combination of the major narrative strands was the result of the continued development of the Passover legend of the Jerusalem Temple or of literary activity apart from the cultus proper. More recently, Georg Fohrer has given a more straightforward literary-critical analysis of the exodus narrative, emphasizing the historical elements behind the primary units of tradition and greatly reducing the role of the cultus in

To focus the point of the present discussion more precisely, it is the effect of the cultus upon the dramatic *structure* of larger narrative complexes to which attention is directed. Pedersen sees such larger narrative complexes as *legenda*, the spoken parts of cultic observances. The whole story constituting such a legend, and the place within it of each episode, reflects the structure of the observance itself. The sequence of moods — gloom and despair, anxiety and suspense, release and joy — and the sequence of significant persons and actions — the evil Pharaoh, the Israelite deliverer, the false start (Exod. 5), the crescendoing tests of strength (plagues), the climactic divine blow — these must have corresponded to the sequence of moods and real or symbolic actions in the cultic celebration. In Noth's understanding, on the other hand, some individual episodes are recognized to have had cultic origins, but the structure of the final exodus narrative is only the result of the latest stage in the editing of the older documents. That structure is significantly different from the simpler structures of action in the older documents and is due in no respect to the function of the literature in the cultus.

This paper is a study of another narrative complex, the interpretation of which can be significantly affected by one's judgment about the relation between the dramatic structures of such narrative complexes and the structures of action of major cultic observances. The complex in question is that contained in Joshua 1–6, a section dealt with in detail by Noth in his commentary on Joshua.[9] What is offered here is an interpretation of the passage from the perspective of Pedersen's judgment about the relation of Israelite literature and cultus. Considerations are presented to support the view that the structure of action in the total narrative originally derived from and had its rationale in a major cultic observance at and in the vicinity of the old Israelite sanctuary of

shaping the content and structure of the final narrative, *Ueberlieferung und Geschichte des Exodus*, BZAW, no. 91 (Berlin: Töpelmann, 1964).

[9] Noth, *Das Buch Josua*, 2d ed., Handbuch zum Alten Testament (Tübingen: J. C. B. Mohr, 1953).

Gilgal.[10] Within the total narrative, particular attention is given to the place of the Passover observance (5:10–12), for the Passover marks a transition point between two major parts of the total narrative, that concerned with the crossing of the Jordan River and that concerned with the capture of Jericho. Both these parts of the total narrative have been recognized by some scholars to be in part cult legends and to reflect traditional ceremonial observances. The possibility exists, therefore, that these two major events of the narrative, and the episode of the Passover observance that now links them, were not first associated with each other by writers putting together previously independent traditions, but rather that the relationships between them now presented by the total narrative structure were themselves part of the cultic traditions of the old Israelite sanctuary of Gilgal.

## The Narrative of Joshua 1–6

The first six chapters of Joshua present a continuous and interconnected narrative, the action of which is complete and self-contained. It is a narrative that extends from the assumption of leadership in Israel by Joshua following Moses' death to the capture, destruction, and cursing of the city of Jericho. While the narratives in the following chapters (7–11) are in some respects continuous with the story line of chapters 1–6, the latter chapters show internal connections and an interdependence that they do not share with chapters 7–11. What is anticipated in chapters 1 and 2 — the crossing of the Jordan River, the establishment of Joshua's leadership, and the conquest of Jericho — is not complete until the end of chapter 6, but at that point it is complete. The later chapters form relatively self-contained episodes with little or no internal connection with each other or with chapters 1–6.[11] Further, the time scheme composed

---

[10] On Gilgal, *ibid.*, pp. 25–27; J. Muilenburg, "Gilgal," in *Interpreter's Dictionary of the Bible*, ed. G. A. Buttrick *et al.*, 4 vols. (Nashville: Abingdon, 1962), vol. E-J, pp. 398–99; and C. U. Wolf, "The Location of Gilgal," *Biblical Research* 11 (1966): 42–51.

[11] Joshua's warning about the *ḥerem* in 6:18 no doubt anticipates the

by the time references within chapters 1–6 (see the next section) is not continued into chapters 7–11. Finally, while Gilgal is occasionally mentioned after chapter 6,[12] the scene of the action moves to other places in chapters 7–11.

While there is a single, self-contained story line in Joshua 1–6, it is not a very neat and straightforward one. It is crowded with digressions, parenthetical comments, repetitions, and expansive variations on details of the action. This gives the narrative a cumbersome and awkward appearance, and literary historians and exegetes have commonly assumed that there must have been one or more earlier forms of the whole narrative or several of its episodes that were simpler, more coherent, and less cluttered by such digressions and apparent inconsistencies.[13]

This cluttered appearance that the total narrative has in a number of places is well illustrated by the narrative of the circumambulations of the city of Jericho in chapter 6. A disproportionately large part of this narrative is taken up with detailed instructions for and descriptions of the order of march, the blowing of horns during or at the end of the seven-day period of circumambulations, and the sounding of the war whoop ($t^e r\bar{u}\acute{a}$). Not only are these matters treated repeatedly and in detail, but what is said about the horns and war whoop in one place sometimes contradicts

---

story of Achan in chap. 7. It is noteworthy, however, that chap. 7 never mentions where the *ḥerem* Achan took came from; all that story requires is that he have taken some *ḥerem*. The connection with Jericho is external to the story itself.

[12] In 9:6; 10:6, 7, 9; cf. 14:6.

[13] J. Wellhausen, *Die Composition des Hexateuchs und der historischen Bücher des Alten Testaments*, 2d printing (Berlin: Reimer, 1889), pp. 119–25; C. Steuernagel, *Deuteronomium und Josua*, Handkommentar zum Alten Testament (Göttingen: Vandenhoeck und Ruprecht, 1900), pp. 170–72; Hugo Gressmann, *Die Anfänge Israels*, 2d ed., Die Schriften des Alten Testaments (Göttingen: Vandenhoeck und Ruprecht, 1922), pp. 234–44; G. A. Cooke, *The Book of Joshua*, The Cambridge Bible for Schools and Colleges (Cambridge: At the University Press, 1918), pp. xiv–xix, 1–52; and more recently, Jan Dus, "Die Analyse zweier Ladeerzählungen des Josuabuches (Jos 3–4 und 6)," *ZAW*, 72 (1960): 107–34; and E. Vogt, "Die Erzählung vom Jordanübergang, Josue 3–4," *Biblica*, 46 (1965): 125–48.

what is said in another place. These repetitions and contradictions indicate, in fact, that there are three different presentations in the narrative of the auditory parts of the circumambulation of Jericho. In one presentation, seven priests carry horns that they are to blow only at the end of the seventh day (6:4–5, 16a, 20b); in another, Joshua gives a vocal command for the people to raise the war whoop, also at the end of the seven days (6:10, 16b); and in a third presentation, the rear guard (*m<sup>e'</sup>assēp*, vss. 9, 13), as well as the priests, carry horns, and these horns are blown continuously during all the circumambulations of the seven days (6:8–9, 13).

When this chapter has been interpreted by means of documentary analysis, two documents and extensive redactional additions have been identified on the basis of the variations here described. This was the result reached in the analysis of the chapter by Julius Wellhausen and followed by others since.[14] Wellhausen took verse 20 as a starting point for dividing the chapter into two originally independent narrative strata. Each of these strata was conceived as having presented a coherent and simple version of the story. But it then becomes apparent that when these originally independent strata were edited together and further redacted to form the present chapter, some portions of the original strata were omitted, for the chapter does not contain two or more versions of all parts of the story. It is, as a matter of fact, only those parts of the story that deal with the war whoop, the horn blowing, and the processions in which repetitions and inconsistencies are found. The great and colossal event that is the climax of the story, the fall of the walls of Jericho, is reported in one very brief and unadorned statement (vs. 20b). Thus, on the assumptions employed in this kind of documentary analysis, the editors who put together the final version of the story must have preserved from their sources several versions of the processions, horns, and war whoop,

---

[14] Wellhausen, *Die Composition*, pp. 123–25, followed by Gressmann and Dus.

while they eliminated all but one version, and that a very brief one, of the main event of the narrative![15]

The Jericho story has also been interpreted from a "supplementary" or "fragment" view of its literary history, particularly by Martin Noth.[16] It is Noth's judgment that there never was more than one independent version of the story, but that version was greatly elaborated at different times by the additions of such elements as the ark, the horns blown by the priests, and connecting links with other stories in the early chapters of Joshua.[17] This view of the literary history of Joshua 6 overcomes one problem raised by the documentary analysis, why there should be only one conclusion to the story but several versions of the circumambulations. Later writers simply had nothing to add about the fall of the city. Noth's understanding of this process of supplementation and expansion of the single original narrative, however, is that it was a purely literary process. Writers added things to the story to make it fit into their own conceptions of the events or to be compatible with other parts of a larger literary work into which the Jericho story was to be incorporated. This supplementary view of the formation of the present narrative, when conceived as a purely literary process, gets no further than the documentary view toward explaining why certain parts of the narrative have been greatly elaborated and complicated and others left perfectly blunt and simple.

Both the documentary and supplementary analyses of the

[15] It could be assumed that three different versions of the story had identical statements of the fall of the wall but differed in the details of the circumambulations. Editors then would have given the common version of the fall only once but all versions of the circumambulations. This still leaves unanswered the question why there should be such interest in and various elaboration of the details of the circumambulations and no such interest in and elaboration of the fall of the wall — unless there were continuing cultic reasons for this disproportionate interest in the details.

[16] Eissfeldt, *Old Testament*, pp. 143–44, describes Noth's view under the heading "fragment hypothesis." Noth's treatment of Joshua 6 alone, however, assumes a supplementary process of formation.

[17] Noth, *Josua*, p. 41.

Jericho story begin with the very sound observation that the materials contained in the narrative are heterogeneous, that they cannot very well have all been composed originally to go together to form the present story. Both analyses assume however, that this heterogeneous character of the materials can only be explained as the result of literary editing and supplementing. They do not give sufficient consideration to the motivations that would have led men to either greatly complicate and disfigure originally smooth and consistent narratives of Jericho or to supplement such an original narrative in so inept a manner as to produce the present cumbersome account. That is, they do not ask what would have been the life setting in which the particular complicating and elaborating of which the story now gives evidence would have been a sensible and serious procedure.

There are stories in the Old Testament, and in the book of Joshua, that make it clear that ancient Israelite narrators could tell a reasonably smooth and self-consistent story (e.g., II Sam. 9–20; Judg. 16:4–31; and Josh. 9). There are other stories, however, which show the kind of repetitiousness and inconsistency observed in the Jericho narrative, and which, therefore, give very strong evidence of having received their present forms through the combining of heterogeneous narrative materials. Many prominent examples of this latter group of stories narrate spectacular and miraculous events, often including divine appearances or actions; for example, the flood story in Genesis (chaps. 6–9), the narrative of the plagues in Egypt and the escape at the Reed Sea (Exod. 7–11, 14), the narrative of Yahweh's theophany and covenant at Sinai (Exod. 19–20, 24), the narratives of rebellions in the wilderness (Num. 13–14, 16), and here in Joshua the narratives of the crossing of the Jordan River and the capture of Jericho (Josh. 3–4, 6). The final narratives of these topics are apparently the result of a different process of formation than are other narratives that do not show the same unevenness and diversity of materials. Instead of retelling the old story in a single self-consistent narrative, these topics are treated by preserving and arranging older elements and units of narrative that pertained to them. Thus the present narratives are composed of heterogeneous traditional materials that do, indeed, form a distinct general narrative structure or plot, but only at the cost of some repetition and inconsistency.

The heterogeneous character of the materials composing this kind of narrative poses two questions that bear on their interpretation: In what life setting would the traditional narrative materials have been preserved and gradually combined to form the final narrative? and, What is most likely to have been the origin of the basic plot, the story line, of such a narrative? The example of the narrative of the circumambulations of Jericho provides an important basis for an answer to the question about the life setting in which such narratives reached their final form. This in turn will suggest an answer to the question about the origin of the basic plot of such narratives.

As was already noted, the narrative of Joshua 6 dwells at length upon matters of the order of the procession, the enumeration of groups and times, and the auditory and ceremonial details of the circumambulations, while the falling of the wall of Jericho is given in one cursory statement. It is in these matters of the groups, the processions, and the sounding of the horns and war whoop that the variations and repetitious elaborations are found. Why should it be such matters as these that were of special concern to the men who shaped the tradition? In what context and for what reason would successive narrators have so greatly complicated these features of the narrative while leaving the climactic event a blunt and unadorned statement?

It is evident that these narrators or writers had their attention firmly fixed upon the circumambulations, and even upon the details of the circumambulations. These circumambulations are very ritualistic and ceremonial actions. It may be inferred from this that the Jericho story had its greatest interest, for those who preserved and ordered its narrative, as a ritual action. While the fall of a great city, especially in the manner that Jericho falls in the story, is not an event that would occur frequently, the same is not necessarily true of the circumambulations upon which the narrative bestows so much attention. These circumambulations are actions that could be repeated at regular times as cultic and ceremonial observances. The distribution of attention, and thus of importance, among the several actions in Joshua 6 can be readily understood if it is assumed that the circumambulations described there were ritual actions regularly practiced at different times or by different groups at Jericho. Such ritual circumambulations may have been done somewhat differently at the same sanctuary on different occasions, or at different sanctuaries with similar cultic traditions containing such circumambulation rituals and legends of the fall of a great city. What may be seen, then, in the three conflicting descriptions of the circumambulations in Joshua 6 are three slightly different forms of this circumambulation ritual. The three forms of the ritual now appear to be merged in Joshua 6, though not too happily, since one of them seems to describe the circumambulation as carried out in silence until its final climactic outburst (6:5, 20*b*, cf. vs. 10), while another of them assumes a continuous blare of horns throughout the seven-day circumambulation (6:8–9, 13). The purpose of merging the three forms of the ritual in the story, instead of eliminating two of them, was presumably to retain all three as legitimate alternative forms of the ritual based upon the story of the fall of Jericho. On any single occasion, however, only one of the forms must have been selected.[18]

This explanation of the repetitions and inconsistencies in the Jericho narrative, and also of the fact that these repetitions and inconsistencies are confined to the ceremonial or

---

[19] That the circumambulations of Jericho reflect actual and regular cultic actions has been recognized by Jan Dus. At the end of his analysis of the Jericho narrative he suggests that an annual or semiannual ritual circumambulation of the Jericho mound was made from the Gilgal sanctuary, and that this would probably have gone on during the seven days of one or both of the two seven-day festivals in the year. He seems not, however, to have noted the extent to which this hypothesis removes much of the ground for his strictly literary-historical explanation of the repetitions and inconsistencies in Joshua 6, ZAW, 82:119.

ritual aspects of the narrative, points strongly toward the cultus as the life setting in which the narrative was preserved and given its ultimate or penultimate form. The heterogeneity of the materials of the narrative may be understood as the result of the desire to preserve old and revered cultic practices and traditions within the one cult legend that sanctioned each of those practices. This is to say about the Jericho narrative something like what Sigmund Mowinckel said of the Sinai narrative[19] and Johannes Pedersen of the exodus narrative.[20] These narratives relate not only spectacular events and divine actions, but detailed instructions for what different persons and groups are to do by way of cultic actions in connection with those events; for example, the Passover observance in connection with the exodus (Exod. 11–12:42), cultic purifications, the fixing of sacred precincts, and sacrificial actions at Sinai (Exod. 19:10–13; 24:3–8), and the circumambulation rituals at Jericho. It was in the cultic traditions of important sanctuaries that special interest would be maintained in the cultic actions that complemented and had their rationales in major cult legends of the sanctuaries. It would also be in the cultic traditions of such sanctuaries that the uneven and somewhat

[19] Mowinckel's conclusion about the Sinai narrative: "ce que J et E rapportent comme récit des événements du Sinai n'est autre chose que la description d'une fête cultuelle célébrée à une époque plus récente, plus précisément dans le temple de Jérusalem, description présentée dans une forme historique et mythologique et adaptée au cadre historique et mythologique des récits de l'Exode," *Le décalogue* (Paris: Felix Alcan, 1927), p. 120. Thorir Thordarson has analyzed the cult legend structure of the Sinai pericope in Exodus 19–24 without making use of the documentary analysis as Mowinckel does, "The Form-Historical Problem of Ex. 34:6–7" (Ph.D. diss., Divinity School, University of Chicago), pp. 30–64.

[20] Pedersen, *Israel*, III–IV:393–412; "A firm and compact plan holds together the legend, in spite of irregularities in the details," p. 402; "As mentioned above, there are features of the legend which show that the great events were reexperienced at the festival through mimetic acts. It is not possible to estimate the extent of these. But we have seen that the entire legend forms a unity, the coherence of which is due to the ritual purpose. It contains the events which were given renewed life in the cult, and thus were identical with what was created in primeval time and was revived by the cult," p. 411.

confusing forms of the present narratives could be understood and appropriately interpreted with reference to the
cultic actions to which the various elements of the narrative
pertained. Unlike simple and straightforward narratives,
these cult legends are not immediately clear and intelligible
on a first reading; they presuppose a setting in which explanation by knowledgeable men was readily available and
was transmitted orally from generation to generation.

The Jericho narrative, however, is not the only part of the
total narrative in Joshua 1–6 in which such heterogeneous
narrative elements point toward a cultic life setting for the
background and formation of the story. The narrative of the
crossing of the Jordan River (chaps. 3–4) shows the same
prolonged interest in precisely the liturgical aspects of the
action; for example, the order of march and distance from
the ark (3:2–4), the detailed and repetitious attention to the
twelve stones from the river and the twelve men chosen to
carry them (3:12; 4:1–8, 20–24), the attention to the precise
standing place of the priests' feet in the river bed and the
timing of the action according to the moment the priests'
feet touched the water or the dry land (3:13, 15; 4:3, 9,
18).[21] Similarly, the speeches of Joshua's inauguration at
the beginning of the story (1:1–9, 12–18), while they probably have been reworked somewhat by the deuteronomic

[21] H.-J. Kraus has developed the view that the narrative of the crossing of the Jordan in Joshua 3–4 is a festival legend for an observance
commemorating the passing through the waters of the Reed Sea after
the exodus (cf. Josh. 3:14–17; 4:23) as well as the entry into the land,
"Gilgal, ein Beitrag zur Kultusgeschichte Israels," *VT*, 1 (1951): 181–
99; "Zur Geschichte des Passah-Massot-Festes im Alten Testament,"
*Evangelische Theologie*, 18 (1958): 47–67, esp. pp. 54–58; and *Worship in Israel*, trans. Geoffrey Buswell (Richmond, Virginia: John Knox
Press, 1966), pp. 152–65. This interpretation of Joshua 3–4 is followed
by G. Henton Davies in "Ark of the Covenant," in *IDB*, vol. A–D,
p. 223; Hans Wildberger, *Jahwes Eigentumsvolk*, Abhandlungen zur
Theologie des Alten und Neuen Testaments, no. 37 (Zürich: Zwingli
Verlag, 1960), pp. 59–62; and, with slight but important variations,
Vogt, *Biblica*, 46:125–48. See now also F. M. Cross, Jr., "The Divine
Warrior in Israel's Early Cult," in *Biblical Motifs*, ed. A. Altmann,
Studies and Texts, no. 3 (Cambridge, Mass.: Harvard Univ. Press,
1966), pp. 26–27, who sees a "ritual Conquest" in Josh. 3–5.

historian, may reflect ceremonial backgrounds;[22] and, in the story of the spies and Rahab in Joshua 2, Noth has pointed out that the three dialogue scenes in the story make up most of the narrative,[23] thus giving it a rather theatrical or dramatic character. Such features of the narrative units within Joshua 1–6 suggest that these materials presuppose various liturgical and ritual actions, that actions and speeches like those presented in the text were actually done and spoken at appropriate moments in a complex Israelite observance at Gilgal. E. Vogt has pointed out that cultic actions symbolically representing the crossing of the Jordan River could have been carried out somewhere other than in that river itself.[24] Also, it may be noted that, quantitatively, a very large percentage of the text of Joshua 1–6 consists of speeches, speeches that could have been spoken in cultic celebrations and symbolic reenactments of the great events of the total narrative. The total narrative, then, would provide both the sanction and the rationale for observance by Israelites of the ceremonies and rituals reflected in the narrative materials.

But if the several parts of the total narrative in Joshua 1–6 had their origin and background in the cultic traditions of the sanctuary at Gilgal, it may be asked whether the origin of the basic story line according to which these parts are now organized would have differed from the origin of the parts. The plot of the story may have derived from and had its life setting in cultic traditions and observances just as much as the individual elements of the narrative. In this case, of course, the total plot of the story would have provided the sanction and rationale, not simply for single cultic actions, but for the traditional structure of a whole series of

[22] E. Nielsen, "Some Reflections on the History of the Ark," *VT Suppl.* 7 (1960): 71, maintains, following Ivan Engnell, that Joshua 1:5–9 bears the marks of an enthronement liturgical tradition in which the king was presented with a written document that set forth the righteousness that he was to maintain. He finds traces of the same tradition in Ps. 1, the law for the king in Deuteronomy, and passages in Chronicles.

[23] Noth, *Josua*, p. 29.

[24] Vogt, *Biblica*, 46:141–43.

cultic actions that together composed a complex cultic observance such as a festival of several days' duration. The narrative line of the legend would have served to relate different specific cultic actions to each other in their proper sequence and durations. Time relationships within the narrative would in this case be significant not only for the telling of the story but for the time relationships between different cultic actions within a total cultic observance or festival. Pedersen observed that, in the exodus narrative, the plot of the total story is prior to many of the elements now contained within that plot, such as the activity of the figure of Aaron alongside the figure of Moses or the number and exact manner of execution of the different plagues worked in Egypt.[25] This view of the priority and cultic background of the basic plot of the story, applied to Joshua 1–6, would mean, for example, that the explanation of the meaning of the twelve stones at Gilgal (4:20–24) or the tradition and practice of a group circumcision at "the Hill of the Foreskins" (5:2–3) presupposes a whole sequence of actions within which they always had a particular place. That is, the word about the twelve stones and the cultic action at the place of circumcision were always parts of a larger frame of reference that included the river crossing and the capture of the city.

This view of the cultic origin and background of the total narrative plot as well as the individual narrative units is in contrast to the view of the formation of Joshua 1–6 held by Albrecht Alt and Martin Noth. They regard the earliest form of the total narrative as the outcome of a literary stringing together of several originally unconnected traditions and etiologies from the locale of Gilgal and Jericho.[26] In Noth's

[25] Pedersen, *Israel*, III–IV:731–36.
[26] See A. Alt, "Josua," *Kleine Schriften zur Geschichte des Volkes Israel* (München: Beck, 1953) 1:176–92; and following him, K. Möhlenbrink, "Die Landnahmesagen des Buches Josua," *ZAW*, N. F. 15 (1938): 238–68. Noth describes the situation in the preliterary stage of the traditions as follows: "Anfangs waren diese Stücke je in sich geschlossene Ueberlieferungen ohne Zusammenhang untereinander, nur durch ihr Haften an Orten derselben Gegend und wohl schon durch ihre Bezugnahme auf Ereignisse aus der Landnahmezeit mitein-

view, the "Collector" who put together the original narrative of Joshua 2–11 was the first to provide a framework in which each of the specific units of tradition had a rationale. What is here called into question is, not that there was such a Collector, but that the framework of the narrative was purely the result of his compiling and editing activity; that the origin of the basic story line was purely literary. The evident cultic and ceremonial interest of the materials of the narrative and the total cultic structure and time scheme that they compose (see the next section) suggest that such a Collector already had the festival legend of Gilgal (the plot of Joshua 1–6) at his disposal, and that he used it without destroying its coherence. Each of the individual units of tradition had already been formulated as a part of this legend and its cultic schematism.[27] It may be that this Collector was responsible for the all-Israelite orientation that the total narrative now presents, rather than a more local orientation to Gilgal or the tribe of Benjamin, but it is not apparent either that the individual cultic traditions existed apart from a larger traditional cultic context prior to the Collector's work or that the Collector would have paid no attention to the narrative structure of the Gilgal cult legends in which many of these individual traditions had their previous rationales.[28]

---

ander verwandt," *Josua*, p. 21. In addition to the critique of this view by Kraus, cited below, John Bright has strongly criticized the excessive reliance upon etiological interpretation of the narrative units in Alt's and Noth's work, *Early Israel in Recent History Writing* (London: SCM Press, 1955).

[27] At different points in a complex cultic observance, certain men would have known the appropriate things to say. What was said at each moment would tend to become stylized and fixed in its basic features, and this fixed speech would be transmitted from generation to generation. Much of Joshua 1–6 consists of such stylized speeches.

[28] Kraus, who in many respects follows the methods of Alt and Noth, differs sharply from Noth's view that the overall structure of the legend in Joshua 3–5 is secondary and artificial as compared to the individual etiological elements: "Es ist m. E. methodisch nicht richtig, von den vielen ätiologischen Einzelelementen in Jos. 3–5 auszugehen, um dann nachträglich die Frage nach der Bedeutung des Lade-Durchzuges

The view here taken, in contrast to Alt and Noth, that the basic narrative is presupposed by the individual episodes or topics, does not assume that each component presupposed the present form of the total narrative in Joshua 1–6. The heterogeneity of the narrative materials points to their formation somewhat independently of each other, but not necessarily independently of the one basic story line according to which they are now organized. That story line consists of an essential sequence of actions that is presupposed throughout as the significant frame of reference for each item. That sequence of actions, the basic plot of the total narrative, may be identified as follows: (1) the inauguration of the leader at Shittim, chapter 1; (2) the spying out of Jericho and agreement with Rahab, chapter 2; (3) the miraculous crossing of the Jordan by means of the ark, an event that established the leader's authority (cf. 3:7 and 4:14), and the setting up of twelve stones in Gilgal, chapters 3–4; (4) the circumcision and the Passover at Gilgal, 5:1–12; (5) the leader's meeting with the heavenly general, 5:13–15, in preparation for (6) the capture of Jericho by means of the circumambulations of the ark and army for seven days, chapter 6. The point emphasized here, over against the interpretation that stresses unduly the original independence of the individual traditions, is that *the basic narrative framework may itself be as primary a datum for tradition and cultic history as the individual items and units that have been employed in elaborating that framework.*

If the total narrative plot had its rationale in a complex cultic observance, some aspects of the total narrative may be significant in quite different ways than they would be in a work produced simply by writers and editors. Episodes

durch den Jordan aufzuwerfen. In einem Heiligtum dominieren in der Orts-tradition immer die kultischen Vorgänge, all anderen Lokalüberlieferungen haften sich die gottesdienstlichen Bräuche an. So kann in Jos. 3–5 doch kein Zweifel bestehen, dass die Lade-Prozession das herausragende Hauptelement ist. *Geht man jedoch von den ätiologischen Einzelelementen aus, dann zerfällt sogleich das Ganze in eine unmotivierte Anhäufung von Ortstraditionen." Evangelische Theologie,* 18 (1958): 55–56, n. 17. Emphasis has been added.

may be related in ways that would be cumbersome and confusing in a straightforward literary production but that become quite clear when it is seen that they reflect cultic realities and schematisms. This is particularly true of temporal relationships between episodes, and in the case of Joshua 1–6 it becomes evident that there is an overall time sequence presented that is almost certainly schematic, that is, significant for cultic and traditional reasons rather than for realistic historical ones. The point is of sufficient importance to be developed in its own right.

### The Time Scheme of Joshua 1–6

Time indications, either dates or durations, are given at several points in the narrative of Joshua 1–6. In a straightforward narrative of ordinary events such time indications would serve the purpose of clarifying the passage of time during or between incidents. As was indicated in the preceding section, however, Joshua 1–6 does not narrate ordinary events in a straightforward manner, and some of the time references in the narrative do not readily clarify the chronology of the action. This is probably due to the fact that these time references have their real significance, not in the chronology of narrated events, but in the temporal sequences and durations of a complex cultic observance the pattern of which is contained in the cult legend.

The central event in the first five chapters of Joshua is the crossing of the Jordan River in 3:14–4:19. Most of the other actions of these chapters (at least as far as 5:12) are parts of the preparation for or sequel to this crossing. (Chapter 2 is an exception to the extent that it is a preparation for the fall of Jericho rather than the crossing of the river.)

The whole series of events constituted by the crossing, its preparation, and its sequels occupies a seven-day period. The crossing comes at the end of a three-day period of preparation (1:10–11; 3:1–4). On the first of those three days, the Israelites are camped at Shittim east of the Jordan when Joshua announces that within three days they will cross the river. On the next day (3:1) they journey to the river and on the following day cross it. At the conclusion of the narrative of the crossing, an exact date for the event is given: the tenth day of the first month (4:19).[29] Then, after Joshua had erected the twelve stones that had been brought from the Jordan (4:20–24) and after he had circumcised all the Israelites born during the forty years of the wilderness period (5:2–9), events that are connected with the founding and the naming of Gilgal, the Israelites observed the Passover on the fourteenth day of the first month (5:10–12), that is, four days after the crossing. Thus, from the beginning of the preparation for the river crossing to the observance of the Passover after the establishment of the sanctuary of Gilgal seven days passed and, since the crossing was on the tenth of the month and the Passover on the fourteenth, the whole period extended from the eighth through the fourteenth days of the first month.

The capture of Jericho (chap. 6) also occupies a period of seven days, though in this case the main action extends over the whole period and does not fall at a certain point within it. As with the crossing of the river, there are events that prepare for the capture of the city. The story of the two spies who visited Jericho and were hidden by the harlot Rahab (chap. 2) is such a preparation. That story has its conclusion, the saving of Rahab's household, at the end of the Jericho story proper (6:22–23). While most of the action of the story in chapter 2 takes place during a single day and the evening following it, there is a three-day period also involved. When the spies, with Rahab's help, escape from Jericho, they hide for three days in the hills before returning to report to Joshua (2:16, 22–23). In the total narrative, this three-day period of the spy story can, and apparently should, be understood as identical with the three-day period of preparation for the

[29] The two exact dates in the total passage are usually regarded by commentators as late additions, e.g., Noth, *Josua*, p. 39. The schematic time relationships of the total narrative do not depend simply on these two dates, however. The dates render the total time scheme specific in terms of a certain calendar and place the total time period in the spring.

river crossing.[30] Thus Joshua and the sons of Israel are at Shittim when Joshua announces that in three days they will cross the river (1:10–11; 3:1). On the next day they leave Shittim for the river crossing. The spies, however, are sent out from Shittim (2:1), and, in the sequence of the present narrative, after the announcement of the crossing in three days has been made (2:1 following 1:10–11). The whole series of actions then is as follows: On the eighth day, Joshua announces the crossing of the river in three days and sends out the spies, who meet Rahab, escape, and hide in the hills. On the ninth day, Joshua and the Israelites go to the Jordan while the spies are hiding in the hills. On the tenth day, the spies return and the river crossing is made. The three day period in both the crossing preparation and the spy story is reckoned inclusively, so that "three days" actually means "part of today, tomorrow, and part of the next day."[31]

Other events that are preparatory to and sequels of the Jericho conquest do not contain time references, but they may be understood as falling within the seven-day period of the conquest itself. The first of these is the appearance of "the Commander of the army of Yahweh" to Joshua (5:13–15). In the present narrative sequence, it is apparent that this warlike heavenly figure with his drawn sword is sent to Joshua to convey to him the message that Jericho is in his power and to give him instructions for its miraculous capture (6:1–5).[32] No passage of days is suggested between this ap-

---

[30] So Cooke *The Book of Joshua*, p. 18. This understanding of the duration of the spy story is possible only on a morning-to-morning reckoning of the day, so that the nocturnal action of the story still belonged to the first of the three days. A detailed study of the time relationships in chaps. 1–3 and 5:10–12, which could not be included here, indicates a consistent morning-to-morning reckoning of the day in the Hebrew text of these chapters.

[31] Cf. Edwin R. Thiele, *The Mysterious Numbers of the Hebrew Kings*, 2d ed. (Grand Rapids, Michigan: Eerdmans, 1965), p. 28 and n. 12 there. Clear examples of such inclusive reckoning of three-unit periods, days or years, are: Gen. 40:13, 19, 20; 42:17, 18; Exod. 19:10, 11, 14, 15; and II Kings 18:9–10.

[32] There are other cases of a "messenger" or "man" who appears and speaks in the person of Yahweh, e.g., Gen. 18:1–14; 22:11–12; Exod. 3:2–5; Judg. 6:11–24; cf. G. W. Ahlström, *Aspects of Syncretism in*

pearance and the beginning of the circumambulations of Jericho, so that this appearance may be understood as occurring on, or during the night preceding, the first of the seven days of the Jericho conquest.

After the city has fallen and its plunder has been disposed of, including the rescue of Rahab and her family by the two spies (6:20–25), Joshua pronounces a curse upon any man who might rebuild Jericho (6:26).[33] There is no indication here of a passage of time beyond the seven-day period of the conquest, and thus all the events concerning the conquest are presented as parts of a single seven-day period.

The whole narrative of Joshua 1–6, then, covers two seven-day periods, one at whose center is the crossing of the Jordan, and one occupied by the circumambulations of Jericho. Unlike the first period, the second one contains no exact dates and no references that make explicit how it is related to the first period. When the observance of the Passover on the fourteenth day of the month has been narrated, the appearance of the Commander of Yahweh's army immediately follows and the seven-day Jericho period begins. It seems, therefore, that, from the point of view of the final narrative, the two seven-day periods are understood to be continuous, the second following immediately upon the first.

There is another consideration that strongly suggests that the two seven-day periods were indeed thought of as continuous with each other. If the two periods were continuous, the Jericho period, with its carefully prescribed ritual circumambulations, would have exactly corresponded to the seven days of the spring Festival of Unleavened Bread. In the prescriptive materials of the P Work (Exod. 12:3–20; Lev. 23:5–8; Num. 28:16–25), in the festival legislation of Deuteronomy (16:1–8), in the Passover prescription in Ezekiel (45:21–25), and in other narratives of the observance of the Passover (II Chron. 30:15, 21; 35:1, 17; Ezra 6:19, 22), the

---

*Israelite Religion,* Horae Soederblomianae no. 5 (Lund: C. W. K. Gleerup, 1963), pp. 17–18.

[33] Cf. Stanley Gevirtz, "Jericho and Shechem: A Religio-Literary Aspect of City Destruction," *VT*, 13 (1963): 52–62.

Festival of Unleavened Bread immediately follows the Passover, the latter coming on the evening of the fourteenth day
of the first month, the Festival of Unleavened Bread on the
fifteenth to the twenty-first of the first month, where the
numbered-days-and-months reckoning is used. In some prescriptions for the festival, special significance is attached to
the first and seventh days (see the P passages listed above).
If the appearance of the Commander of Yahweh's army to
Joshua occurred on the first of the seven days of the siege of
Jericho, that is, on the fifteenth day of the first month, then
that event on the first day and the fall of the city on the
seventh day correspond to the special importance of the first
and seventh days of the Festival of Unleavened Bread. Thus,
the narrative of the circumambulations and fall of Jericho
would be the legend for the Festival of Unleavened Bread as
observed at Gilgal, a festival at which, presumably, ritual
circumambulations of the mound of the old city of Jericho
formed a regular part of the seven-day observance.

What the whole narrative of Joshua 1–6 contains, then, is
a festival legend for traditional ceremonial observances in
and around the sanctuary of Gilgal. The legend covers events
of two seven-day periods, one containing a ritual or symbolic
crossing of the Jordan river by the ark and people and commemorating the entry into the land, and one repeating, during the festival period, the miraculous conquest by the
people and the ark of the great Canaanite city of Jericho, the
mound of which stood not far from Gilgal as a witness of that
ancient and awesome event. The first of the two seven-day
periods prepared for and led up to the festival period; it
reached its conclusion and transition to the second period in
the Passover observance at the sanctuary of Gilgal on the
evening of the fourteenth day of the first month. The Passover, therefore, would appear to have had a particular significance within the whole complex of observances reflected in
this legend of the Gilgal sanctuary. Something of that significance may be discerned by observing the character of the
actions within each of the two periods separated by the Passover.

## Narrative Structure and Cult Legend

### The Passover in the Narrative

The Passover observance in 5:10–12 marks the conclusion of the first of the two seven-day periods contained in the total narrative. Its relation to the other events of this first period may be considered first, and then the relation of the period concluded by the Passover to the following period.

All the principal actions of the first seven-day period are preparations for and initiations into life in the promised land. The Passover is thus the final such initiatory action. In chapter 1, Yahweh sanctions Joshua's leadership in the conquest of the land (1:1–9), and the military contingents from the East Jordan tribes agree to follow and enforce Joshua's leadership (1:12–18). The moment of the miraculous crossing of the Jordan publicly establishes this leadership in the eyes of the rest of Israel (3:7 and 4:14) and is the moment when the Israelites actually set foot in the promised land. After this introduction of the people into the land, two further initiatory actions are narrated before the Passover observance at the end of the period. These are the erection of the twelve stones at Gilgal, together with an explanation of their significance (4:20–24), and the circumcision of the men of Israel who had been born in the wilderness (5:2–8).

It is evident from other parts of the Old Testament that the Passover was not an observance done only at the time of Israel's entry into the land; it was an annual observance (Exod. 12:3–14; Lev. 23:4–5; Deut. 16:1; Ezek. 45:21). There are considerations that suggest that the same was true of practices reflected in the two actions narrated immediately before the Passover in Joshua 4–5. These actions were preparatory to the full exercise of life in the land by the men of Israel.

The passage about the significance of the stones in Gilgal has the form of a "catechism,"[34] a question addressed by a son to his father about the meaning of these stones, and the answer that the stones witness the action of Yahweh in drying up the Jordan for Israel to cross just as he had dried up

---

[34] Cf. J. A. Soggin, "Kultätiologische Sagen und Katechese im Hexateuch," *VT*, 10 (1960): 341–47.

the Reed Sea for Israel to cross at the beginning of the wilderness period. From this deed, witnessed by the stones, the people of the land were to learn that the hand of Yahweh is strong, and the sons of Israel were to learn to fear Yahweh their God always (4:24). This "catechism" passage is like others of the same form; for example, Exod. 12:26–27 explaining the Passover ritual by reference to Yahweh's plaguing the houses of Egypt, and Exod. 13:14–15 explaining the redemption of the firstborn sons by reference to Yahweh's sparing the firstborn sons of Israel when he killed those of Egypt. These passages have the appearance of recitations or liturgical exchanges used in the cultus to transmit from generation to generation the meaning of religious actions and objects. Thus, what Josh. 4:21–24 may represent is a formal declaration used on occasions when the divine establishment of the sacred site of Gilgal was commemorated and culticly confirmed.

The declaration about the meaning of the stones at Gilgal shows a concern that the young men be instructed in the sacred traditions of the Israelite sanctuary at Gilgal. The narrative that follows, the circumcision of the Israelite men at "the Hill of the Foreskins" (5:2–8), reflects a similar concern, and probably an old Gilgal custom, for the presentation and incorporation of young men into the life of adult men in the land. It has long been inferred that the presence of a place named "the Hill of the Foreskins" near Gilgal reflects an old Gilgal custom of performing circumcisions there. Further, since in the narrative it is the men of Israel who are circumcised at that place, it must once have been the custom at Gilgal to circumcise the males, not in infancy, but when they approached the age for marriage and warfare, as modern ethnologists have observed is done in some African tribes.[35] Such a circumcision would have been a regular,

[35] Bernhard Stade, "Der 'Hügel der Vorhäute' Jos. 5," ZAW 6 (1886): 132–43, seems to have been the first to adduce a group of ethnological parallels and to interpret the passage as reflecting an old custom of the Gilgal area. He was followed by Steuernagel, *Deuteronomium und Josua*, p. 158; H. Holzinger, *Josua* in *Kurzer Hand-Commentar zum*

probably annual, practice. Young men in groups would, by undergoing the ritual of circumcision, pass from the community of boys into that of men. The present circumcision narrative, then, would be an Israelite adaptation of such a local Gilgal custom in which the circumcision of young men at the Hill of the Foreskins is applied to all Israelites, since in the story all Israelites (except the East Jordan tribes) are at this point entering into the life of the land and the life of warriors. The extraordinary circumcision is explained by the theory that there had been no circumcisions during the forty-year wilderness sojourn (5:4–7). Whether this was the background and origin of the circumcision episode or not, in the whole narrative this circumcision is a form of initiation into the full exercise of and participation in a new stage of life, that in the land instead of that in the wilderness, and it is an action taken immediately upon setting foot in the land and prior to the Passover observance. That it precedes the Passover may be explained by the requirement elsewhere in the Old Testament that only households whose men were circumcised could take part in that observance (Exod. 12:44–48).[36]

As the narrative presents it, the Passover observance is the action that concludes the stage in the life of the people marked by their wilderness sojourn. Immediately following that observance they begin to live off the produce of the land of Canaan, and the miraculous food on which they lived during their years in the wilderness, the manna, ceases to come.

> And the sons of Israel camped in Gilgal and observed the Passover on the fourteenth day of the month, in the evening, in the plains of Jericho. And they ate from the grain of the land on the morrow of the Passover, un-

*Alten Testament*; (Tubingen: J. C. B. Mohr, 1901), p. 12; and Gressmann, *Anfänge Israels*, pp. 140–41.

[36] Cf. J. B. Segal, *The Hebrew Passover from Earliest Times to A.D. 70*, London Oriental Series no. 12 (London: Oxford University Press, 1963), p. 3. It may be significant of older practice that in the book of Jubilees those required to observe the Passover are the male adults, twenty years and older (Jub. 49:17). Thus, in that practice, the Passover was required of those included in the military census, cf. Num. 1:1–3 and Segal, pp. 135 and 233–34.

leavened bread and roasted grain, on this very day. And the manna ceased on the morrow, when they ate from the grain of the land, and they ate from the produce of the land of Canaan in that year.

(Josh. 5:10–12)[37]

Thus, the conditions of the divinely supported wilderness life are terminated only at the time of the Passover observance, and not simply at the moment when the sons of Israel first set foot in the promised land. The entirety of the seven-day period that concludes with the Passover represents that wilderness condition of life. The second seven-day period, on the other hand, corresponding to the seven days of the Festival of Unleavened Bread, marks the first participation by the people in the benefits of the promised land as well as the first marvelous military success against the people of that land.

That full military life begins for the people only with the second seven-day period is indicated by a number of features in the total narrative. There is a military contingent present before and at the time of the crossing of the Jordan River, but that contingent consists only of men from the East Jordan tribes of Reuben, Gad, and Manasseh (1:12–18; 4:12–13). These tribes have already received their land, and their dependents are already settled upon it. At the crossing of the river they have the appearance of a military escort for the rest of the Israelites: they cross "before the sons of Israel," forty thousand of them, armed for battle, crossing "before Yahweh for war" (4:12–13). No military bearing on the part of the rest of the Israelites is indicated in the narrative prior to the conquest of Jericho.

The unwarlike character of the Israelites entering into possession of the land comes to an end immediately following the Passover. What directly follows the cluster of events related to the Passover observance — the observance itself, the eating of grain from the land, and the cessation of the

[37] This translates MT without change. LXX text varies in some respects, particularly on spatial and temporal aspects of the action. The issues are too complex to broach here. Suffice it to say that the presentation of the action in LXX is consistent with itself but not with MT.

manna — is the appearance of the Commander of Yahweh's army to Joshua with the statement, "Now I have come," and the announcement of Yahweh that he has put Jericho and its king in Joshua's hand (5:14; 6:2). In the processions performing the circumambulations of Jericho during the second seven-day period, the bearing of the people is very much that of an armed company. Apparently, the point in the action at which the people become the army of Yahweh for the conquest of the foreign city is the Passover observance. This "army," which conquers Jericho, performs essentially a ritual and ceremonial action, and that conforms to the character of the actions in the preceding seven-day period and, indeed, to the character of the total narrative as a cult legend.

If, now, the whole sequence of events of Joshua 1–6 is viewed as the order of actions in a complex cultic observance at Gilgal, the actions of the two seven-day periods would have been as follows: On the eighth day of the month, the leader received an oracle from Yahweh confirming his position and promising divine support on the condition that he scrupulously obey prescribed divine requirements, and the military men took oath to follow and enforce the leader's authority. This action took place on the east side of the Jordan, at Shittim, and on the same eighth day arrangements were made for (symbolically) spying out the city of Jericho and for crossing the river. On the tenth day, the river was crossed in some manner that signified a mighty deed of Yahweh in leading the people into the land. This apparently involved a cultic procession in which, as in the later processions at the conquest of Jericho, the ark of Yahweh played a prominent role. When the wondrous event of the river crossing had been thus memorialized, action was taken for the instruction of the young in the significance of that event for the life of the community, and circumcision rituals were performed at the Hill of the Foreskins upon those who had reached the age for war. When a few days had passed for healing from the circumcision (5:8), the Passover observance was held in Gilgal, concluding the initiatory actions of the first seven-day period, and on the following day (the first day of the Festival of Unleavened Bread) the people ate unleavened bread from the grain of the land for the first time (that year), and the army, now including the newly initiated young men, went forth to begin the seven days of ritual circumambulation of the city (or mound) of Jericho.

If, finally, inferences are drawn about the context and function of the Passover from this total narrative, as a narrative, it may be said that the Passover marks the conclusion of one period in the life of the whole people, a period in which by a series of preparatory and initiatory actions they enter into the possession of the land, and that the Passover is immediately followed by a second period in which the people enjoy the benefits of the land and enter into warfare in it. If the total narrative is also viewed as a cult legend of the sanctuary of Gilgal, the seven-day period concluded by the Passover would be an annual observance by means of which the divine basis for Israelite life in the land was renewed. The people of that sanctuary ritually reentered and repossessed the land each year and, by the annual observance of the Passover, reconstituted themselves as Yahweh's people in the land he had given them.[38]

[38] The complex question of what kernel of historical events may lie behind the Gilgal traditions in Joshua 1–6 has not been broached here because it is a different order of problem from that here addressed. To the extent that Joshua 1–6 does show signs of having been a cult legend, as many features of the narrative as possible must be understood as parts of such a legend before the question can be properly posed as to what events served as the original basis for an Israelite celebration of their conquest of the Jericho region. It is patent that the narrative has as its present purpose the magnification and "glorification" of Yahweh's action in giving Israel the land of Canaan. Such magnification and glorification is not accomplished by reciting normal human events; it requires a portrayal of events on a higher plane. The modern historian cannot work directly with events on that higher plane, and the present form of the narrative offers little else. Still one need not doubt that some striking success, perhaps including military victory, made possible the occupation and dominance of the Jericho region by Israelite groups, and that in time that success came to be magnified on the scale now represented by Joshua 1–6. Cf. G. E. Mendenhall, "Response to Roland de Vaux's 'Method in the Study of Early Hebrew History'," in *The Bible in Modern Scholarship*, ed. J. Philip Hyatt (Nashville: Abingdon Press, 1965), p. 33.

# 3

## *Tension and Harmony between Classical Prophecy and Classical Law*

### WALTER G. WILLIAMS

The phrase "Law and the Prophets" is equated in Matt. 7:12 and 22:40 with the golden rule. It suggests unity, yet it also suggests different aspects of the religious life. As used, it seems to signify all Scripture and all religious demands on life. Yet it also divides. On the one hand are the rules and precepts by which one must be governed; and on the other the hopes and expectations of the fulfillment of God's purposes. So often we associate law with regulation and the prophet's word with challenge. It is the purpose of this study to investigate possible relationships between legislative process and prophetic challenge in ancient times.

Specifically, examination will be made of antagonisms and rapport, tension and harmony, in classical law and classical prophecy. The reversal of the order to prophecy and law in the title is deliberate and indicates something of the conclusion to which the study has come, namely, that there is some evidence of the dependence of law upon prophecy.

The study is of necessity limited in the case of the prophets to the prophetic messages which have been preserved in the Later Prophets and in the case of law to that which is embodied in the Pentateuch.

The English common noun "law" is purposely used throughout this study. In Hebrew, as in English, there are many technical designations and types of law. The Hebrew term תורה "Torah," however, includes far more than is generally understood by the English world "law." In addition, the two great decalogues ( Gen. 20:2–17; Deut. 5:6–21)

71

are introduced by the simple phrase "these are the words," not legal phraseology except as scholars have recognized that the phrase by implication means divine law.

Much attention has been given in recent years to studies of the origin and development of law among ancient people, and special attention has been given to development of law among the Hebrew people. J. M. P. Smith's *Origin and History of Hebrew Law*[1] was one of the early publications. It has been outdated in content because of the enormous amount of legal documents recovered in recent years from many countries in the ancient Near East, but it has not been outdated in method.

Professor Smith and others called attention to the significantly parallel laws in Exodus 21–23 and the Hammurabi Code.[2] Since that time the dependence of the Hammurabi Code on other codes has been noted. In the last part of the third millennium B.C. Urukagina of Lagash may have established laws of social significance.[3] The law of Urnammu of the third Dynasty of Ur gave us the oldest extant code of law (*ca.* 2050 B.C.). Bilalama of Eshnunna (*ca.* 1980) gave to his people a new code which is parallel to that of Urnammu. This was followed by the Code of Lipit Ishtar of Isin who ruled from 1934 to 1924. Hammurabi's Code was by no means original. It shows dependence upon the above named predecessors. Other law undoubtedly will come to light.

The word "code" is unfortunate. It implies activity of a legislative body or enactments by a monarch. The term "collection" is a more proper description. These so-called codes are collections of cases which have been settled by reputable judges and are designed to be guides for less experienced judges.

[1] J. M. P. Smith, *Origin and History of Hebrew Law* (Chicago: University of Chicago Press, 1931).

[2] *Ibid.*, pp. 181 ff.

[3] James G. McQueen, *Babylon* (New York: Frederich A. Praeger, 1965), p. 58, credits Urukagina with having written a law code. Samuel N. Kramer recognizes that Urukagina was a reformer but makes no mention of a law code.

It is now recognized that many of the bodies of law in the Old Testament were borrowed from the sociological and religious context in which the tribes of Israel found themselves, such as the Canaanites or other neighboring peoples. Albrecht Alt and others have, on linguistic and historical grounds, differentiated "Das Kasuistisch Formulierte Recht" and "Das Apodiktisch Formulierte Recht."[4] Apodeictic or categorical law could more closely be attributed to divine command. The word actually means "demonstrably true." Casuistic, procedural, or case law had its origin from the customs of people and from their disagreements with neighboring people. To assume that law could only be considered "divine" if it was dictated to a religious leader would have been incomprehensible to the ancient Semite. Life could not be and was not divided between the sacred and the secular.

In the Old Testament, law was believed to have its origin with God. This was true also of neighboring people. Witness the prologue to the Hammurabi Code. A possible exception is Hittite Law, but since the top of the inscription is broken away, the evidence is incomplete. With the Hebrews, however, in no instance is there any consideration of "state law," and no king was ever credited as a "law maker." The king could on occasion be the final judge or supreme court (II Sam. 15:2–6). This was not new. This was recognition that the king was the supreme leader, just as Moses had been, and should therefore be given the same authority in matters of law.

The Old Testament is the end result of a long and complicated process of writing and editing. Its present form shows that it has undergone much revision and editing, particularly in the postexilic period. In that late period editing was theologically motivated. The Jewish community accepted the basic principle of the divine origin of Torah. Attempts to trace the origins of law codes must begin with a recognition of this theological orientation.

[4] A. Alt, "Die Ursprünge des Israelitischen Rechts," *Kleine Schriften zur Geschichte des Volkes Israel* (München, 1959), 1:278 ff.

Literary analysis and some knowledge of the processes by which law is compiled for the benefit of society will enable us to recognize changes which came in Old Testament law. Distinction must be made between the literary form in which law came to us from the postexilic period, and the sources of that law. For the purpose of this discussion we shall center our attention upon the functional origins of law. These will be considered under two aspects: (1) the immediate recipient of the law, and (2) the purpose of the law.

The immediate recipients of law in the ancient world included the judges who settled cases of dispute. Sometimes the judges were the heads of clans. At other times the priests were recipients and functioned as judges.[5] For judge and priest the records of previously settled cases were invaluable. The priests needed information concerning the offering of sacrifices, proper procedures at the altar, and ceremonials. The people were taught small collections of law, and the many instances of decalogues and pentads would seem to fit that pattern. A handful or two of rules could readily be memorized or quickly called to mind.

The purposes and sources of law are many and thus study makes no pretense of being exhaustive. It is hoped, however, that the approach will be conducive to further investigation. Six major sources of law were available.

First, there were ancient bodies of law, which we have already noted. These were readily available and where necessary could be adapted for the borrowing group.

Second, the developing religious institution, and its leadership, was aware of the necessity of rules and regulations to protect the institution and its functions. The priests were quite capable of developing such law.

Third, as the community faced its neighbors, it was aware that certain religious practices among its neighbors were not compatible with its own ideals and teachings. Much reli-

[5] Ezekiel specifically names the priests to be judges (44:24); cf. Exod. 18:22, 26.

gious law has its inception in protest against a competing religion. The tribal religious leadership framed many rules prohibiting the practices of Canaanite Baalism. It is quite possible that prohibition against eating the flesh of swine had such origin. The command "Thou shalt not boil a kid in its mother's milk" (Exod. 34:26*b*) is not a late humanitarian provision, but protest against a magical practice of Baalism, as evidenced by the materials recovered from Ugarit.

Fourth, the changing political structure necessitated new law for a new society. As change was made from control by judges to rule by monarch, provision was made for the change including new patterns of support for the monarchy. Ultimately, the extremely heavy financial burden of Solomon's reign brought further changes, and in the end a protest against this kind of expensive monarchy.

Fifth, the concept of covenant people stressed by the prophets demanded a new type of covenant law. Early in Israel's residence in Canaan such law was associated with the Mount Sinai tradition. In time the concept came to be applied to the entire collection of Torah, and Mosaic authorship was assumed for the whole body of the law.

Sixth, prophetic challenge and leadership produced individuals and groups in society which sought to incorporate into practice what the prophets taught. It has been generally recognized that there is prophetic influence in parts at least of the book of Deuteronomy. One prophet, indeed, (Zech. 7:12) specifically credits the earlier prophets with bringing "the law and the word" from God to the people.

It is to the fifth and sixth sources just enumerated that this study is specifically directed. These will be discussed in relationship to each other, but it will be helpful if we give special attention first to the concept of the "covenant people." This will involve a brief examination of the terminology used, especially the legal phraseology, and some etymological considerations.

George E. Mendenhall, in his article "Covenant" in the *Interpreter's Dictionary of the Bible*, and in his earlier article "Covenant Forms in Israelite Tradition," [6] has compared practices in Israel with those of neighboring peoples, particularly the Hittites. Of necessity, he has given major attention to legal and political definitions. It is useful for our purposes to review briefly his major findings and then relate their significance for our understanding of covenant community.

He defines a covenant as "a solemn promise made binding by an oath, which may be either a verbal formula or a symbolic action. . . . Since the covenant usually had sanctions of a religious nature, it was usually connected with religion." Mendenhall uses the terms "covenant" and "treaty" interchangeably.

The classic literary pattern for a political covenant included the following characteristic elements: (a) the preamble, (b) the historical prologue, (c) the stipulations, (d) the deposit and public reading, (e) the list of witnesses, and (f) the blessings and curses. The element d holds special interest for an understanding of the practices of the tribes of Israel with respect to covenant law. In treaties or covenants there was provision that a copy of the treaty document be deposited in the sanctuary of the contracting parties, and that it be read at specific intervals. Note the treaty between the Hittite Hatusilis and the Egyptian Ramses II.

With respect to secular covenants, Mendenhall observes four types: (1) the suzerainty covenant, in which a superior power binds an inferior one to obligations defined by the superior (references are made in several cases in the Old Testament); (2) the parity covenant, where parties of equal power are bound by oath; (3) the patron covenant, a type in which the party in the superior position binds

[6] *Interpreter's Dictionary of the Bible*, ed. G. A. Buttrick *et al.* (Nashville: Abingdon Press, 1962), vol. A–D, pp. 714–23; *Biblical Archaeologist*, 17 (1954): 50–76; cf. Klaus Baltzer, *Das Bundesformular* (Neukirkener Verlag, 1965); Dennis J. McCarthy, *A Study in Form in the Ancient Oriental Documents and the Old Testament* (Rome: Pontifical Biblical Institute, 1965); E. Gerstenberger, "Covenant and Commandment," *JBL*, 84 (1965): 38–51; and Basil E. Pinto, "The Torah and the Psalms," *ibid.*, 86 (1967): 154–74.

himself to some obligation for the benefit of an inferior; and (4) the promissory covenant, in which no new treaty is made, but where promise is made of future performance of obligations already stipulated. Mendenhall would see a close connection between the patron covenant and the covenant relationship between Yahweh and Israel.

Certainly it is worth noting that in each instance of covenant between Yahweh and Israel, the event is presumed to have been initiated by God, and while there are binding responsibilities upon man, the covenant is for man's benefit, not God's. Here then would be the basis for concept of the grace of God and God's prevenient grace. Gerhard von Rad would recognize that the word "covenant" is often associated with ceremonial acts, but that it should also designate relationship.[7] He follows J. Begrich[8] who shows that "covenant" has usually been interpreted as relationship between equal parties, but that it may be understood as a relationship between two parties of unequal status; however, there is not complete freedom of action for the lesser partner, because he would refuse at his own peril to accept the terms of the treaty imposed by the stronger power.

The literal meaning of the descriptive Hebrew term *karath berith*, to "cut a covenant," suggests that it comes from ancient times. It has been noted that the term is not too frequently used in Old Testament accounts dating prior to the seventh century. The term *karath* usually means "to cut" but it may mean inscribe. Two explanations of this term have been made: (1) that contracting parties passed between the severed parts of the sacrificial animal used in the covenant ceremony, and (2) that the contracting parties participated in the sacrificial meal and cut their meat from the same animal. Both suggest participation in a covenanting ceremony and meal. There is a third possibility, that the terms of the treaty were cut or inscribed as a written document. Etymologically there is validity to this suggestion,

[7] Gerhard von Rad, *Old Testament Theology*, trans. D. M. G. Stalker (New York: Harper & Brothers, 1962), 1:129.
[8] J. Begrich, "Berit," ZAW, 60 (1944): 1–10.

but it must be admitted that not all covenants were written; some were oral. In any case, the term does suggest some form or ceremony of binding agreement.

Increasingly the Greek term "amphictyony" is being used in reference to the confederation of clans of tribes which later became the people Israel. Originally the term *amphictyones* mean "neighbors," but the term amphictyony came to mean "a league of tribes associated to protect, and maintain worship in, the temple of a deity" (Webster's Dictionary). As used by Old Testament scholars in recent years, it defines a community of clans having a common deity or religious allegiance. I find no evidence in the Old Testament of guarding a shrine, although a common meeting place is implied. Any defense mentioned seems to be of themselves and each other. The important aspect of the term amphictyony as used by Old Testament scholars is religious, not political or military. The common bond was unity of religious belief, not ancestry or common terrain. The biological and geographical aspects were introduced artificially at a later date.

There is increasing evidence, too, that the Hebrew confederations were established at two different centers, Shechem and Hebron. John Bright associates Shechem with the amphictyony and Hebron with the patriarchal period.[9] On the other hand, Murray L. Newman, Jr. has demonstrated that two varying concepts of the monarchy had their origins in different centers, Hebron and Shechem.[10] At each center there seems to have been a confederation of clans or tribes. In both cases, the association was through common acceptance of religious loyalties, not blood. Blood ties were introduced into the tribal legends long centuries after blood lines were no longer traceable.

Father Roland de Vaux, in his magnificent study *Ancient Israel: Its Life and Institutions*,[11] has given a realistic pic-

[9] John Bright, *A History of Israel* (Philadelphia: Westminster Press, 1959), pp. 128 ff.
[10] Murray L. Newman, *The People of the Covenant* (Nashville: Abingdon Press, 1962), pp. 8–9.
[11] New York: McGraw-Hill Book Co., 1961.

ture of ancient Hebrew life and careful pictures of tribal and clan structures, not as they later were assumed to have been, but as they probably were. The clan name could be and was adopted by those who married into the clan and by those who sought membership in the clan. Submission to the law of the clan and acceptance of the clan gods were the tests of admission. It was assumed that the newcomers, once admitted, were of the blood line and legally entitled to carry the clan name.

These various lines of evidence suggest strongly that unity was brought about by cultural ties, especially religious allegiance. Certainly there is much evidence to suggest that in times of danger or dissolution of solidarity, appeal was made in the name of religious loyalty and there was guarantee of divine leadership if the tribes and clans would again affirm such loyalty. Abraham, Moses, Joshua, and many of the judges fit this pattern. When we come to the period of the monarchy, we must note that other elements entered into the motivations of the leader and the people. The prophets of the eighth and seventh centuries, however, appealed once more to religious allegiance, not to patriotism — to divine law, not to royal decree.

It is to be noted, however, that no specific mention of covenant relationship or covenant God is made in the writings of the eighth century prophets, with the exception of Hosea (6:7; 8:1). In both cases in Hosea, the word covenant is used as a synonym for "law," especially 8:1, which reads "because they have broken my covenant, and transgressed my law." This seems to be significant to our understanding of the relationship between covenant people and covenant law.

Gerhard von Rad, in *The Problem of the Hexateuch*,[12] asserts that differentiation must be made between the Sinai tradition with the giving of covenant law, and the "settlement tradition" or conquest of Canaan.

[12] G. von Rad, *The Problem of the Hexateuch and Other Essays* trans. E. W. T. Dicken (New York: McGraw-Hill Book Co., 1966) pp. 13–48.

How early the concept of covenant law was held is difficult to ascertain, but both the J and the E records relate
the giving of the law to the making of the covenant while
P relates the covenant to Abraham. It is apparent that the
eighth century prophets did stress the matter of religious
and moral responsibility of God's people. Clash came between the prophets and the people because the people had
accepted the idea of "chosen people" and interpreted this
to mean that God had accepted the tribes of Israel as a
chosen people, and that responsibility lay upon God to
deliver his chosen ones. The prophets were the first teachers
to stress (1) that Yahweh was the Lord of History, (2)
that Yahweh had purpose in history which he was seeking
to accomplish through Israel, (3) that God's people had responsibility in history, and (4) that whatever happened in
the future was dependent upon what men and leaders were
thinking and doing currently. The prophets also said that
this meant specifically that there was responsibility upon
God's people to live as the people of God. It was from this
viewpoint that later Judaism developed more fully the concept of covenant law, and when Scripture was edited and
organized, Torah, or law, was put into the context of requirement for the covenant people.

This viewpoint, whenever it may have been developed,
put law into the pattern of "the terms of the covenant." In
this case, "the stipulations" were imposed by a superior
power upon an inferior, but since the law was for the
benefit of the inferior power, the type was not that of
suzerainty, but patron covenant, as Mendenhall has stated.

A study of Old Testament law reveals that much early
law was specifically regulation of religious ceremonial. The
early decalogue (Exod. 34:17–26) deals entirely with ritual
patterns and conduct in relationship to deity. The body of
law in Exodus 21–23, derived directly or indirectly from
Mesopotamian background, is, in its present form, credited
to the E writer, except for some fragments from J. It was
presumably accepted by the tribes after entry into Palestine.
This body of law deals in large part with person-to-person

relationships, but it does include repetition of material from the previously mentioned primitive decalogue. We have purposely refrained from using the term "code" in this instance, a term which implies codification by a legislature or systematization or control by a ruling body. In the case of the ritual decalogues the teachings and controls of the religious authorities are reflected.

The decalogues of Exodus 20 and Deuteronomy 5 deal first with man's relationship to God, then with man's relationship to man. Further study indicates that as man became more deeply conscious of his responsibility to God he deepened his sense of responsibility to and for his fellowman.

A major criticism of the Graf-Wellhausen school is that it overemphasized the flowering of Judaism in the postexilic period under the influence of the priestly school and that it assumed that the writings and laws of the priests were, in the main, new to the postexilic period, with little or no dependence upon the preexilic prophets. Preexilic emphasis upon the chosen people and the necessity to live as a chosen people cannot be minimized. The E record equates Law with the Book of the Covenant (Exod. 24:3–8). Millar Burrows says, "A true Christian or Jew, whose chief desire is to know and do the divine will, would not think of questioning God's right to command. If he should be asked, however, by what right God demands obedience, the answer of the Old Testament would be, first of all, that Israel in accepting the covenant promised to do God's will" (Exod. 24:7f.; Deut. 27:11–26).[13] Burrows goes on to say, "Rabbinic theology makes much of Israel's voluntary commitment as the basis of the authority of the law."[14] But law and covenant were believed to be intimately related to each other.

The books of the Pentateuch have been known to Judaism as "Torah," or law. To be sure, "law" includes custom, but, even so, it is difficult to account for Genesis as one of the Books of the Law except as one sees its record as con-

[13] M. Burrows, *An Outline of Biblical Theology* (Philadelphia: Westminster Press, 1946), p. 13.
[14] *Ibid.*

81

taining the presuppositions upon which law is based. It is
here that the origins of covenant relationship are given, and
while it is admitted that much of this material is written in
the days of normative Judaism, there is considerable material
from the J and E documents upon which the P interpretation
could be built. Judaism has regularly taken the position that
covenant law cannot be understood apart from the records
of the making of the covenant.

It was not until the eighth century B.C. that any concept
of the moral nature of God was an important consideration.
Amos is the first teacher of record to be concerned with this
issue. In the preceding period, a concept of amoral deity,
such as is found in the story of Micaiah ben Imlah (I Kings
22), was readily accepted.[15] Two hundred years later, Jeremiah protested against what he believed to be his unjust
treatment by God. Still later, the book of Job raised serious
questions concerning the moral justification of the punishment of a "righteous" man, and challenged the whole basis
of the Deuteronomic philosophy of good and evil. The commonly accepted position among Jews and Christians today
is that "of course God is moral." Yet, the contrast between
the positions of Judaism and Christianity with those of Islam
are marked. In Islam, the essential nature of God is power
and Moslem law has its origin in the edict of Allah. He has
both the power to announce it and the power to enforce it.
Judaism and Christianity believe that moral law has its
origin in the nature of God and of his creation. It is not,
therefore, surprising that the Hebrews were aware of the
justice of God before they discovered the love of God.

Even though some of the punishments meted out in the
name of justice and religion seem to have been quite harsh,
little question was raised, because it was recognized that
the wrongdoer himself had known what the penalty for violation would be, just as he knew what the reward for
obedience would be. This was justice. Yet it was early believed that justice was coupled with mercy. Just as man

[15] F. Walter Harrelson, *Interpreting the Old Testament* (New York:
Holt, Rinehart and Winston, 1964), p. 211.

could be compassionate, so could God. The various words in Hebrew which may be translated grace, mercy, compassion, goodness, long-suffering, abiding-love, show how widespread and deeply held the concept of mercy was.

G. Ernest Wright, in a study "The Terminology of Old Testament Religion and Its Significance," called attention to the fact that God the king and ruler had characteristics parallel to those of a father. He indicated that although the father-son relationship is infrequently used in the Old Testament, the master-servant relationship is marked by awareness of the covenant bond between God and the people.[16]

There was tension between priests and prophets with respect to the use of rituals and sacrifices. In a religion where it is possible for man to offer a burnt offering or other sacrifices in atonement for his sins there is danger that the officiating priest or the communicant himself will be considered the agent responsible for atonement and forgiveness. It was here that the prophet issued his word of warning. The prophet believed and taught that salvation was God-initiated and God-given.

Conflict arose also because of the stress in Deuteronomic teaching which has been summarized "Piety brings prosperity; sin brings suffering." Hosea stressed that material prosperity never justifies sharp practices, and that material success cannot be accepted as proof that one has moral conviction and is no defense of the violation of a moral law.

There was tension, too, as obedience to the law was accepted as a mark of superiority instead of an expression of loyalty by a son of the covenant. The prophets were opposed to the substitution of ritual for confession and of ceremonial for penitence. This is particularly marked in the message of Amos.

One of the major steps in man's understanding of the nature of his relationship to God was taken by Jeremiah. He has been called "the prophet of individual responsibility."

[16] G. E. Wright, "The Terminology of Old Testament Religion and Its Significance," *Journal of Near Eastern Studies*, 1 (1942): 404–14.

That description fails to understand the true nature of Jeremiah's message.

Many things happened in society during Jeremiah's lifetime to give new significance to the individual. A new pattern of money economy had been developed. Greater emphasis was placed upon personal ownership of property, especially land. Spread of empire had brought need for new officers in government, many of whom were not of royal blood. But this new importance of the individual was not the major issue in Jeremiah's new understanding. The prophet was convinced that organized religion in Jerusalem was inextricably bound up with the fate of the political structure. He was aware that the Judean state was going down to political defeat and with that inevitably all the structures, political, social, and religious, would perish together. He therefore began to ask the question, "What is the fundamental nature of religion?" He came to the conviction that its essence was man's sense of relationship to God — that the individual was at the heart of religion. This led Jeremiah to two other convictions: (1) that religion should be a matter of inner conviction, not outward compulsion, and (2) that man as an individual should be responsible directly to God for his conduct, not responsible through community. The first position was expressed through his statement of the new covenant (not a new law) which was to be "cut" or inscribed upon the heart of the individual. The second position was stated in the passage which leads up to "the new covenant" (Jer. 31:29–30), "The fathers have eaten sour grapes . . . everyone shall die for his own sins."

So long as it was believed that the covenant was written with and for the community, then the individual was held responsible to the community and through and with the community to God. A community sought to purge itself of all unrighteousness, sometimes by ruthless punishment and death. Just as the community's health was protected by expelling individuals who had communicable diseases, so the community kept itself morally pure in the eyes of God by expelling or killing the sinner. Only as we understand this principle of procedure is it possible for us to understand, at least in part, the seeming ruthlessness of ancient Hebrew trials.

A case can be made also showing that there is greater likelihood that moral levels will be lifted when man senses his direct responsibility to God than when he is content to meet the demands of the society of which he is a part. On the other hand, his sense of responsibility to and for his fellowman is also deepened by his sense of responsibility to God. This is because he recognizes his fellowman as the creation of God as he himself is. The concern is not simply kindness which he might feel toward animals, but a concern for one who belongs to that special group for whom God has a special purpose.

Ezekiel, like Jeremiah, placed emphasis upon the individual's direct responsibility to God, not responsibility through society. He stressed far more than Jeremiah the pattern of individual forgiveness based upon changed conduct (chaps. 18 and 33). It was Ezekiel who taught that there can be no such thing as transfer of moral credits (14:14, 20) and that each individual is responsible for his own sin, not those of his parents or of his children.

On the other hand, Ezekiel had far greater faith in organized religion than had Jeremiah, and if chapters 40–48 reflect the thinking of Ezekiel, he gave to Judaism an ecclesiastical constitution for a Utopia. For this in particular he has been called "Father of Judaism."

Ezekiel seems to have believed that man, being what he is, needs all the help that organized religion can bring to him. The difference between Jeremiah and Ezekiel seems to have arisen from their different experiences with organized religion, as well as from their different personalities. Jeremiah knew an institution which was apparently unchanging and essentially corrupt. Ezekiel participated in an institution which had been modified and purged by exilic conditions. It had dared to change in order to meet the new religious needs of men, but it had done so without giving up any of its basic beliefs. Ezekiel saw the institution as serv-

85

ant or instrument. Such an institution could live. It would have usefulness in the restored society and could be the instrument of God to mediate salvation.

The prophet of the exile, Deutero-Isaiah, used the term "covenant" in ways unique to himself. First of all, he specifically identified the servant with the covenant (42:6; 49:8) and announced that God had given the servant, elsewhere identified as Israel, to be a covenant and a light to the nations. However, he also identified the term covenant with the promise first made to Noah (54:9–10), and with the promise of succession made to David (55:3; cf. II Sam. 7). In the later chapters of Isaiah the principle of vicarious suffering is added to that of the covenant (61:8). In addition, promise is made that eunuchs and foreigners will be included in the blessings of the covenant (56:4, 6), as also will be the repentant sinner (59:21).

It is to the concept of servant as a means of the covenant and to the related concept of vicarious suffering that we must now turn our attention. We have indicated elsewhere [17] that II Isaiah never identified in the same person the functions of servant and messiah. This identification is made first of all in the New Testament and has been projected back into Deutero-Isaiah. Once this distinction is recognized, then identification of the servant can be less emotionally made, as can identification of the messianic king. In Isaiah 44:28–45:1 Cyrus is specifically called the "anointed" or "messiah." His function is military and political, that of liberator of the people of God from exile. The servant is specifically named in several places and is to be identified with Jacob or Israel (41:8, 44:1–2, 21, etc.). However, the question still remains whether or not the poet-prophet meant the whole of Israel, an idealized Israel, or the returning remnant from exile which had been purged by the experiences of the captivity. Such specific identification is unnecessary, however, for the purposes of the present inquiry.

Some understanding of the function of the servant is

[17] Walter G. Williams, *Prophets, Pioneers to Christianity* (Nashville: Abingdon, 1956), pp. 110 ff.

apropos to our discussion. Deutero-Isaiah did teach that his people could and should be the servant of God and a light to the Gentiles (49:6). The message of God as salvation was not to be confined to Judah. This missionary task, however, was not accepted, and attempts were made later by the writer of the book of Jonah to revitalize II Isaiah's message, but without success.

Deutero-Isaiah also enunciated the principles of vicarious suffering; but this too was doomed to extinction until it was revitalized in the mission of Jesus and the message of Paul. The Jews in exile were quite willing to admit that they had sinned and that punishment for sin should be expected, but they protested that the punishment was all out of proportion to the size of the sin. It was in an attempt to explain this supposed discrepancy that Deutero-Isaiah enunciated the principle of vicarious suffering, that perhaps the Jews were suffering so that others could be spared suffering. This was proposed neither as substitution nor as transfer of moral credits. He believed it to be a basic law of history. More important, it was recognition of an obligation upon a covenant people.

Distinction should be made between vicarious suffering and martyrdom. A martyr is willing to die for his faith or his principles. He is not necessarily dying for others, though this sometimes happens. The man who is willing to suffer vicariously is undergoing pain, torment, or even death so that others might be spared. He may lose his life, but his concern is that he may thereby save the life of someone else.

The term "covenant" also carried political and nationalistic connotations. It was early associated with the military and political fortunes of the Hebrew people. The ark of covenant became a symbol of the presence of God and this ensured victory so long as it remained a possession of the Hebrews. Its loss resulted in defeat. It was early believed that there would be no break in the lineage of David as occupants of the throne of Judah. Care was taken in structuring the chronicles of Judah and Israel so as to point up this mark of distinction.

A significant aspect of the reform under Josiah is that the king led the people in entering into a renewed covenant with Yahweh (II Kings 23:2–3). The king initiated and led the covenant ceremony. And in the postexilic period increasing attention was given to the political interpretation of the covenant promise. There were hopes and dreams of a restored and greatly enlarged political power. To be sure, the very structure of the postexilic community, vassalage first to Persia then to Greece, forced Judaism into a pattern of theocracy, but the dream of a restored monarchy was never lost.

In spite of the political overtones, Judaism retained and developed the characteristics of a covenant people. There were two aspects of their covenant responsibility. The first was their relationship to God. The second was their responsibility for other members of the covenant group.

The law by which they lived was not the enactment of a legislature but the assembled teachings of religious leaders. These, they believed, had divine origin, at least divine consent. Much of their law was idealistic, as in Deuteronomy, and in many cases carried no specific penalties for violation, which are usually a part of civil law. No distinction, in fact, is made between civil and religious law. Man was subject to God for all acts of his life.

Phillip Hyatt has noted well the centrality of divine law in the life of Israel. He says:

> A distinctive feature of Israelite worship in this [early] period, according to some scholars, was an annual festival of covenant renewal at the central sanctuary. This type of ceremony is not described in detail, but is suggested by passages such as Joshua 8:30–35; 24; Deut. 11:26–32; 26:1–11; and 27. In this festival, there was a recital of the mighty acts of Yahweh on behalf of his people, such as the exodus from Egypt and the conquest of the land of Canaan; a reading of the Law, such as the Ten Commandments; and a renewal of the covenant through a reaffirmation by the people of their in-

tention to obey Yahweh's commands. In this type of worship, emphasis was laid upon a recognition of what Yahweh had done for Israel, and upon Israel's response to him by obedience to his law.[18]

Hyatt's position is in agreement with the earlier work of von Rad, originally published in 1938, now available in English translation.[19]

Questions may be raised concerning whether or not covenant renewal was an annual festival and whether or not it was a ceremony which involved all the people. There is much evidence, however, to support Hyatt's contention that covenant law was central to Hebrew thought.

Obedience to law involved relationships to man as well as to God. Certain aspects of the law concerned themselves with the conduct of a covenant people. Characteristic of Hebrew society was its concern for less fortunate members of that society. Laws were spelled out which made provision for the indigent members of society, the widowed and the orphaned. It is true that a widow, at least in the early times, could not inherit property, but she did become the immediate responsibility of the husband's next of kin. Much has been written about the institution of levirate marriages and the producing of children who should bear the deceased's name. Equally important was the fact that the family *Go'el*, or redeemer, assumed financial responsibility.

Indigent members of society who were not otherwise cared for had legal rights guaranteed to them. When a field was harvested, the owner was required to leave the corners of the field uncut. This part of the field belonged by right of tradition to the poor, and since this was now a right, they were not beggars. Likewise a man would not rework his field. If grain had been missed in the first cutting, it belonged to the gleaners. The same was true of fruit of the tree or the vine which had been missed. All fallen fruit came under the same restriction. Windfallen fruit was a gift

[18] J. Philip Hyatt, *The Heritage of Biblical Faith* (St. Louis: Bethany Press, 1964), p. 64.
[19] Von Rad, *The Problem of the Hexateuch.*

of God to the poor, not the possession of the owner of the tree.

The whole economy was poor and hired labor had immediate need for wages earned. It was therefore provided in custom and law that no wages could be held back, not even overnight. Wardrobes were scanty, and outer garments, the ancient equivalent of overcoats, served a dual purpose. During the day they were worn as an outer dress garment, but at night they were bed-covering for the family. It was therefore provided that no such garment could be kept by a pawnbroker overnight as security for a loan. Even though the loan was still unpaid, the garment had to be given to the borrower to protect his children from the cold of night. It was the borrower's duty to return the garment to the pawnbroker the next morning. Custom and pressure of public opinion were the only guarantees the pawnbroker had.

Another aspect of covenant community is to be found in laws which pertain to moneylending. It was illegal to charge interest to a member of the group. Some interpreters have tried to make distinction between usury and interest condemning the first but allowing the second. No such distinction was made in Bible times. All interest rates were extremely high and would be classified as usury. The pattern of lending without interest is still practiced by some Christian groups today.

Still another aspect is the law of tithing. Beginning as a method of redeeming nine-tenths by giving one-tenth, the pattern of giving was sublimated and became a basic law of religious expression. As a matter of fact, the Jews gave more than a tenth. One-tenth belonged to God. Any gift must go beyond the tenth.

The tithes and offerings provided not only for the support of the temple priests, the Levites, and the upkeep of the temple: they provided for the charitable work of the community. All charitable work was the direct responsibility of the community as a religious entity. No member of the covenant community, not even the "stranger within the gates," could go uncared for. The sign at the entrance to the National Jewish Sanatorium in Denver has been a great inspiration to me: "None may enter who can pay; none can pay who enter." And from the time of its founding until now, the majority of patients in that hospital have been non-Jews.

We have noted that the concept of covenant seems to be quite old, but that the technical terminology and the formal statements of covenant seem to be fairly late. However, many of these statements are associated with people of great antiquity. Perhaps the answer lies in the fact that the concept of covenant grew out of a conviction of election. Otto Baab says, "By constant reference to this covenant and its ethico-legal demands, Israel fixed its attention upon a common history, a common practice, and a common hope. This history was dominated by the event of Israel's election; the practice centered in obedience to God, which involved all the interests and relationships of life; and the hope was for the realization of the divine promise. By this fixation of attention the community became conscious of itself, its peculiar relationship to God, and its special destiny." [20] Whatever the historical and religious origins may have been, Israel, through its sense of relationship to God and to God's purpose in creation and history, developed a pattern of religion related to life which had never before been known and which has been paralleled only by Christianity. This concept of covenant God and covenant people is unique in the history of religion. In the development of this concept the prophets and the law were partners.

[20] Otto Baab, *Theology of the Old Testament* (Nashville: Abingdon, 1949), p. 61.

# 4

## Prophets, Deuteronomy, and the
## Syncretistic Cult in Israel
### DONALD E. GOWAN

The attitude of the canonical prophets toward the cult has been a perennial subject for discussion, and in recent years it has been particularly lively.[1] Normally it has dealt only with those great, classical statements about sacrifice in the prophetic books, as if they were the sum of what the prophets have to say about the cult, and as if we understood well what kind of cult they were talking about. The history of the discussion from Wellhausen to the present day is well known, and need not be summarized here, except to note that a near consensus has been reached by scholars who have approached the subject from several directions.[2] It is that passages such as Amos 5:21–27 and Isa. 1:11–15 do not condemn sacrifice wholesale as a mode of worship, but rather deal with a false understanding of worship,[3] or state the preconditions for acceptable worship,[4] or warn that wor-

[1] Useful, brief, recent summaries may be found in R. E. Clements, *Prophecy and Covenant*, Studies in Biblical Theology no. 43 (Naperville, Ill.: A. R. Allenson, 1965), pp. 86–102; R. J. Thompson, *Penitence and Sacrifice in Early Israel outside the Levitical Law* (Leiden: Brill, 1963), pp. 161–66.

[2] Exceptions are Richard Hentschke, *Die Stellung der vorexilischen Schriftpropheten zum Kultus*, BZAW, no. 75 (Berlin: Alfred Töpelmann, 1957); C. F. Whitley, *The Prophetic Achievement* (Leiden: Brill, 1963), pp. 63–92.

[3] E.g., H. W. Hertzberg, "Die prophetische Kritik am Kult," in *Beiträge zur Traditionsgeschichte und Theologie des Alten Testaments* (Göttingen: Vandenhoeck und Ruprecht, 1962), pp. 81–90.

[4] E.g., Rolf Rendtorff, "Priesterliche Kulttheologie und prophetische Kultpolemik," *TLZ*, 81 (1956), cols. 339–42; Hans Wildberger, *Jesaja*, Biblischer Kommentar, no. 10 (Neukirchen-Vluyn: Neukirchener Ver-

ship cannot avert the approaching doom.[5] It seems very likely that this kind of interpretation is near to the correct one, at least for most of the "antisacrifice" passages. Yet this does not settle the matter, for it leaves at least two problems unsolved.

First, a great deal of work has been done in recent years to demonstrate the close affinities between the prophets and the cult. That there was an institution of cult prophecy is unquestionable;[6] that the literary forms and messages of the canonical prophets were influenced by the liturgy of the sanctuaries is becoming more and more clear,[7] that at least some of the canonical prophets were cult officials is presently a matter of debate,[8] but is believed by some. Yet despite the trend toward associating the prophets with the cult, what they explicitly say about it is so thoroughly negative that it is still possible for men such as Hentschke and Whitley to present a strong case for the total repudiation of sacrifice in favor of a spiritual religion, and one is left with the

lag, 1965), p. 38; Ernst Würthwein, "Kultpolemik oder Kultbescheid?" in *Tradition und Situation*, ed. E. Würthwein and O. Kaiser, Festschrift A. Weiser (Göttingen: Vandenhoeck und Ruprecht, 1963), pp. 115–31.

[5] Richard Press, "Die Gerichtspredigt der vorexilischen Propheten und der Versuch einer Steigerung der kultischen Leistung," ZAW, 70 (1958): 181–84; Douglas Jones, "Exposition of Isaiah Chapter One Verses Ten to Seventeen," SJT, 18 (1965): 457–71.

[6] Aubrey Johnson, *The Cultic Prophet in Ancient Israel* (Cardiff: University of Wales Press, 1944); Alfred Haldar, *Associations of Cult Prophets among the Ancient Semites* (Uppsala: Almqvist & Wiksells, 1945); Hans-Joachim Kraus, *Worship in Israel*, trans. Geoffrey Buswell (Richmond, Va.: John Knox Press, 1966), pp. 101–12.

[7] Sigmund Mowinckel, *Psalmenstudien III. Kultprophetie und prophetische Psalmen* (Kristiania: Jacob Dybwad, 1923); Ernst Würthwein, "Der Ursprung der prophetischen Gerichtsrede," ZThK, 49 (1952): 1–16.

[8] Pro: A. H. J. Gunneweg, *Mündliche und schriftliche Tradition der vorexilischen Prophetenbücher als Problem der neueren Prophetenforschung*, FRLANT, no. 55 (Göttingen: Vandenhoeck und Ruprecht, 1959); H. G. Reventlow, *Das Amt des Propheten bei Amos*, FRLANT, no. 80 (Göttingen: Vandenhoeck und Ruprecht, 1962). Con: H. W. Wolff, "Hoseas geistige Heimat," TLZ, 81 (1956), cols. 83–94; idem, *Amos' geistige Heimat*, WMANT, no. 18 (Neukirchen-Vluyn: Neukirchener Verlag, 1964).

feeling that the relationship of Amos, Isaiah, and Jeremiah to the cult has not yet been adequately explained.

Second, a great deal of work has been done to elucidate the forms of worship in ancient Israel, with stress on the cult as the preserver and, to some extent, the creator of the sacred traditions.[9] Yet at the same time other scholars are making it more and more clear to us that religion as it was actually practiced in Israel during the monarchy was strongly influenced by the myth and ritual of her neighbors, and was indeed in many respects very little different from other religions.[10] This raises the question of how, and by whom, a form of Yahwism relatively free of the influence of the nature cults (such as we find enshrined in the Torah) was preserved.[11]

It may be that our recognition of the extent to which syncretism had mingled Yahwistic and Canaanite elements during the monarchy can provide one way of resolving the problems just mentioned, and this paper will attempt to show how this is possible.[12] It suggests that the evidence which can be found in the prophetic books, and secondarily in the book of Deuteronomy, concerning the extent of syncretism in the Israelite cult leads to the following conclusions:

[9] Gerhard von Rad, *The Problem of the Hexateuch*, trans. E. W. Trueman Dicken (Edinburgh: Oliver and Boyd, 1966), pp. 1–78; Artur Weiser, *The Old Testament: Its Formation and Development*, trans. Dorothea M. Barton (New York: Association Press, 1961), pp. 81–99.

[10] G. W. Ahlström, *Aspects of Syncretism in Israelite Religion*, Horae Soederblominae, no. 5 (Lund, 1963); Frank E. Eakin, Jr., "Yahwism and Baalism before the Exile," *JBL*, 84 (1965): 407–14; Raphael Patai, "The Goddess Asherah," *JNES*, 24 (1965): 37–52; J. A. Soggin, "Der offiziell geförderte Synkretismus in Israel während des 10. Jahrhunderts," *ZAW*, 78 (1966): 179–204.

[11] Peter R. Ackroyd, *Continuity: A Contribution to the Study of the Old Testament Religious Tradition* (Oxford: Basil Blackwell, 1962); Norman Porteous, "The Prophets and the Problem of Continuity," in *Israel's Prophetic Heritage*, ed. B. W. Anderson and W. Harrelson (New York: Harper, 1962), pp. 11–25.

[12] It is an effort to document a point of view very similar to that expressed by Clements, *Prophecy and Covenant*, pp. 86–102.

1) The cult during the period of activity of the canonical prophets was *universally* syncretistic; i.e., the Israelite people did not have a choice between a cult which preserved the true spirit of Yahwism and cults which were dominated by nature worship. Their only choice was between a highly syncretistic Israelite-Canaanite cult and certain completely foreign imports.

2) Thus the cult which is called apostate by the prophets and the Deuteronomist actually did preserve authentic traditions of Israel's past; did celebrate, among other things, the exodus and the covenant, because it was not really apostate (in our sense of the word), but was a mixture of religions.

3) The prophets are well acquainted with the language of this cult, then, because it is the only place they have ever had to worship Yahweh. They never give a clue that there is any place or any group in Israel where a better kind of worship than that which they condemn can be found.

4) But they do repudiate this cult, and it would seem, wholeheartedly, because they have found that this attractive blend of religions is completely inadequate to convey to the people of Israel a knowledge of Yahwism as they understand it. Such opposition, however, tells us nothing about their views of cult *in general*; nothing about how they would have judged the kind of worship described in Leviticus or Deuteronomy, e.g., for they had never witnessed such worship. Indeed, some evidence will be brought forth to show that the prophets and the Deuteronomist shared exactly the same view of the worship of their day, despite their differences in other respects.

## Syncretism in Israelite Religion

The phenomenon of syncretism scarcely needs extensive discussion in this paper. One need only read the books of Judges, Samuel, and Kings to be convinced that Israelite worship from the conquest on was thoroughly mingled with aspects of the Canaanite fertility religion, and that this was not, for the majority of Israelites, considered apostasy, but was the commonly accepted thing.[13] It is surely clear enough, also, that the temple in Jerusalem, far from being a center of unsyncretistic Yahwism, offered the worshiper a far greater variety of worship experiences than the country sanctuaries, due to the importation of foreign cults to add to the Israelite-Canaanite forms. The extent to which this was true is being made all the more clear by the numerous studies of Canaanite influence on the Old Testament which have been appearing in recent years. This much is indisputable; the idea which requires some proof here is that the *only* cult the prophets knew was one so highly imbued with Canaanite elements that they rejected it for that reason alone, on the basis of their adherence to an old, very conservative, Yahwistic tradition.

Before saying any more about the prophets and "syncretism," however, it is clearly necessary to be precise about how that term is being used in this context. We cannot handle the problem of syncretism in Israelite religion as satisfactorily as we could handle the same phenomenon in the mystery religions, for example. With the latter we have some information which enables us to say that the deity and myth of a certain cult came from Egypt, and that certain of the initiation ceremonies are of Greek origin. But we cannot, as yet, affirm what the presettlement religion was like with much confidence. We do know something about Canaanite religion, of course, and can, from that knowledge, identify some of those elements in the Old Testament, but to be able to separate from them a "pure" form of Yahwism, unaffected by Canaanite religion is, I think, impossible. Indeed Yahwism at all times must have involved some syncretism with other religions.

This means that our use of the term "syncretism" in a pejorative sense to describe the objections of the prophets and Deuteronomist to the cult must be carefully defined.

[13] Ahlström, *Syncretism*, pp. 10–12, 54 f., 86 f.; Eakin, *JBL*, 84:414. The studies by Kraus and others of the cult in Israel probably present us with a somewhat distorted picture of what worship was actually like during the monarchy because of their tendency to concentrate on what was distinctive in Israelite religion, and thus to devote too little attention to the pervasiveness of syncretism.

First, we can say that from *our* point of view the religion of Israel during the monarchy was syncretistic; i.e., it involved an uncritical acceptance of elements from two or more religions. But to the prophets this was apostasy; their monotheistic understanding of Yahweh led them to consider involvement with anything associated with another god tantamount to rejection of Yahweh, though certainly this is not what the majority of Israelites believed. And if this last is true, we are justified in calling syncretistic all the practices the prophets condemn, since from the people's point of view those practices did not involve making a choice between Yahweh or Baal, but merely the acceptance of everything that seemed attractive and useful. I thus differ from scholars who speak of a Canaanite cult in one place, a syncretistic cult in another, and a "legitimate Yahwistic cult" in another. During the monarchy the pervasiveness of syncretism meant there was no clear distinction between "Canaanite" and "Yahwistic" cult. What existed was, for most people, a "legitimate Yahwistic cult," but for a few (of whom the prophets are representative) it was not.

The matter is further complicated by the fact that, from our point of view, there is a good deal of syncretism in the prophetic books and Deuteronomy themselves. Many features of Canaanite religion became a part of the orthodoxy of postexilic Judaism, as the Psalms show especially clearly. I account for both this fact and my statement that the opposition to the cult on the part of the prophets and Deuteronomy was based on their conviction that it had become hopelessly syncretistic in this way:

These people were faced by an Israelite religion which was a great conglomeration of beliefs and practices of various origins. Some parts of it had for centuries been associated with the worship of Yahweh. Other parts had originated in the worship of fertility gods, and were still associated to a greater or lesser extent with those deities. But no matter what its origin, most of it was, in the prophets' day, at least nominally Israelite. Then, for some reason or other, a few Israelites became convinced that certain *parts* of the Israelite religion were normative for all of it. It will be suggested later that this may be accounted for by indications that in circles outside the cult the ancient, Yahwistic traditions had been preserved without many Canaanite accretions, so that it would be fairly easy for a thoughtful man to recognize that certain aspects of the religion did have a character which set them apart from the rest of it. These Israelites, from whom our prophetic books and Deuteronomy have come, became convinced that what this part of the religion taught about the nature of Yahweh and his will for Israel was the truth, and therefore that all the rest of the religion must be judged by it. They set about to do so. They found a severe ethic in this religion, which was being ignored by most of their people, but which they came to believe to be essential to Yahwism; and so it became a central part of their message. They were impressed by the jealous nature of Yahweh, and thus were disturbed when his worship was combined with that of other gods. And so forth. But they did not undertake historical research, as we do, to find out what was Canaanite and what was not. They merely judged their religion according to certain standards which they believed to be normative, rejecting all that conflicted with those standards, but finding no reason to question aspects of the religion which did not conflict. Some of the latter were also Canaanite in origin (and we still have them in our Old Testament), but the prophets were probably not aware of that. Certainly they were not enlightened syncretists, consciously choosing certain foreign elements because they were useful and compatible. No, they were dealing with that which had been the religion of *Israel* for many years and were simply saying, there are certain things in our religion which are irreconcilable with that which is essential to it, and they must be done away with. Because of the fact that these elements were clearly associated with the fertility religions of Canaan, this became the principle by which they were rejected: they are foreign, and do not belong to the worship of Yahweh. Now, this paper will attempt to show that the entire cult came under that judgment. The prophets have concluded that although the mighty acts of Yahweh *are* celebrated in the cult, there is so much there which obscures who he is and what he requires, that it no longer serves adequately as the source of the "knowledge of God" (Hos. 6:6) for his people.[14] Jeroboam's activities provide a straightforward example of this. He celebrated the exodus at Dan and Bethel ("Behold your gods who brought you up from Egypt," I Kings 12:28), but in a form completely unacceptable to the Deuteronomist. His was a syncretistic cult, according to our definition, but to the Deuteronomist, syncretism meant apostasy.

There is no complete agreement among these severe Yahwists as to what parts of the religion are incompatible with their understanding of Yahwism, however. As we shall see, Jeremiah and perhaps Amos have concluded that sacrifice does not convey the knowledge of God; probably because as practiced, it taught man's participation in the renewal of the fertility cycle, typical of nature religions. So they say this cannot have been a part of true Yahwism. The other prophets may not have seen sacrifice as completely inadequate, since they apparently do not condemn it as being against God's will. And the Deuteronomist considers a *proper* form of sacrifice to be an acceptable way of serving God and conveying the knowledge of God, so he seeks to regulate it carefully.

### Evidence in the Prophetic Books for the Extent of Syncretism in the Israelite Cult

It has been suggested that whenever the prophets speak about the cult they refer to it as it is practiced in their day, and not to worship in general; and further, that the cult as they knew it was, by their standards, so affected by Canaanite beliefs and practices that Yahweh, as they knew him from the ancestral traditions, could not be worshiped there at all.[15]

To substantiate this, it is clearly necessary to survey all that the prophets have to say about the cult. The first part

[14] H. W. Wolff, "'Wissen um Gott' bei Hosea als Urform von Theologie," *EvTh*, 12 (1952/53): 533–54.

[15] A similar stress on the corruption of the cult by syncretism as the basis for the prophets' judgments of it may be found in A. S. Kapelrud, "Cult and Prophetic Words," *StTh*, 4 (1951): 7–8; L. Rost, "Erwägungen zu Hosea 4, 13 f.," in *Festschrift Alfred Bertholet*, ed. W. Baumgartner *et al.* (Tübingen: J. C. B. Mohr, 1950), pp. 451–60.

of that study can be done quickly; it merely requires a listing of those elements of Israelite worship which are condemned by the prophets as foreign, and then a consideration of the number of such passages as an indication of what concerned the prophets most about worship in their day. The second part requires a study of those passages which do not, at first reading, clearly refer to a highly syncretistic cult; to determine whether they do, in fact, contain evidence for the existence of a "pure, Yahwistic, sacrificial cult" in the prophetic period. A third part of the study presumably ought to deal with the favorable references to the cult, but these are so few, so much debated, and contribute so little to our subject even if they are preexilic, that it seems safe to omit them from consideration.

1) The practices of which the prophets disapprove are so well known that little discussion of them is needed. They condemn worship of idols, of the host of heaven, of other gods; worship by means of altars, pillars, Asherim, child-sacrifice, prostitution, burning incense, planting of special gardens (Isa. 1:29; 17:10–11); and worship at high places and under green trees. We can document easily the origin of these practices in Canaan, or in certain cases, among Israel's neighbors. Some figures will show what the weight of the prophets' concern with the cult was.[16] (They are only approximate.)

|  | References naming the elements just listed | References which do not name any of the elements listed |
| --- | :---: | :---: |
| Amos | 4 | 2 |
| Hosea | 21 | 3 |
| Micah | 3 | 1 |
| Isaiah | 11 | 1 |
| Zephaniah | 4 | — |
| Habakkuk | 1 | — |
| Jeremiah | 45 | 4 |

[16] Ezekiel is omitted because this book differs from the others listed in containing several positive statements concerning the cult of the future. It provides good support for the position taken here, however, in that it contains not one favorable reference to the cult of the past or the present.

These figures are given only to suggest that those few great, classical statements about sacrifice which are so well known represent only a small part of what the prophets have to say about the cult, and probably ought not to be interpreted outside the context of these concerns, which are so frequently expressed, about the corruption of the cult by things foreign.

2) The passages in which syncretism is not obviously an issue may be divided into three groups:

a) Those where the actual basis for disapproval *is* syncretism, although they have sometimes been interpreted otherwise (Amos 4:4–5; Hos. 2:11; 8:11–13; Jer. 7:21–23; 11:15).

b) Those where the main issue is something else, but which still indicate the presence of syncretism in the cult referred to (Amos 5:21–27; Hos. 6:6; Jer. 6:16–21).

c) Those which contain no trace to the cultic practices elsewhere condemned by the prophets (Micah 6:6–8; Isa. 1:11–15; Jer. 14:12).

A few words should suffice to explain the classification of most of these texts, although some justification must be offered for some of them. It is obvious that if the passages have been classified properly, only those under *c* can possibly provide any evidence for the existence of a cult which is not repugnant to the prophets because of its Canaanite elements. They must be examined to see whether they do provide any such evidence.

*Group a.* Little needs to be said about Amos 4:4–5, which refers to worship at Bethel and Gilgal, the syncretistic nature of which is documented by Hosea 4:15 and 9:15; or about Hosea 2:11, which speaks of the feasts, the New Moon, and Sabbath as having become days for the worship of Baal; or about Hosea 8:11–13 and Jer. 11:15, in which the context indicates the extent of syncretism in the worship referred to. Jer. 7:21–23 requires some discussion, however.

> Add your burnt offerings to your sacrifices and eat flesh.
> For I did not speak to your fathers and I did not command them in the day when I brought them out of the land of Egypt concerning matters of burnt offering and

sacrifice. For with this word I commanded them: Hear my voice and I will be to you a God and you shall be to me a people, and you shall walk in all the way which I command you so that it may be well with you.

This seems to be a complete rejection of the sacrificial system as a human invention which was never commanded by God. Many interpretations of the passage have been offered, of which several are worth listing:

1) It proves there was no sacrificial code in Jeremiah's day.[17]
2) It means a repudiation of the entire cult in favor of obedience in ethical behavior.[18]
3) It is not to be taken literally, but is "exalted poetry."[19]
4) The לא has a comparative, rather than absolute meaning, so the passage establishes a scale of values.[20]

My suggestion is this: Although there probably were some sacrifices offered in the wilderness, Jeremiah is almost correct, in that most of the sacrificial system was Canaanite. Without postulating too much knowledge of ancient history on Jeremiah's part, might it not be true that he had some knowledge of the Canaanite origins of the Israelite sacrificial systems, and rejected it all on that basis, saying this was not a part of the ancestral faith? If, as Mauchline says of the sacrifices in Isa. 1:10–17, "Such forms of worship . . . were regarded as means by which the beneficial rhythm of nature might be maintained for their own interests and advantage,"[21] we have further support for thinking Jeremiah repudiated all such forms because he found them expressing a Canaanite understanding of God and nature. The other

[17] Julius Wellhausen, *Prolegomena to the History of Ancient Israel*, trans. J. Sutherland Black and Allan Menzes (New York: Meridian Books, 1957), p. 59.
[18] Wilhelm Rudolph, *Jeremia, HAT*, no. 12 (Tübingen: J. C. B. Mohr, 1958), p. 53.
[19] C. Lattey, "The Prophets and Sacrifice," *JTS*, 42 (1941): 155–65.
[20] Albert Strobel, "Jeremias, Priester ohne Gottesdienst? Zu Jer 7, 21–23," *Biblische Zeitschrift*, 1 (1957): 214–24.
[21] John Mauchline, *Isaiah 1–39*, Torch Bible Commentaries (London: SCM Press, 1962), p. 53.

prophets (except possibly Amos) do not do this, but it seems possible that Jeremiah did.

If verse 24 is by the same author as verses 21–23,[22] then the word שרירות (stubbornness) supports our interpretation of this passage as a declaration that Israel's cult has been hopelessly syncretistic ever since the conquest, for of its ten occurrences, six are used of those who worship false gods, and three others are in the same context with such references (leaving Jer. 23:17, which is noncommittal).

*Group b.* These three texts are alike in providing some additional information about the prophets' disapproval of syncretistic worship, and in the fact that this information is secondary to the main point they are trying to make.

Amos 5:21–25:

I hate, I despise your feasts,
and I am not appeased by your solemn assemblies.
For if you offer to me burnt offerings and your
cereal-offerings, I will not approve;
and peace-offerings of your fat cattle
I will not look upon.
Take away from me the tumult of your songs,
and to the melody of your harps I will not listen.
But let justice roll down like waters,
and righteousness like an ever-flowing stream.
Did you bring sacrifices and cereal-offering to me
in the wilderness forty years, O house of Israel?

I take verse 25 as a valid commentary on verses 21–24, and thus as a clue that this passage is to be interpreted much the same as Jer. 7:21–22; as a declaration that all these forms of worship are Canaanite in origin, and are to be repudiated for the same reasons ritual prostitution is repudiated (2:7b–8). However, this passage has been placed in group *b* because while Jer. 7:21–22 apparently must be taken as a judgment of cultic practices themselves, many scholars believe the

[22] Accepted by Rudolph, *Jeremia*; doubted by J. P. Hyatt, "Jeremiah," in *The Interpreter's Bible* (Nashville, Tenn.: Abingdon Press, 1956) 5:876.

main point of Amos 5:21–24 is not, "How should one worship?" but, "What does God desire of man?"[23] In that respect it is to be compared with group *c*.

Jer. 6:16–21: There are two points made in this passage.
A displeasure with syncretism is expressed by saying that
innovations in worship will make no difference.[24]

> For what purpose does frankincense come to me
>     from Sheba, and good cane from a distant land?
> Your burnt-offerings are not acceptable,
>     and your sacrifices are not pleasing to me.

But the main point is the affirmation that no offering of any
kind can avert Yahweh's wrath, because of Israel's rejection
of the law (vs. 19). Here, as in Amos 5:21–27 and elsewhere,
the concern of the prophet is not cult at all, but obedience
to the moral law.

Hosea 6:6:

> For *ḥesed* delights me and not sacrifice,
>     and the knowledge of God more than burnt-offerings.

There is a problem of syntax here. Are both sacrifice (זבח)
and burnt offerings (עֹלוֹת) repudiated,[25] or is sacrifice
repudiated and burnt offerings given relative value, or are
both given relative value?[26] Whichever it be, two factors
must be considered in interpreting the verse: (1) If verses
7–10 are a part of the same oracle, our crucial verse then is
closely connected with denunciations of corrupted sanctuaries. Then, whether לֹא and מִן are absolutes or not, the
verse could be a repudiation of sacrifices by which "knowledge of God" is not conveyed, because of the corrupt priest-

[23] W. O. E. Oesterley, *Sacrifices in Ancient Israel* (New York:
Macmillan, 1937), p. 194.

[24] Wellhausen, *Prolegomena*, p. 65, believed the use of incense was
borrowed from paganism late in the cultic history of Israel. M. Haran,
"The Uses of Incense in the Ancient Israelite Ritual," *VT*, 10 (1960):
118–21, shows that archeological evidence does not decide the matter,
but believes that Deut. 32:10 is sufficient to refute Wellhausen.

[25] W. R. Harper, *A Critical and Exegetical Commentary on the
Books of Amos and Hosea* (New York: C. Scribner's Sons, 1905), p. 287.

[26] Strobel, *BZ*, 1 (1957): 217.

hood which Hosea condemns.[27] (2) The second factor cannot be omitted, even if (1) is true. It is that the essential question Hosea deals with is not, "What is the proper kind of worship?" but, "What does God desire of man?" and that question is always answered in terms of ethics in the Old Testament.

*Group c.* Micah 6:6–8 contains no hint that sacrifice is repudiated because of its Canaanite origins. In fact, sacrifice is not actually repudiated at all.

> With what shall I appear before Yahweh,
>> shall I bow myself to God on high?
> Shall I appear before him with burnt offerings,
>> with yearling calves?
> Will Yahweh be pleased with thousands of rams,
>> with myriads of rivers of oil?
> Shall I give my first-born for my transgression,
>> the fruit of my loins for the sin of my soul?
> He has told you, O man, what is good;
>> and what does Yahweh require of you,
>> but to do *mishpaṭ* and love *ḥesed* and walk
>> submissively with your God.

The question again is, What does Yahweh desire of man? and the exaggerated rhetoric of the initial options presented seems to indicate that the prophet is not seriously weighing two possible ways of pleasing Yahweh, then abandoning one in favor of the other. Surely he did not intend anyone to consider verse 7 a live option. So this passage may be read as containing no judgment about the cult at all. It is valuable to observe that Deut. 10:12 ff. asks the same question, "What does Yahweh ask of you?" and answers it the same way, in terms of ethical obedience; but since the Deuteronomist would not like to present sacrifice in a disparaging light, omits the rhetorical contrast. If the question and answer in Micah involve a judgment about the cult and whether sacrifice is valid or not, I do not see how Deuteronomy could

[27] H. W. Wolff, *Hosea*, Biblischer Kommentar, no. 14:1 (Neukirchen Kreis Moers: Neukirchener Verlag, 1961), p. 153.

speak in essentially the same language. The two differ in their attitude toward sacrifice, surely, but Deuteronomy agrees perfectly with Micah in giving the same answer to the question, "What does Yahweh really want of man?"

Since this passage cannot be taken as a judgment of the cult in general, it is not a real exception to the view that when the prophets *did* judge the cult, it was because of syncretism.

In Isaiah 1:11–15 nothing is said explicitly of syncretism, although it may be significant that Isaiah used terms which elsewhere are used to condemn corruptions of the cult.

What good to me is the multitude of your sacrifices,
    says Yahweh.
I am satiated with burnt-offerings of rams and
    fat of fed cattle,
and blood of bulls and lambs and
    he-goats does not delight me.
When you come to appear before me, who seeks these
    from your hand, the trampling of my courts?
Bring no more vain cereal-offerings,
    incense is an abomination to me.
New moon and Sabbath, calling of assembly –
    I cannot stand iniquity and solemn assembly.
Your new moons and your appointed times my soul hates.
    They are a burden upon me;
    I have become weary of bearing them.
And when you spread out your hands, I will hide my
    eyes from you.
    Even though you multiply prayer, I will not listen.

The word שָׁוְא (vain) is used of idols in Jer. 18:15, Ps. 31:7, and Jonah 2:9. The word תּוֹעֵבָה always seems to refer to cultic irregularities, and thus is not an ethical judgment (cf. I Kings 14:23–24). Not too much can be made of this, however. Essentially, this is a list of forms of worship which *could* become legitimate for Yahwism, according to the rest of the Old Testament. But once again, modern interpreters have found in this passage (as in Amos 5 and

Micah 6) not so much a judgment concerning how one ought to worship God, but of who is fit to worship.[28] References to "iniquity and solemn assembly" and to prayers by those whose hands are full of blood support this.[29] The condemnations of Canaanite elements in worship to be found elsewhere in the book of Isaiah do not permit us to take this single text as evidence for the existence of a cult which was free of those elements.

No extended discussion of Jer. 14:12 is necessary, since it simply says that no amount of ritual can avert the doom which is coming to a rebellious people, and does not say anything about how the obedient are to worship.

We conclude from our study of the prophetic references to the cult that when they explicitly condemn it, it is because it is syncretistic. In those few texts which refer to the cult without any mention of syncretism, the point of the passage is not what is wrong with the cult, but what is wrong with men in the present day that cannot be alleviated by worship. The existence of two, or even more, passages in the prophetic writings which talk about the cult without mentioning any of the practices we have called syncretistic would scarcely be good evidence for the existence of a "legitimate Yahwistic cult" under other circumstances; but when the point of these passages is something other than the validity of certain cult practices, as modern research has shown, we ought to be justified in considering them as not providing evidence for the existence of a type of cult which is never referred to elsewhere.

### Evidence in Deuteronomy for the Israelite Cult during the Monarchy

The much-discussed questions of the origins and affinities of Deuteronomy cannot be dealt with here, nor is it possible even to go into detailed consideration of the problem of the relationship of that book to the prophetic movement. But

[28] Mauchline, *Isaiah 1–39*, p. 53; Wildberger, *Jesaja*, p. 38.
[29] A different interpretation is given by Hentschke, *Schriftpropheten*, p. 97 f.

two points can be made from a brief study of Deuteronomy which contribute something further to our knowledge of what Israelite worship was like when the prophets were active, and to our understanding of the basis for their opposition to that cult.

First, it should be clear from what the prophets and the book of Kings say that the cultic practices condemned in the book of Deuteronomy as Canaanite were not things which Israel was *in danger of* adopting, but things which *were* adopted by Israel. So it seems valid to compare the prohibitions in the cultic realm which we find in this book with those things condemned by the prophets as a way of comparing their attitudes toward the cult of the monarchic period. Deuteronomy condemns the worship of idols, of the host of heaven, of other gods; the use of altars, pillars, Asherim; child-sacrifice, divination and sorcery, cult prostitution, worship at high places and under green trees; and prophecy by other gods. This list is nearly identical with the one compiled from the prophetic books, with only minor differences. This agreement is, I believe, significant, and cannot be attributed entirely to a Deuteronomic editing of the prophetic books.

Second, two positive admonitions in this book are important to us. Deut. 10:12–22 asks the same question as prophetic passages we have dealt with, and it gives the same positive answer:

> And now, Israel, what does Yahweh your God ask of you, but to fear Yahweh your God, to walk in all his ways, and to love him, and to serve Yahweh your God with all your heart and with all your soul; to keep the commandments of Yahweh, and the statutes which I command you this day for your good? (vss. 12–13)

The answer is phrased differently, without a contrast between worship and obedience, and this is to be expected, since the Deuteronomist is also interested in prescribing a proper form of worship for an obedient people. But we have seen that the negative words about the cult which do appear in Deuteronomy and the prophetic books are the same, and that in this first of two positive statements about what God requires of man, the prophets and Deuteronomy offer a common answer.

In the other passage, 12:4–14, 26–27, Deuteronomy and the prophets differ. Both detest the Canaanite influence on their religion, but while the prophets only condemn such practices, the Deuteronomist seeks to show how reform can take place. Recognizing that worship must continue, he creates a plan for worship which will be acceptable to God — granted the people obey that which both parties know God desires most. The prophets (until Ezekiel) do not look ahead in this way; they do not like what they see, but they have no program to replace it. Modern studies have shown they do not advocate a "spiritual religion" in its place; they seem, rather, to have left program planning to more systematic souls. The eschatology of these two parties may account for the difference; the Deuteronomist is essentially optimistic, trying to create a community which will be fit to occupy the promised land, while the prophets see no point in reforming worship at sanctuaries which will soon be destroyed.

*Sacred Tradition in Cult, Deuteronomy, and the Prophetic Preaching*

It has been suggested that the ancient, sacred traditions of Israel had been preserved for and by the prophets and the Deuteronomist in conservative circles to which both belonged. Can we identify and describe more accurately such circles? Many scholars today find the locus of preservation of the sacred traditions in the cult, and believe the prophets to be dependent on it for both the form and the content of their message.[30] But others see serious problems with this, for some of the reasons which have been discussed here, and have been looking elsewhere for a realm of continuity, espe-

[30] Würthwein "Kultpolemik"; Reventlow, *Das Amt des Propheten; idem, Israel,* BZAW, no. 82 (Berlin: Alfred Töpelmann, 1962); Walter Beyerlin, *Die Kulttraditionen Israels in der Verkündigung des Propheten Micha,* FRLANT, no. 72 (Göttingen: Vandenhoeck und Ruprecht, 1959).

cially to the Levites, or to groups composed of Levites and prophets.[31] It does not appear that a fully satisfactory answer to so specific a question can be given as yet, but on the basis of the work done here some suggestions in general terms about the preservation of the sacred traditions may be given.

This paper has stressed that the cult was normally and nominally Yahwistic. That this is true is shown by an exception, Jezebel's cult, which was anti-Yahwistic, and which was repudiated by Israel. A Yahwistic cult of any sort will then be expected to preserve in some form the early traditions of the religion. We have seen evidence that they would be combined with Canaanite myths and rituals; that is clear from the Psalms and even the prophets. But the liturgical sources in the Bible show us that in at least some sanctuaries the early traditions were not completely obliterated by nature-myths. For most people, all this material, exodus-tradition, Sinai-covenant, and nature-myth, was fully acceptable.

As recent studies have shown, the prophets had close contacts with the cult. They had to worship somewhere, though probably without taking part in all that went on in the sanctuaries. So the cult may have been the source of much of their knowledge of Yahweh. However, they differed from most of their contemporaries in concluding that a part of what was done and taught in the cult was to be judged by another part of cultic teaching which clashed with it. They selected certain materials and made them normative, and this led them to react against the cult as being hopelessly corrupt in its present form.

Such a selection of parts of cultic teaching was not arbitrary, nor was it completely original with the prophets. There may have been other, more private sources of knowledge about the early Yahwistic traditions. Here the recent studies of the Levites, of the early prophetic associations,

---

[31] Wolff, *TLZ*, 81 (1956), cols. 83–94; *idem, Amos' geistige Heimat*; G. von Rad, *Studies in Deuteronomy*, Studies in Biblical Theology no. 9 (Naperville, Ill.: A. R. Allenson, 1953). Those who disagree with the Levite theory include Martin Noth, in a review of von Rad, *TLZ*, 73 (1948), cols. 536 ff; Otto Bächli, *Israel und die Völker*, AThANT. no. 41 (Zurich: Zwingli, 1962), pp. 181–84.

and of wisdom teaching in early periods are helpful in filling some of the blanks in our understanding of this aspect of Israelite life.[32] It is also possible that the written documents, J and E, were available to some. But there is a strong probability that in the living community there existed highly conservative factions (such as the Rechabites) which contributed little to the ongoing life of the people, and nothing to the problem of how to keep up with the changing times, but which did preserve. with only slight changes, the tradition of how things used to be. Without trying to make too close a connection between the Deuteronomist and the prophets, it seems safe to say that both of these parties were strongly influenced by what they learned from this realm of their society, although they did not belong to that realm themselves.[33]

Both the prophets and the Deuteronomist adhered to a syncretistic type of religion. That was inescapable, since they were concerned about the *ongoing* life of their people. The cultural changes brought about by life in Palestine made it essential for Israelite religion to change, or it would die. These men tried to find a way between two dangers; that of becoming like the Rechabites, a cultural remnant, and that of becoming like the priests of the high places, who had modernized the religion so thoroughly that they had lost all that was of value in the old way. Some syncretism was essential because of that cultural change, and it was of value, for surely both the systems of the Deuteronomist and the prophets represent a more adequate form of the faith of Israel than that which had been brought into Canaan in the distant past.

[32] As, e.g., the works of Wolff and Porteous, cited above.
[33] Cf. Gerhard von Rad, *Old Testament Theology*, trans. D. M. G. Stalker (New York: Harper, 1962), 1:66.

# 5

## Some Remarks on Prophets and Cult
### G. W. AHLSTRÖM

The subject of the relationship between law and cult in Israel has been defined in various ways. In a recent study R. E. Clements has maintained that the failure of Israelite cult was responsible for the failure of the law. Since the cult did not "make known a true knowledge of Yahweh," the law did not "prevent a dissolution of moral standards in Israelite society."[1] To this rather dubious statement Clements adds the assertion that the law "failed to be an effective force in governing Israelite behaviour, because the cult failed to make known the true demands of the covenant."[2] This is scarcely credible; in fact, it is a rationalization which does not accord with the facts. We do know that the cult had to "establish and renew the covenant" and that this included a recitation of the holy ordinances. Obviously, what disturbed the prophets — and for that matter, modern scholars as well! — was the divergence between the religious ordinances of the law and the moral behavior of the people. It is doubtful that the cult was responsible for this. This is merely the truism of human life, that ideals and realities do not always go hand in hand. To hear a demand is one thing; to *do* it is another.

On the other hand, I agree with Clements that the assertion of Gerhard von Rad[3] concerning the law cannot be wholly accepted as true. He contends that "it was in the

[1] R. E. Clements, *Prophecy and Covenant*, Studies in Biblical Theology no. 43 (Naperville, Ill.: A. R. Allenson, 1965), p. 86.
[2] *Ibid.*
[3] G. von Rad, *Old Testament Theology*, (New York: Harper & Row, 1965), 2:176 ff. (German ed., 2:187 ff.)

eighth-century prophets that for the first time the law took on a threatening aspect."[4] In my opinion this so-called threatening aspect of the law of Yahweh was inherent in the covenant ideology. Ps. 89:31 ff., with its covenant ideology, attests this. If the sons of David do not follow Yahweh's *tōrāh* and *mišpāṭîm* as laid down in the covenant, Yahweh will punish them. This means that also the people will be punished. In this ancient psalm, as in many other psalms, the threat of judgment is found in an old liturgical setting where the creation of the cosmos and the defeat of chaos is prominent. Here the cult prophet declared the divine words of blessing and well-being which would "create" the ideal status for the people of Yahweh, and which, conversely, would mean death and destruction for their enemies. This style of blessing and cursing, bringing fortune or misfortune, light or darkness, can be traced back to very ancient times in the Near East.[5] Moreover, this style is not only well known, appearing in many Israelite psalms, but has been employed very frequently by the prophets. However, what the prophets "inaugurated" was the use of this cultic form not only in the cultic setting, where it was invoked on behalf of the people, but also in public preaching, where it pronounced evil and doom upon the people as a punishment. The cultic formula, with its negative foreboding, became an instrument of judgment in the mouth of the prophets as it had been in the mouth of the cult prophets.

In this regard, Clements has also considered another related phenomenon, the importance of the so-called *tōrāh*-entries or *tōrāh*-liturgies. He maintains that by these "the cult sought to regulate access to the sanctuaries and to prevent unsuitable persons from presenting themselves before Yahweh."[6] However, when the prophetic attitude toward cult and ethics is discussed, these *tōrāh*-liturgies ought to be

---

[4] Clements, *Prophecy and Covenant*, p. 81.

[5] Cf. H. Güterbock, "Die historische Tradition und ihre literarische Gestaltung bei Baybloniern und Hethitern bis 1200," *Zeitschrift für Assyriologie und vorderasiatische Archäologie*, 42 (1934): 15 ff.; F. M. T. Böhl, *Mitteilungen der altorientalischen Gesellschaft*, 2:3 (1937), 2 ff.

[6] Clements, *Prophecy and Covenant*, pp. 82 f.

considered and also compared with what is called the "prophet-*tōrāh*."[7] From very ancient times the divine words had been uttered by special priest-prophets or cult-prophets in a liturgical setting.[8] Here we find the natural "starting-point" for the prophetic criticism of the cult and the moral standards of the people. The later prophets could use these, and by expanding the form of such cultic oracles and *tōrāh*-liturgies, adapt them to their own preaching.[9] An example of such a prophetic *tōrāh* is found in Isa. 1:10–17. Notably, it ends with the admonition to the people to remove the evil from the eyes of Yahweh that they may

> learn to do good, seek justice, correct oppression,
> defend the fatherless, plead for the widow (vs. 17).

This last sentence is so old that we can assuredly say that it is older than the Israelite religion itself. This idea, found in Sumero-Accadian royal ideology (cf. *Codex Ham.* R XXIV:59 ff.), has become a part of the Israelite tradition, cf. Pss. 34:15, 68:6, 82:3 f, Amos 5:15, Jer. 22:15 f.[10] Here, as in so many other instances, it can be shown that the Canannites are the mediators of this idea, passing it on to the Israelites. In the Krt text found at Ugarit we read that king Keret's son Yaṣib accuses his father, using the following words:

> You have not decided the case of the widow
> You have not judged the oppressed

[7] S. Mowinckel, *Psalmenstudien* (Kristiania: J. Dybwad, 1922), 2:118 f.; *idem, Le Décalogue* (Paris: F. Alcam, 1927), pp. 141 ff.; J. Begrich, *Die priesterliche Tora*, BZAW, 46 (1936): 63 ff.; K. Koch, "Tempelanlassliturgien und Dekaloge," in *Studien zur Theologie der alttestamentlichen Überlieferungen*, Festschrift G. von Rad (Neukirchen: Neukirchener Verlag, 1961), pp. 45 ff.

[8] Cf. E. Würthwein, "Kultpolemik oder Kultbescheid?" in *Tradition und Situation*, ed. E. Würthwein and O. Kaiser, Festschrift A. Weiser (Göttingen: Vandenhoeck & Ruprecht, 1963) pp. 127 f.

[9] Koch, "Tempelanlassliturgien," pp. 53 ff.; Clements, *Prophecy and Covenant*, p. 84.

[10] Cf. E. Hammershaimb, "On the Ethics of the Old Testament Prophets, *SVT*, 7 (1960): 80 f. See also F. Ch. Fensham, "Widow, Orphan, and the Poor in Ancient Near Eastern Legal and Wisdom Literature," *JNES* 21 (1962): 129 ff.

You have not driven away those who prey on the poor
You have not given bread to the fatherless.

(UM 127:46 ff.) [11]

Keret is accused of not having fulfilled his royal duties. Obviously we have to acknowledge the fact that the ethical demands in this text are as outspoken as in some of the Israelite texts. Moreover, this should remind us of the unfairness of some scholars who accuse the Canaanite religion, asserting that it was immoral and posed a threat to the Israelites.[12]

The tōrāh-liturgies which I have mentioned already[13] are an indication that the cult did stress the ethical side of religious life.[14] This fact has too often been neglected or denied in the scholarship of past generations. The appearance of this ethical element in the prophetic message shows that they employed this along with other liturgical forms and cultic ideas. In fact, it is not at all a great leap to pass from these tōrāh-liturgies to the parenetic style of preaching so often found in the prophetical books and in the book of Deuteronomy.[15]

[11] Cf. II 'Aqht V:4 ff. where the same motif in a positive way is used about Danel.

[12] Cf. G. E. Wright, who considers the Canaanite religion to have been "the most dangerous and disintegrative factor which the faith of Israel had to face." The Old Testament against Its Environment, Studies in Biblical Theology no. 2 (Chicago: H. Regnery, 1950), p. 13. According to the deuteronomistic view and interpretation of history this is correct. Nevertheless, that is not the same thing as saying that it was a historical fact.

[13] As examples of such liturgies, one may mention Pss. 15 and 24, cf. also Ps. 81. As prophetic tōrāh-oracles see Mic. 6:6 ff., Isa. 1:10–17, 33:14–16. See among others Aage Bentzen, Introduction to the Old Testament (Copenhagen: G. E. C. Gad, 1949), 2d ed. 1:189; O. Eissfeldt, The Old Testament: An Introduction, trans. P. R. Ackroyd (New York: Harper & Row, 1965), p. 74; H. Gunkel, "Jes. 33, eine prophetische Liturgie," ZAW, 42 (1924): 177 f. Ps. 15 is by J. L. Koole considered as a royal liturgy, "Psalm XV-Eine königliche Einzugsliturgie?" Oudtestamentische Studiën, 13 (1963): 98 ff.

[14] Cf. S. Mowinckel, The Psalms in Israel's Worship, trans. D. R. Ap-Thomas (New York: Abingdon, 1962), 2:70 f.

[15] I. Engnell, Gamla Testamentet (Stockholm: Svenska kyrkans diakonistyrelses bokförlag, 1945), I:71 f.

We may now return to the idea that the Israelite cult was a failure in teaching "the true knowledge of Yahweh." Clements believes that this was due to the failure of the cult to give the covenant and its statutes a place of importance in worship. (One might add that it would be difficult to prove this.) For this reason, according to Clements, the prophets "insisted" upon the "authentic word of Yahweh's covenant" in the prophecies which they uttered, not relying upon what was spoken through the priests and cult prophets at different sanctuaries.[16] In my opinion, we do have to make a distinction between the official cult personnel and some of the prophets. No doubt, some prophets have interpreted their own revelations and even the religion of Israel in a way different from that of the official priests. Such interpretations would involve far reaching conclusions, the consequences of which would be very different from those envisaged by the priests. The prophets did emphasize that "sacrifice as an external act unrelated to the spirit had no value."[17] But this is not to say that they rejected sacrifice per se. It is true that prophetic objections to certain cult phenomena are due to the growing syncretism in religion. However, since the prophets do not give a *manuale* of Israelite religion and worship, we have no right to conclude that they were hostile in principle toward the cult.

For instance, we do not know much about Amos' conception of the Jerusalemite cult other than from 2:5 f. (cf. 6:1) and from his negative attitude toward the Israelite cult at Bethel. Therefore, when Clements asserts that Amos "was authorized to declare that the cult was a lie, and its blessings were just fictions," he goes too far.[18] Both he and Gowan have missed an important point.[19] Amos is unable to recognize the Jerusalemite Yahweh in the cult at the temple in

---

[16] Clements, *Prophecy and Covenant*, p. 97.

[17] H. H. Rowley, *The Unity of the Bible* (London: Carey Kingsgate, 1953), p. 42.

[18] Clements *Prophecy and Covenant*, p. 99.

[19] See chapter 4, this volume. Cf. A. S. Kapelrud, who maintains that to Amos "all kinds of cult practice seem to have been completely irrelevant," *Central Ideas in Amos* (Oslo: Oslo University, 1956), p. 37.

Bethel. To him it is mostly a baalistic cult; therefore, this particular form of cult is a lie. From this we may conclude that the Yahweh worship at Bethel is different from the Yahweh worship at Jerusalem. It is the deity of Jerusalem, Yahweh of Zion, Amos 1:2, who gives Amos his message and sends him to Bethel, not the Yahweh of Bethel. In the story of Amos' appearance at Bethel we see the conflict between two Israelite religious traditions. Because Amos rejects the cult at Bethel no warrant is given for us to use his book to reject the cult in general.[20] What Amos wants is, as he sees it, a true cult, one which is in harmony with the correct cult place, namely, Jerusalem. To Amos, Jerusalem is the only official cult place of the religion of Yahweh. Of course, this does not imply that Amos could not have criticized the cult at Jerusalem.[21] But at Jerusalem, Yahweh showed himself as he was, and what Amos saw at Bethel he could not recognize or identify with Yahweh. Hosea seems to be of the same opinion. The truth is that neither Amos nor Hosea nor any other "writing" prophet could really conceive a religion without cult, cf. Zeph. 3:18. That would have been something of a *contradictio in adjecto*, which, perhaps, would be much more suitable to a period hostile to cult, such as our own time.[22]

Since I have mentioned one of the tendencies in Amos and Hosea, it is now possible to make a suggestion. In the religio-

[20] Cf. D. L. Williams, who says, "Amos was combatting a popular conception of worship which had become automatic and lifeless," "The Theology of Amos," *Review and Expositor*, 63 (1966): 395. It is, of course, quite impossible to prove the last part of this statement. The first part of it can also be criticized because Amos was not dealing with a "popular" form of cult but with the official Israelite cult at the royal temple of Bethel!

[21] Amos 6:1, cf. Jer. 2:8, 28, 23:13 ff.

[22] When G. Quell says that "das sakrifizielle Tun ist ein Feind der Religion," (*Das kultische Problem der Psalmen*, BWAT, 11 [1926]: p. 59) one cannot help suspect that this is a modern opinion and not the conception of the Israelites. The same can be said about R. Hentschke, *Die Stellung der vorexilischen Schriftpropheten zum Kultus*, BZAW, 75 (1957). For a critic of Quell's opinion see among others S. Mowinckel, *Religion und Kultus* (Göttingen: Vandenhoeck & Ruprecht, 1953), p. 136.

political struggle between Bethel and Jerusalem — and other cult places too — the Jerusalemite religious leaders utilized the idea that their cult place, Jerusalem, was the place which Yahweh had really chosen as his own.[23] In my opinion, this idea has very much been advocated by the prophets. Here they, as well as the religious leaders of Judah, have built upon the tradition referred to in II Sam. 6. When the ark was brought up to Jerusalem this city became the choice of Yahweh as his particular dwelling place.[24] Consequently, after the fall of the northern kingdom, Israel, this conception became one of the ideological foundations of the events which occurred during the time of Josiah. A support for this may be found in a passage which is seldom related to this, namely, Hos. 3:6 (Eng. v. 5):

> Afterwards the children of Israel shall return
>   and seek Yahweh their god, and David their king,
> And they will come in fear to Yahweh and to his
>   goodness in the latter days.

This declaration of the prophet follows his assertion that first Israel will dwell for a long time without king and prince, without sacrifice and *maṣṣēbāh*, without ephod and teraphim. This is the punishment, namely, that things which normally belong to an orderly society and its cult, including sacrifice and *maṣṣēbāh*, will be lacking. The only future the prophet can promise to them is one which demands a Davidic dynasty in Jerusalem with its Yahweh cult. The "sin" of the northern kingdom is thus twofold: it has broken away from the Davidic dynasty, chosen by Yahweh; and its religion with its conception of Yahweh was not the same as in Jerusalem, where Yahweh, according to this prophet, should be worshiped. Again we observe that Hosea is not hostile in prin-

[23] Phenomenologically speaking the deity always chooses his cult place. He belongs there because there he "reveals" himself, there he lives. Cf. also Exod. 20:24.

[24] Cf. Pss. 2:6, 48:2–5, 68:16 f., 87:1 f., 132:13–16, Exod. 15:13, 17, Isa. 2:2 f., 8:18, 18:7, Zech. 1:17, 2:16, 3:2. See also W. Staerk, "Zum alttestamentlichen Erwählungsglauben," *ZAW*, 55 (1937): 15 ff.

ciple toward kingship and cult.[25] He does not condemn cult
per se. For Hosea, as for the other prophets, the question
concerning the cult was twofold: What kind of cult is this?
What does Yahweh want from the people?[26] For the prophets Yahweh of Zion is *the* god, a god different from the "baal-
ized" Yahweh of Bethel or the local Yahweh of some *bāmōt*.[27]

Amos and Hosea are judging the cult of the northern Israel
from the standpoint that it is not really an Israelite form of
religion. The whole kingdom and its cult is apostate. It has
fallen away from Jerusalem where Yahweh and his chosen
dynasty are to be found. In the eyes of these prophets as
well as in the eyes of the Jerusalemite leaders, the religion
of the northern kingdom is an erroneous cult. It is a purely
Canaanite cult which is dedicated to Bethel and to Baal,
not to Yahweh.

Since it has already been mentioned, we may inquire concerning the prophetic criticism of the Judean and Jerusalemite cult. It is possible that the Judahite prophets, men such
as Isaiah,[28] were influenced and inspired by the prophecies

[25] For Hos. 3:4 f. as expressing a main concept in Hosea's attitude
toward religion cf. Ahlström, *Aspects of Syncretism in Israelite Religion*,
Horae Soederblomianae 5 (Lund: Gleerup, 1963), p. 26, n. 4.

[26] According to G. von Rad the concern of the prophets "was not the
faith . . . it was to deliver a message from Jahweh to particular men
and women," *Old Testament Theology*, 2:129. Yes, but the message
from Yahweh was his *dābār*, his word, which also from of old was
heard in the cult, cf. E. Würthwein, *Tradition und Situation*, pp. 126 ff.
Würthwein maintains that the prophets "nicht grundsätzliche, lehrhafte
Ausführungen darüber machen, das Opfer (und Gebet!) mit echter
Jahweverehrung unvereinbar sind, sondern kultische Handlungen und
Gebete bestimmter Menschen in bestimmter Stunde zurückweisen"
because these peoples have abandoned the statutes of Yahweh and
broken with his covenant, p. 130. Cf. A. C. Welch, *Prophet and Priest
in Old Israel* (London: SCM, 1936), pp. 17 f.; H. H. Rowley, "Ritual
and Hebrew Prophets," *Journal of Semitic Studies*, 1 (1956): 343.

[27] Cf. Engnell, "Profeter," *Svenskt Bibliskt Uppslagsverk*, 2d ed.
(Stockholm: Nordiska Uppslagsböcker, 1963), 2, col. 597. This does
not, of course, mean that everything that happened in Jerusalem was
acceptable. What here has been outlined is the principle.

[28] E. Hammershaimb is of the opinion that it is not quite out of the
question that Isaiah has taken over the idea of the remnant from Amos
and made it one of his main conceptions, *Amos* (Copenhagen: Nyt
Nordisk forlag, 1946), p. 83. Cf. also R. Fey, *Amos und Jesaja, WMANT*

of Amos.[29] After all, the two nations were small, proximate territories, and it is very likely that Hosea's sharp denunciations of Israel echoed in Judah. Amos' appearance in the northern kingdom could have become a "signal" and an inspiration for some prophets and their followers in Judah, giving them deeper insights into the religion of their day. Self-criticism, coupled with older Judahite traditions about Yahweh and his worship,[30] could have produced "reinterpretations" of the nature of Yahweh, reinterpretations which could not exclude the cultic development of the people.[31] Perhaps we could say that history is syncretistic and creates syncretism.

To proceed one step further in the discussion, I would like to consider what has been called the old or conservative Yahwistic tradition.[32] Even if we assume the existence of such a tradition, we still have difficulty locating it. Where has it been in existence during the long epoch of time that had passed from the entry of the Israelites into Canaan down to the eighth century? No one would deny that there have been some groups in Israel that have preserved a more conservative attitude toward "Canaanization" of their religion.[33] This is a natural phenomenon. However, to write the history of this tradition and to obtain any measure of objectivity seems impossible. All we can do is point to some

---

12 (Neukirchen, 1963); and K. Budde, "Zu Jesaja 1–5," *ZAW*, 49 (1931): 27.

[29] For the problem of the transmission of the prophetical utterances see my article "Oral and Written Transmission: Some Considerations," *The Harvard Theological Review*, 59 (1966): 69 ff., 80 f.

[30] Of course, we must be aware of the fact that there were several kinds of Yahweh traditions. Every sanctuary contributed to this from its own pre-Israelite traditions as well as through its own history as a Yahweh sanctuary.

[31] As an example of this one can mention the strong emphasis the prophets laid upon the idea that Yahweh was the only real giver of fertility. In preaching this idea they used the language which was connected with the worship of Baal and Ashera, which was the only understandable language in this matter.

[32] Thus Gowan, chapter 4, this volume.

[33] Cf. Johs. Pedersen, *Israel*, (London: Oxford University Press, 1940), III–IV: 515.

groups which we may reckon to have preserved a conservative tradition, such as the Rechabites[34] or possibly some Levitical groups.[35] Another possibility would be an Abiathar group, descendants of the priest Abiathar who was expelled from Jerusalem by Solomon,[36] or possibly some prophetical guilds and the אנשי האלהים.[37] However, it is almost impossible to show how these groups looked upon their own religion and its traditions because the texts we have are not, as far as we know, transmitted to us by these groups, except perhaps for some prophets and Levites.[38]

It has been suggested that the book of Deuteronomy is the product of a group of Levites, that it went "underground" during evil times, and that it was resurrected under Josiah to enter as a new force on the historical scene.[39] This is still

[34] It is perhaps possible to see the Rechabites as especially hostile to the Baal cult, particularly considering their denial of the use of wine. We do, however, not know whether the Rechabites created or influenced what could be called a reform movement.

[35] N. W. Porteous, "Actualization and the Prophetic Criticism of the Cult," in *Tradition und Situation*, pp. 99 f.

[36] Cf. E. Auerbach, *Wüste und Gelobtes Land* (Berlin: Schocken, 1932), pp. 24 ff. K. Budde, *Geschichte der althebräischen Litteratur* (Leipzig: C. F. Amelangs, 1906), pp. 38 ff.

[37] Thus, for instance, I. Engnell, *Gamla Testamentet*, I:148. F. F. Hvidberg thought that in some Judean families "old traditions from the period of the desert had been preserved more purely than was generally the case among North-Israelite tribes," *Weeping and Laughter in the Old Testament* (Leiden: E. J. Brill, 1962), p. 80. This is also a hypothesis that will be hard to prove.

[38] Cf. M. Gertner, "The Masorah and the Levites," *VT* 10 (1960): 244 ff.

[39] A. Alt, "Die Heimat des Deuteronomiums," *Kleine Schriften* (München: C. H. Beck, 1959), 2: 250 ff., cf. Porteous, *Tradition und Situation* pp. 99 f. For the problem of the Levites see among others Aage Bentzen, *Die Josianische Reform und ihre Voraussetzungen* (Copenhagen, 1926); G. von Rad, *Studies in Deuteronomy*, Studies in Biblical Theology no. 9 (Chicago: H. Regnery Co., 1953), pp. 67 f.; G. E. Wright, "The Levites in Deuteronomy," *VT*, 4 (1954): 325 ff.; E. Nielsen, *Shechem* (Copenhagen: G. E. C. Gad, 1955), pp. 276 ff., "The Levites in Ancient Israel," *Annual of the Swedish Theological Institute*, 3 (1964): 16 ff.; G. Minette de Tillesse, "Sections 'tu' et sections 'vous' dans le Deutéronome," *VT*, 12 (1962): 80 f.; J. A. Emerton, "Priests and Levites in Deuteronomy," *VT*, 12 (1962): 129 ff.; A. H. J. Gunneweg, *Leviten und Priester FRLANT*, 89 (Göttingen: Vandenhoeck & Ruprecht, 1965), pp. 213 ff.

a moot question. To assert that the so-called pure Yahwism — whatever is meant by that — should have gone "underground" seems unrealistic. The influence of Canaanite religion upon Yahwism, and the assimilation of Yahwism to the religion of Canaan, presupposes that the Yahwistic tradition did not go underground or disappear for a time. On the contrary, it has mingled with and has been changed by ideas and traditions which expressed the religious life of Canaan to which the Israelites adapted themselves.[40] Some of the old religious phenomena could therefore become more or less inadequate in the new setting, but in some circles the memory of them would be remembered, perhaps in their original form.[41]

Another question may be raised here. Do we have to reckon with a nomadic ideal in order to be able to speak of an "old, conservative Yahwistic tradition?" If we do, we are only making one problem dependent upon another without solving either of them. Of course, my intention is not to deny that the Israelite religion had traditions and religious forms which go back to prehistoric times. However, to equate this with nomadic ideals is impossible, for we know neither to what degree the tribes actually were nomadic, if at all,

[40] When discussing the phenomenon called syncretism one should remember that this term means a merger of at least two streams of traditions; thus a discussion about the syncretism in the history of the Israelite religion must take into account not only that the Israelites have adopted and become assimilated to Canaanite religious phenomena but also that Israelite cult phenomena and ideas may have been adopted by Canaanites and Jebusites living together with the Israelites. Thus, for instance, the "Jebusite component" has "rapidly and smoothly . . . been able to adapt itself to the ancient Israelite tradition, symbolized by the Ark of the Covenant," R. A. Carlson, *David, the Chosen King* (Stockholm: Almqvist & Wiksell, 1964), p. 174. Cf. also I Sam. 5:4 f.

[41] Compare G. Fohrer's opinion about the pre-exilic "Erzähler der Hexateuchschichten." He says that "sie lehnten weder die kanaanäischen Elemente grundsätzlich ab, noch passten sie den eigenen Glauben völlig an die Kulturlandreligion an; vielmehr suchten sie deren lebensfähige, berechtige und dem Jahweglauben nicht wiederstrebende Elemente durch eine entsprechende Interpretation in diesen einzubeziehen," Tradition und Interpretation im Alten Testament," *ZAW*, 73 (1961): 9. If this was the attitude on the part of the narrators, how much more "assimilated" to the Canaanite culture had the whole population and its cult become? Cf. also *ibid.*, p. 12.

nor the nature of the nomadic religious ideals themselves. Perhaps there is some truth in the statement of E. Hammershaimb that "the Israelite religion (or the religion of Yahweh) contained powerful elements deriving from a still older period, by virtue of which Israel did not succumb in its conflict with the religion of Baal."[42] One of the elements which Hammershaimb believes was central to the Canaanite religion, and which appears to be central in the prophetical writings too, was the concept of *mišpāṭ*.[43] I would add to this the fact that it was also central in the Jerusalemite tradition. Thus, the element of *mišpāṭ* cannot be used as an argument for a special "quality" of the original conservative Yahwistic tradition by disassociating the Israelites from the Canaanites.[44]

It may be true, as some have maintained, that the prophets envisaged themselves as bearers of a tradition which stemmed from the earliest period of the Israelite religion. However, this does not justify the conception of a nomadic or desert ideal characteristic of prophetical thought. As a matter of fact, the period of the wilderness wanderings and the place called the desert are no ideal in the prophetic message.[45] The period of wanderings is merely a necessary ordeal to reach something better, cf. Hos. 2:16 ff., 13:5, 15, see also Isa. 6:11 f., Ps. 106:9. The desert is the place of death, *šĕōl*, Ezek. 26:19 ff., Jer. 2:2, 17:6. In fact, according to Amos,

[42] *Some Aspects of Prophecy from Isaiah to Malachi* (Copenhagen: Publications de la Société des Sciences et des Lettres d'Aarhus, 1966), p. 34.

[43] *Ibid.* pp. 70 ff.

[44] H.-J. Kraus asks if Israel when settling in Canaan did "deny its origin" and adopt the entire Canaanite worship, *Worship in Israel*, (Richmond, Va.: John Knox Press, 1966), p. 130. This is too simple a question. Adopting other religious forms or being influenced by them does not imply a denial of one's own origin. The process could, for instance, be seen as an enrichment of the people's own tradition, Cf. G. Fohrer, ZAW, 73 (1961): 6.

[45] I. Engnell, "Profeter," 4, *Svenskt Bibliskt Uppslagsverk* 2, cols. 570 f.; "*Paesaḥ-Maṣṣōt* and the Problem of 'Patternism'" in *Orientalia Suecana* 1 (1952): 45 f.; S. Talmon, "The 'Desert Motif' in the Bible and in Qumran Literature," in *Biblical Motifs*, ed. A. Altmann (Cambridge: Harvard University Press, 1966), pp. 31 ff.; cf. Pedersen, *Israel* I–II:454 ff., III–IV:541.

the period of wilderness wanderings is the beginning of
Israel's apostasy from Yahweh.[46] In Amos 5:25 the prophet
asks:

> Did you bring sacrifices and cereal-offerings to me
> forty years in the wilderness, O house of Israel?

We should notice that the emphasis in this passage is upon
the phrase לִי, "to me." To whom did they bring sacrifices,
to Yahweh or to someone else? The answer expected is given
in verse 26. Israel did not bring sacrifices to Yahweh; they
worshiped other gods. Instead of bringing the proper sacrifices to the "right" god, the people are accused of having
worshiped Sakkut and Kaiwan, names of the Accadian deity
Ninurta, the Babylonian Saturn which was the star of
justice.[47]

In another circle of tradents we can find an example of
the people's apostasy from Yahweh as beginning already
during the wilderness wanderings. In Exod. 32,[48] the high-
priest himself, Aaron, is accused for introducing a "new"
form of worship, the bull-worship.[49] Therefore, this text is
extremely important, giving us, as it does, an insight into
the real nature of Israelite religion.

When now Gowan says that Amos 5:25 f. means that the
concern of the prophets "is not cult at all, but obedience

---

[46] Cf. Hos. 9:10; see also Ps. 106:19 ff., Ps. 78. According to Kraus,
among others, the period of the wanderings in the wilderness was in
the conception of Hosea "the real time of Israel's salvation," *Worship*,
p. 131. But if we notice what the prophet says in 13:5, we see that the
idea of the desert as an ideal time or place to which one should return
is not Hosea's ideal. There the desert is called the land of drought,
that is, the land where nothing can live. Hosea, then, shares the common opinion of the desert as the land of death, and in saying that
Yahweh found his people there, 9:10, he says that Yahweh also saved
them from the desert. This is also in harmony with Deut. 32:10 ff.

[47] Amos perhaps sees in Israel's sacrifices, cult processions, etc. something which he regards as having been done already in the wilderness
wanderings; thus he accuses the nation for continuously having been
an apostate people. To Amos 5:26 cf. E. A. Speiser, "Note on Amos
5:26," *The Bulletin of the American Schools of Oriental Research*, 108
(1947): 5 f.

[48] Cf. also Ps. 106:19 ff.

[49] Cf. Nielsen, *Shechem*, p. 276.

to the moral law," [50] I cannot agree. Rather, it is both. Not only does Amos want the proper sacrifices and the true cult, but also that obedience to the moral law which springs from the cult he considers the true one.

In this connection we recall what is said in Ps. 51. In verse 18 we learn that God (Elohim) has no delight in sacrifices, but rather, as is the case in verse 19, delights in the kind of sacrifice which is a broken spirit. The passage continues in verse 20 asking God (Yahweh's name does not occur in this psalm) to do good to Zion. If he does this, he will receive the right sacrifices, זבחי־צדק, verse 21. Burnt offerings and bulls will be sacrificed on his altar.[51] This is similar to Ps. 4:6, where the text invites the people to trust in Yahweh and to bring, as offerings, the right sacrifices. In these passages one can discover the theological meaning of sacrifices for the Israelites. It is from this fundamental conception that the prophets are speaking and judging the cult.[52]

Another important passage which ought to be considered is Jer. 7:21 ff. Do we not have in this passage an interpretation presented by Jeremiah from a particular situation? Jeremiah is dealing with the temple cult. To the people the temple had become a guarantee for the national existence of Israel; more than that, the temple was inviolable; it would never be desecrated or destroyed. Of course, this is

[50] See chapter 4, this volume. Cf. Kraus who maintains that prophets like Amos and Jeremiah belonged to a stream of tradition in which "the divine law is to the fore and sacrifices are mentioned only secondarily." Here Kraus refers to Deut. 33:8 ff., *Worship*, p. 112. However, Deut. 33:10 has *mišpaṭ* and *tōrāh* as parallel phenomena to *qeṭōrāh* and *kālîl*, thus it will be hard to prove that the sacrificial duties of the Levites are secondary. One could well maintain that they are as important as *mišpaṭ* and *tōrāh*.

[51] For this psalm see among others Geo Widengren, *The Accadian and Hebrew Psalms of Lamentation as Religious Documents* (Uppsala: Almqvist & Wiksells, 1937), pp. 31 f.; Rowley, *The Unity of the Bible*, p. 48; E. R. Dalglish, *Psalm Fifty-One in the Light of Near Eastern Patternism* (Leiden: E. J. Brill, 1962).

[52] It should be emphasized that ethics could not at this time be divorced from the cult, the source of the religious life, because the ethical demands were given by the deity, and at the sanctuary where he lived one had to learn his will and commands.

quite understandable. This religious ideal was not a contemporary invention but had been taught from very ancient times. It was a fundamental religious reality, because the temple, properly speaking, was the place where the deity lived.[53] If the temple was destroyed, it would show that their god was not really a deity at all, or at least, one of little power and influence. Naturally, Judah did not believe they had such a god. For this reason the idea of the inviolability of the temple and its steadfast existence had become a political issue.

Now, however, Jeremiah tells the people something quite different concerning the temple. This object around which the special hope of the people centered would be destroyed. Because the cult in Jerusalem was not directed to Yahweh it was an improper cult. It concerned other gods, because there were non-Yahwistic cult objects in the temple. At this point we observe that it is both the cult and the moral behavior associated with it that are wrong. The prophet now asks for a change of behavior on the part of the people, 7:3. Although the oracle in 7:21 ff. does not mention the commands regarding the sacrifices which Yahweh gave Israel at the time of the Exodus, we also observe that there is no mention of the *pesaḥ* in this oracle. Are we justified, then, in concluding that Yahweh has not even given any commands about the Passover? Obviously Jeremiah does not mean to assert that the Passover is against the will of Yahweh.[54] From the omission of a reference to sacrifices, then, we cannot conclude that he is opposed to these. Rather this passage must be understood against the background of the whole context and situation out of which Jeremiah speaks.

Having considered these evidences, we might ask whether the prophetic criticism of the cult could really have been a denunciation of the cult as such, or a denial of the sacrificial system in principle. The contemporaries of the prophets do not give any indication that this is what they learned from

[53] Cf. above n. 23.
[54] Concerning Jeremiah and the cult cf. Rowley, *The Unity of the Bible*, pp. 40 f.

the prophets. Or are we to conclude that the prophets in this matter had no influence either on the people of their own time or of those who followed in the future?

Finally, we may consider one other related question: Why did the syncretism of which we have spoken exist at all? At this point an important difference, which has not previously been mentioned here, arises. To understand this, we must remember that every religion becomes sterile if it does not receive new impulses to impart life to it. Naturally, the continuous confrontation with changing life must create "changing" phenomena in a religion. With reference to Israelite forms of religion, it is important that we stress the changes which occurred in the cult after Israel settled in Canaan. Israel now confronted a new situation which it had to take into account. The religious life in this new country was not exactly the same, and so it had to follow the customs and rules of Canaan. At this time a process of assimilation begins.[55] The conceptions that were current in Canaan concerning culture and cult, life and religion, deities and holy places, became the possession of the Israelites.[56] Without these a people could not live in the country, for this was the land of the god El. In this land one had to follow El's *mišpāṭ*. This explains why there was such a marked process of syncretism and why eventually some groups representing Israelite religion can hardly be distinguished from the proponents of Canaanite cult and practice.

The basis upon which this syncretism built, or, we might rather say, which made the assimilation of Canaanite ideas possible, was the identification of El and Yahweh. Phenomenologically, Yahweh is another form of the West Semitic El. In fact, it has been suggested a number of years ago that Yahweh's original name may have been Yahweh-El.[57] This

---

[55] Cf. my book, *Aspects of Syncretism in Israelite Religion*, p. 12; A. S. Kapelrud, "The Role of the Cult in Old Israel," in *The Bible in Modern Scholarship*, ed. J. Ph. Hyatt (Nashville: Abingdon Press, 1965), p. 47.

[56] Cf. Mowinckel, *The Psalms in Israel's Worship*, 1:16. See also Hvidberg, *Weeping and Laughter*, pp. 79 f.

[57] Engnell, *Gamla Testamentet*, I: 122 ff., 261 ff. Cf. Ed. Meyer, *Die Israeliten und ihre Nachbarstämme* (Halle: M. Niemeyer, 1906), pp.

idea finds support in Ps. 10:12, where the Masoretic ac-
centuation indicates that we are to read the two names
together, as one, אל יהוה.[58] This also explains why there
is no polemical attitude toward El in the Old Testament.

The existence of widespread syncretism in Israelite religion finds its source not only in the practical matters per-
taining to the religious customs of the people in the land in
which they now live, but also in the identification of El and
Yahweh, the latter being originally another form of El, thus
making possible an ever-increasing adoption and adaption
to the cult and ideology of Canaan. This is the background
against which one has to see the difficult task of the prophets
in their struggle against a "wrong" cult.

---

213 ff.; D. N. Freedman, "The Name of the God of Moses," *Journal of
Biblical Literature*, 79 (1960): 151 ff.

[58] Cf. M. Dahood, "Hebrew-Ugaritic Lexicography III," *Biblica*, 46
(1965): 317 ff.

# 6

## Hort Redivivus: A Plea and a Program
### ERNEST C. COLWELL

Fenton John Anthony Hort needs to be brought back to life. He made a major contribution to the textual criticism of the New Testament in the nineteenth century.[1] He can make a major contribution today.[2]

In that day he presented a carefully reasoned account of textual criticism that was comprehensive in its discussion of method, in its reconstruction of the history of the manuscript tradition, and in its appraisal of text-types. He did not try to be comprehensive in his discussion of the *materials* of textual criticism. He published no catalog of MSS. He cited no manuscript evidence in a critical apparatus. But, having studied what evidence others had accumulated, he applied to its interpretation the powers of a great intellect; and with the help of his collaborator, he produced the best edition of the Greek New Testament that we possess.

Much of the strength of his work derives from its comprehensiveness. He ignored no major facet of the manuscript tradition. Thus, element after element of our later "discoveries" can be found frankly stated in his work. He recognized the early date and wide distribution of the "Western Text" long before its champions did. He leaned more heavily upon patristic evidence than we do. He saw clearly that the "canonization" of the New Testament books did not

[1] Brook Foss Westcott and Fenton John Anthony Hort, *The New Testament in the Original Greek* (London and New York: Macmillan, 1881). The references in this article are to Volume 2 of the reprint of 1896.

[2] Throughout this paper the discussion of manuscript evidence is limited to manuscripts of the Gospels.

result in accurate copying in the first three centuries. His work was comprehensive. The work of the last forty years has often been fragmented. Today we need a fresh comprehensive statement, and it must begin with Hort.

A careful restatement of Hort's work will go far toward correcting the extremist errors of the last forty years. These errors are a by-product of the *Sitz im Leben* of New Testament studies. Historismus is gone. Confidence in the ability of the historian to establish complete objective reality in the past has evaporated. This has led to a radical scepticism as to the value of any historical study. Textual criticism is unimportant today because it is a minor subdivision of historical study. Our fathers classified it as a part of "lower criticism" and regarded it as essential. We classify it as a low form of criticism and regard it as dispensable. In an age in which physical science has redefined itself as probability, historical probability has lost its significance for theologians. This loss has been rationalized into desirability. Concentration upon systematic theology has eliminated interest in grammar and text. Existentialism without a past has helped to produce manuscript study without a history. Whether from these or from other causes, two deplorable conditions have existed in the main stream of New Testament textual criticism in this generation.[3]

A study of monographs and manuals produced in the last forty years shows an amazing number that make no serious effort to reconstruct the history of the manuscript tradition. This can be said of Metzger's recently published manual.[4] Professor Robert Grant says plainly that the task is im-

[3] The exceptions that can be cited to antiobjectivity do not change the general picture. Their influence has been very limited. Quentin's "Rule of Iron" was rejected by the reviewers, and was abandoned in his own project when the New Testament was reached. It can be useful within a tightly knit group of MS, but not elsewhere. Vinton Dearing's objective method is not easily understood, and is still under appraisal. Finally the computer promises objectivity if we can decide subjectively what it is to count. First efforts at its use have failed from lack of rigor in preliminary definition.

[4] Bruce M. Metzger, *The Text of the New Testament* (London: Oxford University Press, 1964).

possible. On second thought, I withdraw the adjective "plainly." What he says is: "The primary goal of New Testament textual study remains the recovery of what the New Testament writers wrote. We have already suggested that to achieve this goal is wellnigh impossible. Therefore we must be content with what Reinhold Niebuhr and others have called, in other contexts, an 'impossible possibility'."[5] Equally extreme is Clark's comment: "In general P[75] tends to support our current critical text, and yet the papyrus vividly portrays a fluid state of the text at about A.D. 200. Such a scribal freedom suggests that the gospel text was little more stable than the oral tradition, and that we may be pursuing the retreating mirage of the 'original text'."[6] And, most recently, Kurt Aland is able to solve finally the problem of one Western noninterpolation after another without reconstructing the history of the manuscript tradition.[7] At the end of his article he does seem to sense a void, for he promises to reconstruct the history of the manuscript tradition in a subsequent article.

I use the phrase "reconstruct the history of the manuscript tradition" with the assumption that the purpose of the reconstruction is to aid in restoring the original wording of the text. Thus I deny that those have salvaged historical value who point out that every variant may tell us something about the history of the church. The current enthusiasm for manuscript variations as contributions to the history of theology has no solid foundation. Granted that a number of variant readings have been theologically motivated, would any serious student of the history of theology turn to these as a major source? Is it not true, on the contrary, that we can be sure of theological motivation for a variant reading only when the history of theology in that MS's time and

[5] Robert M. Grant, *A Historical Introduction to the New Testament* (New York and Evanston: Harper & Row, 1963), p. 51.

[6] Kenneth W. Clark, "The Theological Relevance of Textual Variation in Current Criticism of the Greek New Testament," *Journal of Biblical Literature*, 85 (1966): 15.

[7] Kurt Aland, "Neue Neutestamentliche Papyri II," *New Testament Studies*, 12 (1965–66): 193–210.

place is already well known?[8] For example, in C. S. C. Williams' study of intentional variants contrast the solidity of the Marcionite chapter with the uncertainty and tentativeness of the surrounding material. The much-needed task of relating textual criticism to contemporary biblical theology and hermeneutics must be carried on at a deeper level than this.

What has been said above suggests that the direction needs to be reversed. Instead of talking about "the theological relevance of textual variation," we should discuss "the relevance of theology to the establishment of the text of the New Testament." But textual critics are not competent to discuss this. The technicians are too naïve theologically. For example, in the course of his argument that Luke 22:43–44 (the bloody sweat passage) is an interpolation, Aland says "Who indeed would have omitted these verses if he had found it in the text before him?" Aside from the scribe of MS 13 and Corrector A of Sinaiticus, a review of Christian theology in the early centuries would make the answer easy. Thus C. S. C. Williams, after a long discussion of possible theological motivation for omission of these verses, decides that they were part of the original text.[9] Even Hort can be indicted here in the light of post-*Rechtgläubigkeit und Ketzerei* studies. Hort was never naïve. He did know early Christians who would have omitted this verse, but they were heretics! "Except," he says, "to heretical sects, which exercised no influence over the transmitted text, the language of vv. 43 f. would be no stumbling block in the first and

[8] The *nomina sacra* in their development and variations are an exception. There the data from the MSS carry theological significance on their faces, and may provide fresh witnesses to theological developments.

[9] C. S. C. Williams, *Alterations to the Text of the Synoptic Gospels and Acts* (Oxford: Blackwell, 1951), pp. 6–8. Note that the author understates the extent of lectionary evidence for the transposition, that he quotes without dissent Goguel's claim that the omission in Alexandrian witnesses would date from the time and under the influence of Athanasian orthodoxy, although the subsequent discovery of P[75] which omits the passage makes this doubtful.

second centuries. . . ." [10] This neat division between orthodoxy and heresy is — so I am informed by theologians — no
longer possible.

What the textual critic offers the theologian is the text
as it existed in a specific time and place. But to do this he
needs the help of the theologian who is today, unfortunately,
incapable of textual criticism.

Erich Fascher has had the boldness to attempt a fusion
of hermeneutics and textual criticism.[11] His main thesis in
regard to the history of the manuscript period is weakened
by two limitations. (1) He asserts that Hort's theory should
be changed in three ways — but two of the three are already
in Hort: (*a*) The widespread antiquity of the Western Text,
(*b*) the lack of homogeneity in the Western Text. It is
obvious that he has not read Hort; but if so, he should not
revise him.[12] (2) He deals primarily with isolated readings,
unrelated to the history of the MSS, and relates them to
the history of Christian thought. The work is a valuable
challenge to textual criticism, but it is not a supplement to
it. The rejection of text-types destroys the bridge between
the two disciplines.

The second deplorable condition of our studies in the
last forty years is the growing tendency to rely entirely on
the internal evidence of readings, without serious considerations of documentary evidence.

The two great translation efforts of these years — RSV
and NEB — each chose the Greek text to translate on the
basis of the internal evidence of readings. Frederick Grant's
expository pamphlet on the RSV made this clear. The translators, he says, followed two rules: (1) Choose the reading

[10] Westcott and Hort, "Notes on Select Readings," in *The New
Testament*, p. 66.

[11] Erich Fascher, *Textgeschichte als hermeneutisches Problem*
(Halle: V. M. Niemeyer Verlag, 1953).

[12] Aland confesses that "few of us [Germans] will presumably have
read their [Westcott and Hort's] Introduction . . . in spite of its
primary importance." (Kurt Aland, "The Significance of the Papyri for
Progress in New Testament Research," in *The Bible in Modern Scholarship*, ed. J. Ph. Hyatt [Nashville: Abingdon Press, 1965], p. 325.)

that best fits the context; (2) choose the reading which explains the origin of the other readings.[13] Professor Dodd informed me that the English translators also used these two principles — Hort's intrinsic probability and transcriptional probability. One of the RSV translators while lecturing to the New Testament Club at the University of Chicago replied to a question as to the Greek text he used by saying that it depended on where he was working: he used Souter at the office and Nestle at home. One of the English translators in admitting the unevenness of the textual quality of that translation explained that the quality depended on the ability of the man who made the first draft of a book.

Whether in Early Christian times or today, translators have so often treated the text cavalierly that textual critics should be hardened to it. But much more serious is the prevalence of this same dependence on the internal evidence of readings in learned articles on textual criticism, and in the popularity of manual editions. These latter with their limited citations of variants and MSS actually reduce the user to reliance upon the internal evidence of readings. The documents which these rigorously abbreviated apparatuses cite cannot lead the user to dependence upon external evidence of documents. These editions use documents (to quote Housman) "as drunkards use lampposts — not to light them on their way but to dissimulate their instability." [14]

The scholars who profess to follow "the eclectic method" frequently so define the term as to restrict evidence to the internal evidence of readings. By "eclectic" they mean in fact free choice among readings. This choice in many cases is made solely on the basis of intrinsic probability. The editor chooses that reading which commends itself to him as fitting the context, whether in style, or idea, or contextual reference. Such an editor relegates the MSS to the role of

[13] Frederick C. Grant, *Introduction to the Revised Standard Version of the New Testament*, ed. L. A. Weigle (Chicago: International Council of Religious Education, American Standard Bible Committee, 1946).

[14] A. E. Housman, ed., *M. Manilii Astronomicon; Liber Primus*, 2d ed. (Cambridge: University Press, 1937) p. 1iii.

supplier of readings. The weight of the MS is ignored. Its place in the manuscript tradition is not considered. Thus Kilpatrick argues that certain readings found only in one late Vulgate MS should be given the most serious consideration because they are good readings.

Sometimes, though more rarely, the argument is based on transcriptional probability. Thus Kilpatrick has pointed out that Atticism was rife in the second century and he claims that it affected the wording of some MSS. Interestingly enough, he begins his argument with references to ἀποκριθεὶς εἶπεν, admittedly barbarous Greek, and its variant ἔφη. He says, commenting on six passages in Mark, "Have the scribes changed the good Greek ἔφη to the barbarous ἀποκριθεὶς εἶπεν or the other way about? If we may assume that their intention was to improve the evangelist's Greek rather than to degrade it, then ἀποκριθεὶς εἶπεν will be original."[15] After Plutarch, he points out, Atticism became the norm; and he asks "Did the scribes of this period try to bring the varied Greek of these books more into line with the prevailing fashion?"[16]

But in this matter we may *not* assume the intention of the scribes. Various intentions were possible to them. In four of these six passages, harmonization to Matthew and Luke may have been the intention. Or scribes may have had the intention of changing from the rare to the usual, from secular usage to gospel idiom. In the Westcott and Hort text the barbarous ἀποκριθεὶς εἶπεν occurs 139 times in the four gospels (Matt. 48, Mark 17, Luke 42, John 32), while good old ἔφη occurs only 35 times. These figures strongly suggest that in this matter the scribes were not Atticizing very well. Moreover it is the Beta text-type that reads ἔφη in Kilpatrick's six passages, and the same text-type reads ἀποκριθεὶς εἶπεν 139

[15] G. D. Kilpatrick, "Atticism and the Text of the Greek New Testament," in *Neutestamentliche Aufsätze*, ed. J. Blinzler (Regensburg: Pustet, 1963), p. 126. Gordon Fee presents an independent and significant criticism of this article in his unpublished dissertation (*The Significance of Papyrus Bodmer II and Papyrus Bodmer XIV–XV for Methodology in New Testament Textual Criticism*, Diss. University of Southern California, 1966).

[16] *Ibid.*, p. 128.

times. Attention to Hort's theory would save us from some of the dangers of subjective judgment based on partial evidence. DuPlacy has recently said, "Textual criticism is a historical discipline. As such, its primary duty is to take its sources seriously. . . . I will plead then," he says, "the cause of history, and above all in the name of history, the cause of the documents,"[17] and with this Hortian judgment I am in full accord. We need Hort Redivivus.

We need him as a counterinfluence to the two errors I have discussed: (1) the ignoring of the history of the manuscript tradition, and (2) overemphasis upon the internal evidence of readings. In Hort's work two principles (and only two) are regarded as so important that they are printed in capital letters in the text and in italics in the table of contents. One is "ALL TRUSTWORTHY RESTORATION OF CORRUPTED TEXTS IS FOUNDED ON THE STUDY OF THEIR HISTORY." And the other is "KNOWLEDGE OF DOCUMENTS SHOULD PRECEDE FINAL JUDGMENT UPON READINGS."

In the second place, and it is a second place, we need Hort Redivivus because additional manuscript evidence has become available. Hort's theory and method needs reconsideration in the light of this new evidence. Hort himself said that the discovery of new evidence forces the reconsideration of the old.[18]

But it is not the mass of recently known witnesses that makes this important. Aland occasionally speaks as if the gross amount of witnesses, as such, invalidated all that Hort had done, and forces a new theory upon us.[19]

The discovery of additional MSS, including the early papyri, has not demanded a drastic revision of Hort's two

[17] Jean DuPlacy, "Histoire des Manuscrits et Histoire du Texte du Nouveau Testament," *New Testament Studies*, 12 (1965–66): 125.

[18] Westcott and Hort, *New Testament*, p. 14 "Evidence is valuable only so far as it can be securely interpreted; and not the least advantage conferred by new documents is the new help which they give toward the better interpretation of old documents, and of documentary relations generally."

[19] Most extremely in "The Significance of the Papyri for Progress in New Testament Research," in *The Bible in Modern Scholarship*, pp. 325–46.

basic principles. In saying this I differ sharply from Aland. His counting of heads is ominously reminiscent of scholarly argument in the days when the Textus Receptus was unassailable. The important question is "Where do these heads stand in a plausible reconstruction of the history of the manuscript tradition?" Professor Aland, while deferring attention to this question, has in his actual practice followed Lachmann by a naïve acceptance of documents of early date.

The clearest example of this lies in his deference to P[75]. In Nestle[26] readings, and explicitly in a recent article (as also in the multiple Bible Society edition), he reverses Westcott and Hort on the Western noninterpolations because P[75] disagrees with them in agreeing with Codex Vaticanus. But there is nothing in that agreement that is novel to Hort's theory. Hort did not possess P[75], but he imagined it. He insisted that there was a very early ancestor of his Neutral Text, that the common ancestor of Vaticanus and Sinaiticus was a remote ancestor, not a close ancestor. P[75] validates Hort's reconstruction of the history, but P[75] does not add a new argument for or against that theory.

The comparison to the champions of the Textus Receptus is not entirely fair, for Aland is clamoring about the numbers of *early* MSS; and in general early MSS *are* more important than late MSS. But the crucial question for early as for late witnesses is still, *Where do they fit into a plausible reconstruction of the history of the manuscript tradition?*

The other extensive early gospel papyri fit into Hort's reconstruction of the history as well as P[75] does. Aland exclaims that P[45] shows that the P[75] text-type was but one of the types extant in the second century. But Hort made this same claim. If P[45] fits into what Hort called the Western Text, as it seems to do, we should remember Hort's insistence upon the early date of the Western Text.

The third extensive papyrus, P[66], is almost certainly a slightly corrupted copy of a basic P[75] type of text. But the early existence of a debased form of this text was insisted on by Hort. The exact nature of the early debasement may be shown by P[66] to be somewhat different in detail from Hort's concept, but the basic concept was there.

What forces the revision of Hort, or — at the least — serious consideration of his theories, is the appearance of significant new evidence. Four areas in which this new or better evidence is available are the following: (1) Extensive earlier papyri. P[45], P[46], P[47], P[66], and P[75] carry us back one or two centuries closer to the original. And what is equally important, they are documents containing a large amount of text. Thus they can be appraised as individual manuscripts (as the fragments cannot), and they can be located within the manuscript tradition. (2) The evidence of lectionary manuscripts is now at least halfway available. These documents, ignored by our ancestors, need to be placed in any comprehensive picture. (3) The evidence of increasing numbers of Fathers is available in scholarly, critical editions. (4) The evidence of the versions, notably of the Old Latin, is now available in works of great value. Increases in evidence of this sort indicate that if Hort is to be revived his work must be measured against significant new evidence. It is an understatement to say that this has not yet been done.

Can Hort be revived? Yes, if the focus is on method and history. In the face of a long generation of critical attack this may seem to be a bold statement. From Kirsopp Lake's: "His work was a failure, though a brilliant one," through Kilpatrick's choice of eclectic method, to Aland's "A gulf separates us from them [Westcott and Hort], which can no longer be bridged," and "This much is certain, the presuppositions of Westcott-Hort are no longer valid,"[20] the road is rough. But since I have myself participated in the demolition of one Hortian bastion,[21] my assertion that the task is possible will not be charged to sentimental romanticism.

[20] "The Significance of the Papyri for Progress in New Testament Research" in *The Bible in Modern Scholarship*, p. 329; and "Neue Neutestamentliche Papyri II," *New Testament Studies*, 12 (1965–66): 209.

[21] "Genealogical Method: Its Achievements and Its Limitations," *Journal of Biblical Literature*, 66 (1947): 109–33.

Soon after the appearance of my paper on genealogical method, I read as the presidential address at SBL a paper titled "Biblical Criticism: Lower and Higher" in which the basic assumption is that Hort's theory was to be abandoned.[22] I think now that I was wrong, that Kilpatrick is wrong, and that Aland is wrong. Each of us, obsessed with some one glaring fault in Hort (Colwell, genealogical method; Kilpatrick, overemphasis on MSS; Aland, no Greek papyri) threw out the baby with the bath water.

Improvements on Hort in the statement of theory and the reconstruction of the history are possible. These are contained in the program which follows, but two examples are enough to make the case.

1) Hort organized his entire argument to depose the Textus Receptus. While still a student at Cambridge, 23 years old, Hort clearly indicated in a letter the identity of the villain: "I had no idea till the last few weeks of the importance of texts, having read so little Greek Testament, and dragged on with the villainous *Textus Receptus* . . . and Tischendorf I find a great acquisition, above all, because he gives the various readings at the bottom of his page, and his Prolegomena are invaluable. Think of that vile *Textus Receptus* leaning entirely on late MSS; it is a blessing there are such early ones. . . ." (December 29 and 30, 1851)[23] Two years later (1853), he wrote ". . . I have not seen anybody that I know except Westcott, whom, being with his wife at his father's at Moseley, close to Birmingham, a fortnight ago, I visited for a few hours. One result of our talk I may as well tell you. He and I are going to edit a Greek text of the N.T. some two or three years hence, if possible. Lachmann and Tischendorf will supply rich materials, but not nearly enough and we hope to do a great deal with the Oriental versions. Our object is to supply clergymen generally, schools, etc., with a portable Gk. Test., which shall not be disfigured with Byzantine corruptions. But we *may*

---

[22] *Journal of Biblical Literature*, 67 (1948). See footnote 3 on page 3.
[23] Arthur Fenton Hort, *Life and Letters of Fenton John Anthony Hort* (London and New York: Macmillan, 1896), 1:211.

find the work too irksome." [24] This attack is no longer necessary, and therefore improvements are possible. Hort's formal
use of stemmatics served this purpose alone, and adds confusion to his work. Thus his arguments and his reconstruction start with the mass of recent manuscripts and work
backwards. The chronology needs to be reversed. [25] We need
to begin at the beginning.

2) Hort's reconstruction of the history can be corrected
by our increased knowledge from both ends of that history.
Soden's contribution to the history of the manuscript tradition in the Byzantine period was significant. [26] Better knowledge of patristic habits in quotation in the early centuries,
plus earlier documents, enables us to write more accurate
accounts of the early manuscript tradition.

Yet in this revision we shall not surpass Hort merely by
adding MS to MS. Unless we are as serious and thoughtful
as he was, we labor in vain. Many a scholar, for example,
uses the early fathers as evangelists in America use the
Scriptures — as proof texts. We need to apply the penetrating insight of such questions as Klijn's: "What is the relation
between the kind of text found in these ancient writings (the
Fathers) and the text of the New Testament in the available MSS? Is it possible to say that our MSS went through
a period in which they were as freely handled as the text
used by the authors of the earliest Christian writings? This
impression we do not get." [27]

The program of textual studies requires that the critic

[24] Arthur Fenton Hort, *Life and Letters*, 1:250. Professor I. A. Moir
of Edinburgh brought these passages to my attention.

[25] See E. C. Colwell, "The Significance of Grouping of New Testament Manuscripts," *New Testament Studies*, 4 (1957–58): 90–91.

[26] See, e.g., the summary statement in E. C. Colwell, *The Four
Gospels of Karahissar. I. History and Text* (Chicago: University of
Chicago Press, 1936) pp. xi–xii; David Voss, "Is von Soden's K$^r$ a
District Type of Text?" *Journal of Biblical Literature* 57 (1938):
311–18; and Jacob Geerling's reconstructions of Family 13 and Family II in *Studies and Documents*, Vols. 19–24 (Salt Lake City: University
of Utah Press, 1961–64).

[27] A. F. J. Klijn, "A Survey of the Researches into the Western Text
of the Gospels and Acts," *Novum Testamentum*, 3 (1959): 165.

take five steps. (1) begin with readings, (2) characterize individual scribes and MSS, (3) group the MSS, (4) construct a historical framework, (5) make final judgment on readings.

### Begin with Readings

The readings of individual MSS are the objective data with which the critic ultimately must deal. He should be familiar with a very large number of these, including readings that never find their way into an *apparatus criticus*. This familiarity can be obtained either by making or reading complete collations of a number of documents. These documents should include early papyri, the great uncials, and commonplace Byzantines — among the Greeks. But these documents should also include Old Latin and Vulgate MSS, Old Syriac and Peshitta, Coptic MSS, and Greek and Latin Fathers at least from the early centuries. But at this stage the study of readings is not final, for knowledge of documents should precede final judgment upon readings.[28]

The knowledge derived from a study of these readings will lead to an understanding of scribal habits and practices without which the history of the manuscript tradition cannot be written. We need a series of compendia of corruptions from the Greek MSS, from the individual versions, from the Fathers — comparable to the work of L. Havet on the Latin MSS of the classics. But the knowledge gained from one of these compendia cannot be transferred to another, nor can the knowledge gained from one period be generalized to another, nor can the treatment of one part of the New Testament be generalized to the entire canon.

### Characterize Individual Scribes and MSS

At least for important witnesses (and ideally for all that are used) the peculiarities of the individual scribe need to be known. No one has said this better than Hort — "It . . . becomes necessary in the case of important MSS to observe and discriminate the classes of clerical errors by which their

[28] Westcott and Hort, *New Testament*, p. 31.

proper texts are severally disguised; for an authority representing a sound tradition can be used with increased confidence when its own obvious slips have been classed under definite heads, so that those of its readings which cannot be referred to any of these heads must be reasonably supposed to have belonged to the text of its exemplar." [29] Identifying the scribe as distinct from his source is not easy. Vinton Dearing has pointed out that we are in fact prone to minimize the difficulties and assume that we are looking over the scribe's shoulder when we are in reality looking at his source.[30] Yet the scribe's contribution *can* be identified — notably in singular readings, especially in nonsense readings, or in readings that have won universal rejection not only from other scribes but from all editors as well.[31]

The goals of this study at this stage are to know this MS in so far as it is the product of the scribe who copied it. The scribe's fingerprints upon the codex are the object of search. (1) What units of text did he copy? Single letters, or syllables and short words, or single complete words, or phrases and clauses? (2) What was his pattern of errors? (3) Was he a careful or a careless workman? (4) If careful, was his care limited to exact copying or did it include care for a better expression of the content of his exemplar? i.e., to what extent was he an editor as well as a scribe?

The identification of the scribe's habits in these special readings enables the student of the particular MS to discard variants that otherwise would be regarded as part of the genetic strain of that MS. Textual criticism must return to the position taken by Tischendorf in regard to singular readings — "A reading altogether peculiar to one or another ancient document is suspicious." This primary position of Tischendorf's, which Tischendorf failed to follow with re-

[29] *Ibid.*, p. 36.
[30] In a personal letter to the author.
[31] See E. C. Colwell, "Scribal Habits in Early Papyri: A Study in the Corruption of the Text," in *The Bible in Modern Scholarship*, ed. J. Ph. Hyatt, pp. 370–89. In retrospect, I feel more confident of my own identification of the scribal habits of P[66] and P[75] than I do of those of P[45]. In P[45] few of the "singular readings" meet the two additional requirements stated above.

spect to Sinaiticus and Hort failed to follow with respect to
Vaticanus, merits the most rigorous observance. For example, the fact that the scribe of P[66] copied syllable by syllable,
added to the further fact that he often produced nonsense
by dropping a short syllable, removes all weight from his
omission of the article or of a short preposition. Thus the
characterization of the scribe aids in the characterization
of the MS.

To insist that these are two characterizations is to make
a subtle distinction. But its subtlety does not detract from
its value. Each MS that establishes a landmark in the history
of the MS tradition should have its fingerprints taken, and
its value assessed. The second stage in the program is knowledge of individual documents.

### Group MSS

The third stage is to establish the group relationships of
MSS and to evaluate the groups. As I have argued elsewhere [32] these relationships are of three kinds, and the
resulting groups need to be clearly differentiated from each
other.

*The family* is a group of MSS so closely related to each
other (often from closeness in time and place of origin)
that a stemma can be reconstructed and the archetype, or
its text, reconstructed. Examples are Family 1, and Family
Pi. Note that the use of stemmatics flourished in classical
studies of a controlled text, and that the enduring families
of New Testament MSS also come from the period of a
controlled text.

*The tribe* is a group of families with looser relationships
between families than within families, yet a group whose
interrelationships are relatively close, relative, that is, to
the looser relationships of the members of a text-type. The
tribe is thus defined by its position between the family and
the text-type. It is larger than one, smaller than the other.
More closely related than one, less than the other. The great

[32] "The Significance of Grouping of New Testament Manuscripts,"
*New Testament Studies,* 4 (1957–58): 73–92.

value of this category is that it prevents the confusing identification of these groups with either or both family and text-type. The classic example of confusion in the terms applied is the Caesarean Group, called Family Theta by Streeter and text-type Gamma by Kenyon. It now seems clear that it is neither.

*The text-type* is the largest identifiable group of MSS. It has a longer life span than most families or tribes. Thus it will have some members that may be weaker than the members of either of these smaller groups. Examples of text-types are Kenyon's Beta (Hort's Neutral), and Kenyon's Alpha (Hort's Syrian).

Two steps are essential for establishing the existence of any of these groups of MSS, and a third step is helpful but not essential. This third step (which comes first in the actual process of identification) directs attention to passages in which the attestation divides three or more ways. A study of these multiple readings often provides a clue to group relationships. This is a time-saving device, and is in no way essential to the establishment of group relationships.

Because of my use of this device (or because of the enthusiasm of some of my students for its use), I have been credited with championing something called "the multiple method." I should like to seize this opportunity for acting modestly (an opportunity that comes but rarely to the scholar) and leave any claim that there is a multiple method to the championing of others.

The essential steps for establishing the existence of a group of MSS are (1) demonstrating that the members of the group share the support of a list of readings not found in other groups, and (2) demonstrating that the members of the group support one another in approximately 70 per cent of all cases where variation occurs between Greek MSS. This demonstration is possible for families, tribes, and text-types. Thus it follows that the sporadic readings of a particular type do not demonstrate the existence of the type in a particular time or place.

One word of caution in regard to the grouping of MSS:

in this task we are not concerned with good readings or bad readings, with original readings or corrupt readings, but only with shared readings. Klijn makes this point clear.[33] We concern ourselves with quality of readings at other stages of the program, but not here.

Hort admitted that mixture dealt a fatal blow to the use of genealogical method, but he insisted that the history of the manuscript period could be written in spite of mixture. And he was right.

### Construct a Historical Framework

The task of textual criticism is to establish the form of the text in time and place. This is historical study. Thus the fourth stage in the program is the writing of the history of the manuscript period. Hort's dictum is *"All trustworthy restoration of corrupted texts is founded on a study of their history,* that is, of the relations of descent or affinity which connect the several documents."[34] This history can be written in spite of mixture, but only if stemmatics is abandoned. This abandonment must include the pattern of constructive thought appropriate to stemmatics. Most of our manuals present charts that assume that the method of building a family tree is appropriate to the reconstruction of the total history of the manuscript period. These charts (e.g., the charts illustrating the difference between Streeter's theory of local texts and Hort's theory) need to be thrown away.

Where groups are clearly defined by the methods stated above, mixture itself can be clearly defined. My own study of Leningrad MS 105, a good candidate for the title of "most mixed MS,"[35] showed that where groups had been established, the amount and nature of mixture between groups can be established. But family trees cannot be built! And groups have not been clearly established in the first two centuries. What can be done is to write an historical account of the process of mixture that produced the documents.

[33] Klijn, *Novum Testamentum*, III (1959): 167–71.
[34] Westcott and Hort, *New Testament*, p. 40.
[35] *The Four Gospels of Karahissar. Volume I. History and Text* (University of Chicago Press, 1936), pp. 216–22.

When we approach the larger task of writing the history of the entire manuscript period, we must start with a new characterization of the process. The story of the manuscript tradition of the New Testament is the story of progression from a relatively uncontrolled tradition to a rigorously controlled tradition. The important questions in the writing of this history are, Where were controls applied? When? By whom?

The progression when uncontrolled was characterized by scribal changes — when controlled it was characterized by editorial selection. Each of these includes improvements as well as corruptions; but in general scribal change meant corruption, and editorial selection with its consequent controls meant improvement over the preceding anarchy and meant also the blocking of major corruption.

Certain presuppositions underlie this thesis. Close agreement between MSS is possible only where there was some control. Wide divergence between MSS indicates lack of control. The basic presupposition behind these two is the assertion that scribes do not automatically, as scribes, copy accurately. The early papyri demonstrate this. Even when the scribe was a skilled calligrapher, accuracy in copying could be beyond his ability. In the early centuries of the New Testament period accurate copying was not even a concept. There were scribes capable of making accurate copies when adequately motivated — as for example when copying for a library. But that the New Testament required this kind of treatment was not a common idea. Papyrus 66 has almost two hundred nonsense readings. Papyrus 69 (also from the third century) omits carelessly, mangling a sentence.

Nor were translators more capable of accuracy when they worked without control. The makers of the "Old" versions — both Latin and Syriac — make J. B. Phillips look like a careful workman. The manuscript copies of these early translations continue the tradition of an uncontrolled text. One page of a critical edition of the Old Latin makes this plain to the dullest eye.

The progression from no concept of control for accuracy to some control is clearly visible in the quotations of the New Testament by the Fathers in the early centuries. In the earliest block, quotation is so free that it makes the demonstration of knowledge of a particular book difficult. Moreover, it is highly significant that the first expression of scholarly concern for an accurate text was concern for the text of the Old Testament. The same Origen who produced the Hexapla quotes the New Testament now from one strain of the tradition, now from another. At the beginning, the Old Testament was the Christian Scripture; and that beginning lasted longer than we think. It influenced concepts and attitudes at least into the third century. Granted that the Fathers were worse than the scribes; the scribes still enjoyed a remarkable freedom from control.

The chances are high that the first controls were introduced by scholarly Christians. The controls produced more good than bad. They sought "ancient" and "good" copies. From these they produced reasonably accurate copies. These first efforts must have been sporadic. Without the keen concern and vigorous support of an organized Church they could not establish the authority of a standard text, henceforth to be carefully controlled.

That concern and support became apparent in the fourth century. The Alpha text-type was most probably born then, and the Beta text-type — as text-type — is probably no older.[36] Jerome's Vulgate adorns that century, the classical example of concern for a controlled, standard text. The Syriac tradition was standardized about the same time.

But when did the Delta text-type (the "Western Text") arise? While scholars still speak of its earlier existence and of its almost universal distribution, they no longer speak of it as a text-type. If the term text-type derives its meaning from the Alpha and Beta text-types, Delta is not a text-type. It lacks that homogeneity which gives the others the name text-type. Yet the amount of agreement it possesses calls for explanation.

[36] The Early Koine may have been subjected to a very partial revision toward Beta before the fourth century.

Most students of its content identify it as an uncontrolled text, a popular text rather than a scholar's text. Where is it found? In the earliest translations into Latin and Syriac;[37] in some of the early Fathers; and in bilingual MSS. Is it impossible to turn Streeter's theory around and modify it to say that the Western text is the local texts of the early centuries? The truly provincial texts were those first missionary copies carried to illiterate groups or into the backwoods where Greek was not a language. From these copies came the careless early versions. From them, some church leaders quoted. Some of them appeared in a would-be learned, bilingual dress. They are prerecension texts in their origin. They are corrupted texts due to the uncontrolled nature of their propagation. That the Latin "Westerns" have one batch of readings, and the Syrian "Westerns" another supports the assumption of their provincial origin, or their provincial development.

Any attempt to write a comprehensive history of the manuscript period requires a decision between provincial origin and provincial development. I tentatively choose the latter — provincial development from a common origin of the Western groups. That origin deserves to be called the Early Koine,[38] the popular missionary text of the Christian movement. In sharp contrast to the medieval Koine (the Alpha text-type), it was not an edition prepared by sophis-

[37] Not in Coptic, whose Sahidic version usually agrees with the Beta text-type.

[38] (1) The general nature of the text in the earliest period (to 300 A.D.) has long been recognized as "wild," "uncontrolled," "unedited." (2) MSS from this period and MSS which preserve the text of this period have an unusually large number of singular or subsingular readings, most of which are corruptions. (3) MSS from this period do not cluster into closely related groups. (4) The ancient editors who brought order out of this chaos did so by *selecting* readings from these earlier MSS. They probably began their work by selecting a "good" earlier MS. (5) The agreements among the earliest witnesses are in part due to a shared ancestry, in part to coincidence in corruption. (6) The earliest versions add to the corruption of "primitive" free handling of the text the natural corruption of the translator — which often ran on the same tracks. (7) Therefore, agreements between the earliest versions and the earliest Greek witnesses without substantial Greek support are to be suspected of being agreement in corruption.

ticated scholars. It was, rather, the lay-preacher's Gospel. Again in contrast to the medieval Koine, its copying was not controlled. It was controlled as American preachers and evangelists control their selection and use of Scripture.

The course of its development has been accurately described by Streeter in his theory of local texts. It became differentiated in Syria, in Latin Africa, in Armenia. Streeter's expansion of the so-called Caesarean Text to include practically all of Soden's Western (i.e., Iota) groups was fundamentally sound, but erroneous in one superficial item and one serious item.

His superficial error was that the text he was describing did not come from Caesarea, but the exact location of its origin is of little importance. He was describing the gradual expansion, corruption, and differentiation of the Early Koine.

His most serious error was not his claim for more unity and homogeneity than this group of witnesses contain. His fatal error was his treatment of the Beta text-type as a comparable local text. This it is not. Both Alpha and Beta are editions carefully made and fairly well controlled in copying with a pattern of subsequent corruption quite different from that of the Koine in the early period.

But in this same early period scholars were converted to Christianity. The Paschal Sermon of Melito of Sardis shows us that before the last quarter of the second century men who were masters of rhetoric had entered the Church. From the same period Papyrus 75, containting large sections of Luke and John, is best explained as an attempt at scholarly accurate production of a copy of the Gospels. The format of its page obviously comes out of the book trade, not out of the needs of the mission movement. In length of lines (25 letters) and number of lines to the column (42) it is very close to the pattern of the great fourth century vellum codices, Vaticanus and Sinaiticus (18, 15 letters to the line, 42, 48 lines to the column). The point is that $P^{75}$ looks like a column from a book-roll. Contrast $P^{45}$ with about 48–50 letters to a line. It looks like a page, even though it is a page with 39 lines. P[66] also looks like a page, not like a column — with 24 letters to a line but an average of only 19 lines to a page.

When to this formal resemblance to published books the content relationship is added, P[75] is seen to be one of those "ancient and good copies" which educated Christians sought out in the fourth century as the basis for better editions.[39] It has the closest relation to Codex Vaticanus. This first effort at a good copy almost certainly sprang from scholarly concerns rather than ecclesiastical. And one comment on the editorial work of scribes and editors needs to be made now — capable scribes and editors often left the text closer to the original than they found it.

From what has been said, it follows that the dividing line in the history of the text is the achievement of control. This means editions with sanctions. In the period prior to this achievement, MSS with the same ancestry differ widely. After this achievement, MSS with the same ancestry differ so little that they become almost identical.

For example, from the precontrol period compare 34 verses (John 9:1–34) of P[66] and P[75]. They are basically the same genetic strain, yet they differ from each other 39 times in this short block of text: more than one to a verse. From the control period, take two MSS: the Isaac Gospel and 2322. They belong to Soden's Kappa[r] group: the last of the great Byzantine recensions of the Alpha text-type. In 31 verses (Mark 11) they never differ. Moreover if ten K[r] MSS are compared throughout the Gospel of Mark, "six of the ten agree in 180 variants from Stephanus. Every MS has at least 80% of these variants, and seven . . . have over 90%. . . . And only four of the ten MSS have more than fifteen variants outside of this list of 180" in the *entire Gospel of Mark*.[40]

Examples of this sort can be multiplied many times. They show clearly that one crucial guideline in writing the history

[39] Gordon Donald Fee, cf. note 15 above, has shown as intimate a relationship between P[75] and B as exists within Family 1.

[40] David O. Voss, *Journal of Biblical Literature*, 57 (1938): 317.

of the text is the presence or absence of control in the copying of the text. This will prevent the listing of scribal habits across the centuries as though they were one thing.

In the writing of the history of the text another taboo must be observed. Do not write the history of the entire New Testament. There is a history of the individual gospel. There is a history of the gospels — but the Gospel of Mark seems to have a special history. There is a history of the Letters of Paul, another of Acts, another of Revelation.

Walter Thiele in a recent publication[41] has pointed out that the text of Augustine in different parts of the Bible presents contrasting elements: Non-Western in the Gospels, a little more Western in Paul, much more Western in Acts, and Western in the Catholics. Kirsopp Lake's choice of Mark as *the* Gospel to study was based on the peculiar history of that Gospel in the manuscript period.

Thus the historian will be forced to reconsider the meaning of mixture in the early period as contrasted with the later. In those first centuries, block mixture — as in the Washington Gospels — is common; and it almost certainly derives from the varying histories of the available exemplars, which rarely overlapped in content. A second cause of what we have called "mixture" is that coincidence in corruption which is possible to all uncontrolled, or poorly controlled, texts.[42] But when MSS were numerous and concern for the best text existed, real mixture resulted from the correction of one type or family by another.

## Make Final Judgment on Readings

As the last stage, judgment has to be made on variant readings in the light of the previous stages plus the internal evidence of readings. In the study of internal evidence of readings Hort needs no improvement. His canons for the ap-

---

[41] *Die Lateinischen Texte des I. Petrusbriefes* ("Vetus Latina: Aus der Geschichte der Lateinischen Bibel" 5; Freiburg: Herder Verlag, 1965).

[42] As I have argued elsewhere, the stemmatic, genealogical pattern of thinking keeps us from seeing the large role played by coincidental agreement.

praisal of readings have won continued and widespread approval. Intrinsic probability (fitness to context), and transcriptional probability (choosing the reading that can explain the origin of the others) are an effective and inclusive summary of all detailed canons of criticism. But Hort was more fully aware of their limitations than many contemporary scholars are.

He warns us that the assumptions involved in intrinsic evidence of readings are not to be implicitly trusted. ". . . it is needful to remember," he says, "that authors are not always grammatical, or clear, or consistent, or felicitous; so' that not seldom an ordinary reader finds it easy to replace a feeble or half appropriate word or phrase by an effective substitute; and thus the best words to express an author's meaning need not in all cases be those which he actually employed." [43]

He reminds us that "the basis on which transcriptional probability rests consists of generalizations as to the causes of corruption incident to the process of transcription." [44] These generalizations come from a study "of those readings which can with moral certainty be assumed to have been introduced by scribes." [45] And, with the exception of careless blunders, all readings, including these, have a kind of excellence: a quality that derives from the author or a quality that appealed to a scribe as an improvement. Serious contrast of these two excellences is imperative.

Where intrinsic probability coincides with transcriptional probability the student secures a high degree of certainty. "But," Hort reminds us, "a vast proportion of variations do not fulfill these conditions." [46]

Therefore we need to revive another part of Hort's final procedure as editor. It is briefly stated in a section often overlooked: "the history of this edition" — "No rule of precedence has been adopted; but documentary attestation has been in most cases allowed to confer the place of honor

[43] Westcott and Hort, *New Testament*, p. 21.
[44] *Ibid.*, p. 22.
[45] *Ibid.*, p. 24. The collection of data in this area has only begun.
[46] *Ibid.*, p. 29.

against internal evidence, range of attestation being further taken into account as between one well attested reading and another." [47]

Much of the value of reviving Hort lies in this emphasis. As Professor Sidney Mead once said of the historian's work, "He doesn't claim certainty, but he asks that the witnesses be allowed to bring their evidence to court, and that the evidence will be taken seriously." If Hort is revived, it will be.

[47] *Ibid.*, p. 17.

# 7

## Today's Problems with the Critical Text
## of the New Testament
### KENNETH W. CLARK

In the preface of an edition of the Greek New Testament we read the editor's assurance: "You now have the text which is accepted by all." This well-known statement may be recognized at once as belonging not to a recent critical edition but to one printed three centuries ago, the Elzevir of 1633. That Latin phrase yielded the term *textus receptus,* used ever since of the Greek New Testament text employed in Western Europe for several centuries. In the first Elzevir edition (1624) the term used was *textus acceptus.* The awkward term "Received Text" is a poor translation and might better be replaced by the term "Accepted Text."

The Elzevir brothers have repeatedly been charged with making a presumptuous and erroneous claim, but it must be acknowledged that they wrote only the truth. Comparison of the printed editions beginning with Erasmus and for three centuries thereafter reveals that scores of editors continued to produce the same text with but slight alteration. Furthermore, it is often overlooked that even prior to the printed editions thousands of manuscript copies had been reproducing the same basic text throughout the Byzantine centuries. The editors were truly correct in describing their product as a *textus receptus,* since it was then all but universal among publishers and scholars. It is well known among us that the Era of the Received Text lasted until mid-nineteenth century.

The threat to the long established *textus receptus* began to cast a long shadow even as the Elzevirs coined their term, but the text in common use did not easily yield up its accustomed prestige. The contest was long and often bitter before the text accepted by all was supplanted by what we call today the critical text. The Oxford Press ended its long series of printings of the traditional *Textus Receptus* only sixty years ago. We of the twentieth century are the first in 1500 years of Christian history, i.e., since the fifth century, to possess the critical text which is in general use today. Indeed we are inclined to feel highly gratified that we have recovered this text, through discovery and scholarly processes. It is a common opinion that we now possess the true text, trustworthy for interpretation. This opinion is illustrated in a new book by Fred L. Fisher entitled *How to Interpret the New Testament*: ". . . the text that is now accepted is open to question in very few places . . . of minor significance."[1]

This recapitulation from the history of criticism brings us to the first of today's problems to be noted here. It is this: that the Westcott-Hort text has become today our *textus receptus*. We have been freed from the one only to become captivated by the other. The persistence of the Byzantine text has been repeated in our own rigid adherence to Westcott-Hort. The psychological chains so recently broken from our fathers have again been forged upon us, even more strongly. Whereas our textual fathers, such as John Mill and Richard Bentley, actively debated the character of the text in their day, our generation of theologians finds easy contentment with our current *textus receptus*.

Even the textual specialist finds it difficult to break the habit of evaluating every witness by the norm of this current *textus receptus*. His mind may have rejected the Westcott-Hort term "neutral," but his technical procedure still reflects the general acceptance of the text. A basic problem today is the technical and psychological factor that the Westcott-Hort text has become our *textus receptus*.

Perhaps someone will remonstrate that there have been many critical texts produced since 1881, which is true. Some-

[1] Cf. J. R. Harris, *Four Lectures on the Western Text* (London: C. J. Clay and Sons, 1894), who warned against the "cult" of Westcott-Hort.

one will adduce the Nestle series of twenty-five editions since the beginning of this century. With each new edition we are prone to hasten to the bookstore to obtain the latest text. Our problem lies here, that few scholars are aware that the latest Nestle is a close copy of the 1881 text, and that edition succeeds edition with little or no textual change. All the critical editions since 1881 are basically the same as West-cott-Hort. All are founded on the same Egyptian recension, and generally reflect the same assumptions of transmission.

In order to test this assertion as a hypothesis, eight Duke students have recently collaborated in the collation of numerous critical texts against Westcott-Hort, in two sample passages (Mark 11 and John 12). These passages were chosen because the chances of alteration would seem the greater in the light of researches on the Caesarean text and on recent papyrus acquisitions.

This group has observed that in John 12 Westcott-Hort shows between twenty and thirty changes from the earlier texts of Lachmann and Buttmann, other than orthographic details. But in the many editions after Westcott-Hort only slight alteration has taken place. For example, the British and Foreign Bible Society edition of 1958 (which is the equivalent of the Nestle 1957[23] edition) shows in John 12 only two slight differences from Westcott-Hort. In 12:30 Ἰησοῦς is transposed with καὶ εἶπεν and in 12:32 ἐάν replaces ἄν; and in both instances all or nearly all editions agree in this departure from Westcott-Hort. Again, take the Tasker edition which purports to be the *New English Bible* base. In, John 12 it departs from Westcott-Hort four times. In 12:9 and 12:21 this edition spells two second aorist forms with ov rather than αν. The two other changes from Westcott-Hort are the same two cited above in the BFBS text. All four changes have nearly unanimous agreement in other editions. It is apparent that none of these formal changes can be reflected in the NEB translation. A final example may be seen in the 1966 American Bible Society edition, which is avowedly based on Westcott-Hort and expressly altered wherever the committee determined. In John 12 there are five alterations made, including three of the four just mentioned. Another is the addition of the article in ὁ ἰησοῦς (12:12) and the other is the transposed σὺ λέγεις in 12:34. Can there be any doubt that these editions are a near replica of Westcott-Hort? They are typical of the many editions that have appeared. Since 1881 twenty-five editors have issued about seventy-five editions of the Greek New Testament. The collation of these many "critical" texts consistently exposes the fact that each of them is basically a repetition of the Westcott-Hort text of which we may be permitted to declare with truth: "You now have the text which is accepted by all." Indeed, we have continued for eighty-five years to live in the era of Westcott-Hort, our *textus receptus*.

Psychologically it is now difficult to approach the textual problem with free and independent mind. Where textual emendations are at issue we have literally moved in frequent circle, with alternating favor between two choices. Eclectic experimentation and sporadic emendation constitute the order of our day. Critical alteration in the frequent editions has been slight and amounts only to intermittent patches. The main fabric is still that of Westcott-Hort. A recent expression of Colwell's, though relating to a different factor, is truly applicable here also: "Hort has put . . . blinders on our eyes." However great the attainment in the Westcott-Hort text, the further progress we desiderate can be accomplished only when our psychological bonds are broken. Herein lies today's foremost problem with the critical text of the New Testament.

Another of today's problems with the critical text may be brought to attention by quoting the 1633 Elzevir preface further: ". . . in which text we present no alteration or corruption." This claim we have been unwilling to grant, and yet we are faced with it once again today in the Westcott-Hort claim of textual neutrality. They maintained that "the books of the New Testament as preserved in extant documents assuredly speak to us in every important respect in language identical with that in which they spoke to those for

whom they were originally written."[2] They exalted the text
of Vaticanus because "neither of the early streams [Western
and Alexandrian] of innovation has touched it to any ap-
preciable extent."[3] We realize that theirs is a qualified claim
to originality for the text that is now our *textus receptus,* and
yet we tend to overlook their caution in our own habit of
reliance upon the text now accepted by all.

Kilpatrick describes our common assumption, that "the
Neutral text alone preserved . . . something like its original
purity."[4] At the same time we are all aware that several distinctive recensions circulated in the early church whose relationships were really not as Westcott-Hort described them.
Not only is it true that the modern *textus receptus* is not
always and everywhere original, but it is further true that
we cannot yet explain the origin and the status of any of the
earliest recensions. We recognize recensions that existed but
we are yet unable to trace a course of transmission among
them. The textual history that the Westcott-Hort text represents is no longer tenable in the light of newer discoveries
and fuller textual analysis. In the effort to construct a con-
gruent history, our failure suggests that we have lost the way,
that we have reached a dead end, and that only a new and
different insight will enable us to break through. An acceptable theory of recensional relationships must recognize the
true status of each recension. Kilpatrick has argued for the
originality of certain "Syrian" readings. Tasker has again cau-
tioned that the "Western" text is "much more valuable than
Westcott and Hort supposed." But such contentions are
based upon the evidence of a few individual readings only.
We have not yet been able to discover the pattern wherein
the recognizable recensions were woven in the life of the

[2] B. F. Westcott and F. J. Hort, *The New Testament in the Original
Greek: Introduction,* 2nd ed. (London: Macmillan and Co., 1907),
p. 284.

[3] Westcott and Hort, *New Testament,* p. 150.

[4] G. D. Kilpatrick, "The Greek New Testament Text of Today and
the *Textus Receptus,*" in *The New Testament in Historical and Contemporary Perspective: Essays in Memory of G. H. C. Macgregor,* ed.
H. Anderson and W. Barclay (Oxford: B. Blackwell, 1965), p. 189.

church. The true critical text must be found to be in conformity with the correct account of transmission. This now appears as one of today's chief problems.

There has seldom if ever been a time when more illuminating manuscript resources have come into the hands of textual critics than in our own day. We do recall that fifth-century Alexandrinus reached London a few years after the King James Bible appeared. A century ago fourth-century Sinaiticus emerged from monastic obscurity. But the critic today has for the first time extensive third-century papyrus texts. The Beatty Library in Dublin thirty-five years ago acquired the notable codex of the Pauline Corpus, and portions of the Four Gospels and the Acts, and one-third of the Apocalypse. The Bodmer Library in Geneva recently acquired two copies of John and one of Luke and a fragment of the General Epistles.

Initial examination of these earliest witnesses has shown primarily text in harmony with Westcott-Hort. But more detailed analysis propounds a most difficult problem. These early Egyptian copies do not agree with one another. There is sometimes agreement with Vaticanus, again a distinctive agreement with Sinaiticus, again they attest the Caesarean recension, and yet again some fragments favor Bezae.

What then shall we say of the testimony of these newest and earliest witnesses? They come to light with joyous announcement and high expectation, only to reveal that they further complicate where we hope for clarification. Recensional variety is now seen to have originated as early as A.D. 200. Although we are now enabled to move earlier, the picture does not clear. We have acquired new evidence that textual bifurcations occurred in the earliest stage of transmission. What is more, it is now clear that variant recensions originated *prior* to Hesychius and Lucian. The textual history postulated for the *textus receptus* which we now trust has been exploded. As if this were not enough, we are forced also to admit that the earliest Egyptian text itself was not homogeneous. What now shall we say about our modern *textus receptus?* What solution can be found to this new problem of our day?

Another problem has been newly created by this recent acquisition of extensive third-century papyrus texts, which are both blessing and bane to the critic's labors. More than two centuries ago, John Albert Bengel first classified the manuscripts accessible then. His was a simple twofold division into Asiatic, Byzantine copies of the later centuries, and the more ancient African witnesses consisting of the Old Latin version and Codex Alexandrinus — the last manuscript so named because of its known derivation (and perhaps its origin) in Alexandria itself. Johann Salomo Semler in 1767 developed a threefold classification by further dividing Bengel's ancient African witness into the Western Latin with Codex Bezae, and the Eastern Greek of codices ABCL and Origen which latter he assigned particularly to Alexandria. Finally, in Westcott-Hort's picture this last classification was again divided into the Neutral and the Alexandrian types. Such is the critical background when P⁶⁶ and P⁷⁵ appear in our day as witnesses from Upper Egypt in the early third century. They now provide evidence that the "Egyptian" text of Vaticanus and Sinaiticus was already in use in the distant provincial South no later than A.D. 200, far from the great city of Alexandria. A tendency to center upon Alexandria when discussing cultural origins in Egypt is thus largely nullified. What is more, the Egyptian origin of the new papyri, whose texts bear resemblance to our earliest uncial codices, influences the long debate as to the provenance of the Codices Sinaiticus and Vaticanus. An Egyptian origin becomes the more probable (as long ago urged by Kenyon and Lake), and this too is an important factor in the effort to reconstruct the account of textual transmission.

A problem commonly unrecognized lies in the fact that even now we have recovered no copy of New Testament text prior to the fifth century, except for Egyptian Christianity. Successive discoveries of superior witnesses have created an impression that overreaches the facts. All the manuscripts so far recovered, including the most sensational of recent discoveries, may enable us now to recover no more than the early text in Egypt, whether in Alexandria or in southern communities. No source exists in modern libraries to supply direct knowledge of regional texts elsewhere prior to the fifth century. Since it is not yet possible to recover primitive texts elsewhere than Egypt, we are unable for the first stage of the New Testament text to make geographical comparison, and therefore we cannot discern transmissional relationships between different regions.

We can recognize recensions in fifth-century manuscripts and later in other Christian centers; but it is still a problem in our day that we lack any copies of regional recensions, although there is reason to believe that such variety of text did exist. That we now possess no textual witnesses outside of Egypt prior to the fifth century is completely true for the Greek text. However, it is necessary to acknowledge a slight exception to the general statement, if we should refer to versional witnesses. Two of our copies of Gospel text in the Old Latin may have been written in the latter part of the fourth century: Codex Bobbiensis produced in North Africa, and Codex Vercellensis in Northern Italy; both attest the existence of the Western text prior to Codex Bezae. And from within Egypt a few copies of Coptic text survive from the fourth century; chiefly the Bodmer bohairic papyrus of John, the Michigan sahidic papyrus of John, and a subachmimic papyrus of John published by Sir Herbert Thompson. All of these versional witnesses further affirm that regional recensions existed early and that within the confines of the Nile Valley Christian communities early introduced variety in the text. Although it is a problem that all our earliest copies of New Testament text were produced solely in Egypt, it is yet a prior problem to clarify for Egypt alone the history of the church and the transmission of the text in use there in the earliest centuries.

Still a further oversight has been common; the failure to realize that for much of the New Testament text it is still true that we rest where Westcott-Hort did eighty-five years ago, on the great Codices Vaticanus and Sinaiticus. Despite the exciting discoveries of ancient papyri, a large portion of the New Testament text has not yet been recovered from earlier generations. In the last hundred years there have come to light about forty New Testament papyri written earlier than fourth-century א, B, and W. In these papyri twenty-one New Testament books are represented. The most extensive and best preserved of these are the Bodmer papyri ($P^{66}$ and $P^{75}$) containing two copies of John and one of Luke, all largely preserved. The Beatty papyri of Gospels, Acts, Paul, and Revelation are fragmentary but yet extensive, especially for Paul. But beyond these five papyri, the rest are mutilated and only fragmentary. Actually, there is very little overlapping of text except for the Gospel of John. Although all these papyri come from Egypt, or close by, they yield an assortment of readings difficult to classify and so complicate our problem of recovering the text of the Egyptian Church. Surely these witnesses to the text must some day give direction to textual research, but for the present they present to our limited view conflicting and complicating testimony. But it is quite true that the early papyri offer little in the text of Matthew and Mark, and of Acts and the Catholic Epistles. Therefore for portions of these books and other areas of the New Testament, we are entirely lacking early witness. We possess no papyrus text of the Pastoral and the Johannine Epistles prior to the fourth century.

Another current problem with the critical text today is that emendation has been eclectic and quite sporadic and unsystematic. Since the appearance of Westcott-Hort nothing but eclectic revision has been introduced into any critical edition. Insofar as the original effort continues for the reconstruction of the original text, the method employed has been eclectic exclusively. In contrast to this modern condition, we may note, the course of past criticism has included certain notable breakthroughs, creative innovations. For example, when manuscript gave way to press in 1516 a new comparative method was employed to improve the text by comparing two or more variant copies and making a deliberate selection of the trusted reading. Successive editors enlarged the scope of comparison, not only between an increasing number of copies but even between regional witnesses, and they came to place a greater reliance upon the latter technique (so Griesbach). The introduction of this comparative method reduced the centrifugal factor that was inherent in scribal labors, and countered it with a centripetal influence of the editor-printer. The logic of this method led naturally to still another notable insight and novel method; namely, to weigh the character of each witness. And the climax of this principle was the breakthrough achieved in Lachmann's novel text. Of course, the next high point was attained when Westcott and Hort applied the historical method to produce an orderly account of recensional relationships. Each breakthrough in textual revision has been the result of a new insight that has given rise to a novel method productive of a major change. There has been no such breakthrough since 1881; and this is true in spite of the most illuminating discoveries such as the Caesarean text and family groups and even substantial third-century papyrus copies.

We live in a generation of eclectic criticism, and necessarily so. We have not found emancipation from this limited treatment of the text because we do not yet possess the key to unlock the meaning of our rich resources. We feel the want of an insight that would dictate a different procedure and produce a different result. Therefore we are constrained at present to move in a narrow range of sporadic and unsystematic retouching of the text. The text now received by all has been but slightly and uncertainly patched. Eclecticism has great value but as a method it must be acknowledged to be a concession to the limitations of our time. We cannot approve eclectic emendation as a permanent technique of criticism because it is by its very nature tentative.

Eclectic repair has been subjective and tendentious. In repeating such an allegation we mean to be descriptive rather than disparaging, but it is necessary to recognize the truth about our method today. Colwell recently observed that we have "appreciated the internal evidence of readings" but have mistakenly assumed that we avoid the subjective whenever our conjectures are supported by manuscript testimony. A disciplined subjectivity is a legitimate critical instrument, especially when we do acknowledge our use of it. Nevertheless, it should be recognized that it can never represent the final judgment. Eclectic emendation is always a tentative proposal, subject to weightier overarching evidence whenever such evidence can be discerned. Because of its subjective character, eclectic emendation cannot escape bias, however inadvertent. When one examines a limited textual unit such as a single word or a short phrase apart from the broad context, the selection between variant choices depends upon short-range reasons and therefore partial judgment must be supplemented by private inclination.

If this is the true condition of our textual criticism today, then it is wise to conclude that the best New Testament text at present is indeed our current *textus receptus* plus the critical apparatus. To the degree that the true text still remains unresolved, to that extent we are persuaded to utilize the *apparatus criticus* as an integral part of the text. To the extent that textual judgment awaits resolution, the individual theologian is required to assume personal responsibility for at least a tentative interpretation.

We have now made our way to a final problem of our day. We require a critical history of transmission. The critics of Westcott-Hort's construction have been many, and let it be said that one cannot separate Westcott from Hort. Both were responsible for the text; the text and textual history are one, and both editors must subscribe to the fundamental theory of transmission on which the text is erected. In the foregoing review of current problems we have here recalled some of the evidence that the Westcott-Hort explanation of transmission is untenable, even while it serves as foundation for our *textus receptus*. The traditional complaint is strongly supported by new and additional sources. It is often remarked that the Westcott-Hort text carries us back only to the fourth century. Now we do possess extensive third-century texts which first encouraged the hope that a fresh critical insight might appear. But this hope diminishes when it is revealed that these papyrus texts merely demonstrate the earlier existence of such texts as Vaticanus and Sinaiticus, and our problem is merely moved a century earlier. We still cannot perceive the origins and the influences and the relationships of the variant texts in use as early as A.D. 200. Possibly the best approach to this problem might be through the text of the Gospel of John, for which we do possess more abundant and more varied early witnesses.

A different basis for renewed hope may here be suggested. It is possible that the key we require is to be found in patristic study, especially of the earliest period. Long ago R. M. Grant decried that the necessary collaboration in textual and patristic studies has failed us, in "disintegrative specialization," but we need not be resigned to this condition. Psychologically, it is necessary first to dismantle the Westcott-Hort structure, to abandon the course wherein we have encountered a barrier. Further, we might gain by removing the traditional textual labels that prejudice and confine exploration.

Since our earliest manuscripts, along with the Alexandrian Fathers, have thrown light especially upon textual forms in Egypt, we need to examine particularly the Fathers *outside Egypt*. And as a final suggestion, attention might be turned to the travels of the Fathers: Clement, from Southern Italy to Alexandria; Origen, from Alexandria to Caesarea; Marcion, from Pontus to Rome; Justin Martyr, from Samaria to Rome; Irenaeus, from Ephesus to Rome and to Lyon, and so on. Certainly it is not suggested here that the barrier before us will yield at once to these devices, for in that case a solution must ensue herewith. It is, however, suggested that some such approach, some new angle, some novel experiment must be tried if we would in our time achieve a breakthrough to cast light upon the history of transmission. This is the fundamental need before we may move on to a thorough and systematic renovation of the critical text.

The remedy we need can come only through a better diagnosis. The true diagnosis will of necessity be a new and different one. Such diagnosis should be promoted through the reference work projected by the International Greek New Testament Project. Upon a successful diagnosis depend all the issues of debate which have been discussed above. Perhaps apology should be offered for our occasional review of familiar knowledge, but where the weaving is left unfinished old threads must be picked up. We have sought directions for the completion of the pattern in this conspectus of today's problems.

# 8

## The Motif of Fulfillment in the Eschatology
## of the Synoptic Gospels
### WILLIAM A. BEARDSLEE

Eschatology is a stubborn element in the Bible, refractorily
unmodern and difficult to interpret theologically. We do not
need to review the history of this problem. It will throw
our problem into focus, however, if we quote one of the
many pungent passages in Albert Schweitzer's *Quest of the
Historical Jesus*. Schweitzer is discussing the Son of man
problem, and it was his conviction that Jesus brought the
future into the present by his recognition of himself in his
earthly existence as the future Messiah-Son of man. We are
interested here, not in the historical aspect of Schweitzer's
handling of the Son of man question, but in the following
comment which he makes:

> The Messianic secret of Jesus is the basis of Christi-
> anity, since it involves the de-nationalizing and spiritu-
> alization of Jewish eschatology. . . . It is the primal
> fact, the starting-point of a process which manifests it-
> self, indeed, in Christianity, but cannot fully work
> itself out even here, of a movement in the direction of
> inwardness which brings all religious magnitudes into
> the one indivisible spiritual present, and which Chris-
> tian dogmatic has not ventured to carry to its comple-
> tion. The Messianic consciousness of the uniquely great
> Man of Nazareth sets up a struggle between the present
> and the beyond, and introduces that resolute absorption
> of the beyond by the present, which in looking back
> we recognise as the history of Christianity, and of which
> we are conscious in ourselves as the essence of religious

progress and experience — a process of which the end is not yet in sight.[1]

To me this is one of the seminal passages in Schweitzer's book, since it moves far beyond the Ritschlianism which its references to "spiritualization," for instance, suggest, to a kind of "process" view of the absorption of the transcendent in the immanent which shows how deeply prophetic Schweitzer was of so much that has happened in modern theology. "The resolute absorption of the beyond by the present" — that is the key phrase, and it is important because so much of the later interpretation, in spite of its having a deeper sympathy for eschatology than Schweitzer did, comes back to this same functional point: in much current interpretation of eschatology, the beyond is resolutely absorbed by the present.

Our subject, then, is the motif of fulfillment in the eschatology of the Synoptic Gospels, meaning by fulfillment those ways in which the present is understood as being carried forward into the future. We shall further limit our understanding of fulfillment — and limit it in a way that is not wholly fair to the sources themselves — by concentrating on the fulfillment of human striving rather than the fulfillment of the divine promises, though in fact this distinction may prove to be hard to carry through. The subject is important as a test of the adequacy of the interpretation of "future" in eschatology which resolutely absorbs the future in the present. We shall concentrate on trying to appreciate the form of the relation to the future that appears in the Synoptic tradition. I should like to call this paper a study in the phenomenology of hope if that did not seem like an overly ambitious title. In the conclusion we shall try to point to some theological implications of our study of the phenomena.

Let us first try to be clearer about what we are looking for. "Future," at any rate as *we* approach it, is most immediately meaningful as the projected future of our effort, or of the situation in which our effort is in tension with other, non-

[1] Albert Schweitzer, *The Quest of the Historical Jesus*, trans. W. Montgomery (New York: The Macmillan Co., 1964), p. 285.

controllable factors. That this sensibility is also ancient is shown by the tension between fate and *arete*, virtue, as a classical perception of historical time.[2] From this approach, future is related to striving and thus to deficiency, and it is natural that the movement beyond striving, the movement of pure openness, of receptiveness, of faith, should appear as a movement from the future to the present, so that as striving and the sense of deficiency are transcended, the future is forgotten and the *presence* of the beloved one, or of the object which is being perceived for its own sake, or of God, should be the sole focus of attention.[3] At the same time there is something in this analysis that does not quite seem to do justice to various forms of perception of the future in the biblical tradition. There we find in various ways the faith that there may be future-oriented activity that is comprehended by the receptive stance of faith, in a trans-figured future orientation. Our task, then, is to give attention to the perception of the future in the Synoptic eschatology, to see to what extent the future appears in connection with striving and the completion of deficiency, and to what extent it appears in other structures of perception.

We shall concentrate our attention on two levels of the Synoptic material: Q and Mark. There is no need to apologize for Mark. Personally I do not think that there is any need to apologize for Q either, although of course I recognize the controversial status of the sayings document. But that is not our problem. We are simply going to assume the traditional Q, recognizing, of course, that there are many things we do not know about it.[4]

[2] Cf. Charles N. Cochrane, *Christianity and Classical Culture* (London: Oxford University Press, 1944), pp. 168–69.

[3] This typology is indebted to Abraham Maslow, *Toward a Psychology of Being* (Princeton: D. Van Nostrand, 1962).

[4] A thorough and balanced recent summary of the controversy about the traditional two-source hypothesis, strongly supporting the hypothesis of Q, can be found in Werner G. Kümmel, *Introduction to the New Testament*, trans. A. J. Mattill, Jr. (Nashville: Abingdon Press, 1966), esp. pp. 50–61. Cf. also James M. Robinson "ΛΟΓΟΙ ΣΟΦΩΝ Zur Gattung der Spruchquelle Q," in *Zeit und Geschichte*, ed. Erich Dinkler, Festschrift R. Bultmann (Tübingen: J. C. B. Mohr, 1964), pp. 77–96.

Q was a collection of sayings of the Lord, but it was not *didache* as that term is used to contrast with *kerygma*. Q was, on the contrary, a style of proclamation, and it is one of the oddities of New Testament scholarship that it was so long fashionable to regard it as a collection of "teachings" which were a supplement, coming after the presentation of Christian kerygma, to show men how, once they had responded to the kerygma, they were to behave in daily life.[5] This way of thinking is appropriate to a later stage in the life of the church, but not to that early stage in which Q was gathered together. The only reason why the didache theory of Q was so long-lived was the presupposition that there was only one form of early Christian proclamation, the passion kerygma that appears in different versions in Paul and Mark. Once we set aside this presupposition and listen to what the sayings of Q have to say, it will be very clear that they carry a strong note of proclamation, that they are in fact a different form of early Christian kerygma.

Q centers on the word of the Jesus who is known as the resurrected, exalted Lord, and for the historian of Jesus one of the central problems is to disengage the words remembered from the time of Jesus from the words heard as words of the exalted Lord. The Son of man sayings in Q are those which have attracted the greatest interest in this regard. But we shall not be concerned to analyze Q from this point of view — even though it is clear that this collection of sayings represents a process, a process moving from an early Palestinian community into a Greek-speaking community that had put its impress upon Q before it came into the hands of Matthew and Luke. Rather we shall try to look at the shape of hope in Q itself, leaving open the question of the historical Jesus.

[5] The traditional view that Q was teaching supplementary to the passion kerygma is represented, e.g., by Martin Dibelius, *From Tradition to Gospel*, trans. Bertram Lee Woolf (New York: Charles Scribner's Sons, 1935), pp. 245–46. The view that Q represents a distinct style of Christian proclamation is presented by H. E. Tödt, *The Son of Man in the Synoptic Tradition*, trans. Dorothea M. Barton (Philadelphia: Westminster Press, 1965), pp. 232–69; Kümmel, *Introduction to the New Testament*, p. 56 gives qualified assent.

H. E. Tödt has proposed that Q is to be understood as arising in a community which found its bond with Jesus renewed by the resurrection, and carried his proclamation forward into its own time and situation — without, however, giving particular attention to the meaning of Jesus' death for faith.[6] Though in fact the community mingled remembered words of Jesus and prophetically given words of the resurrected Lord, it did not fuse the figures of the earthly Jesus and the coming Son of man, rather keeping clear the distinction between the earthly life of Jesus as a time of conflict and rejection, and the future total triumph of the Son of man.[7] With this position I am in basic agreement, though not with the details of Tödt's analysis of the Son of man sayings.

It is obvious that the sayings of Q present a most vigorous hope — whatever we are to make of it — a hope cast in the eschatological form of the impending coming of the Son of man and of the Kingdom of God, for both these terms are central in Q. On the one hand, the hope of Q has a strongly dialectical character. The empty present is contrasted with the filled future, as in the Lucan form of the Beatitudes, which are probably earlier in form than Matthew's. On the other hand, Q contains a strong realized-eschatology element, as in the saying, "But if it is by the finger of God that I cast out demons, then the kingdom of God has come upon you" (Luke 11:20), in which hope is the expansion and fulfillment of something already present. Let us look at this pattern of expectation more closely.

First, we note that though the death of Jesus is not a motif of Q — much to the sorrow of those who want to impose a uniformity on early Christianity — the motif of death-through-life *is* prominent and recurring in the collection.

> Whoever does not bear his own cross and come after me, cannot be my disciple (Luke 14:27).
> He who finds his life will lose it, and he who loses his life for my sake will find it (Matt. 10:39).

[6] Tödt, *Son of Man*, pp. 247–50.
[7] *Ibid.*, p. 273.

175

> Blessed are you when men hate you, and when they exclude you and revile you. . . . behold, your reward is great in heaven (Luke 6:22).

This motif of finding-through-losing is not simply presented as a command to the believer; it is presented also as Jesus' way, though through his life rather than his death:

> Foxes have holes, and the birds of the air have nests, but the Son of man has nowhere to lay his head (Matt. 8:20).
> A disciple is not above his teacher (Matt. 10:24).

Thus, insofar as hope is understood as pointed toward the fulfillment of ordinary human goal-directed strivings, the first impact of the message of Q is the negative one: it is only through death that there is life, and only in giving up is there finding. At this point the message of Q is at one with the death-of-Christ centered kerygma of Mark and Paul.

If we look beyond this initial negative note, we find three motifs in the sayings material that engage our attention. First there is the already mentioned motif of realized eschatology. It is a striking fact that if we leave out of account the parables — and of course it was with them that Dodd was primarily concerned — most of the sayings which express a newly present eschatological reality are Q-sayings.[8]

> But if it is by the finger of God that I cast out demons, then the kingdom of God has come upon you (Luke 11:20).
> Woe to you Chorazin! woe to you Bethsaida! for if the mighty works done in you had been done in Tyre and Sidon, they would have repented long ago in sackcloth and ashes. (Matt. 11:21).
> Something greater than Jonah is here. . . . Something greater than Solomon is here. (Matt. 12:41–42).

[8] Cf. C. H. Dodd, *Parables of the Kingdom* (New York: Charles Scribner's Sons, 1936), esp. ch. 2.

As we read them in their setting in Q, those sayings convey an immense sense of the new presence of divine reality, which carries with it a likewise powerful sense that this divine reality is moving forward to its fulfillment. Students who concentrate on the Christological passages in Q may miss the point that this present eschatology is the key to the inclusion in Q of so much of the wisdom-type material about the conduct of the present life. Wisdom was concerned with the understanding and management of life, with the short-time span of human self-consciousness. What happens in Q is that the lore of this tradition is transposed into the radical key of *agape*: This is the new presence of the divine. Openness to the other's future through the route of loss of concern for one's own — that is what gives concreteness to the life-through-death motif of Q that we have sketched. Perhaps we do not need to illustrate this further than to refer to the golden rule, a prudential saying about how to smooth the rough edges of life in one's own interest, which, transposed into the setting of Q, conveys the claim of the other, as does the claim, more radical in itself, of love for the enemy.[9] The shift of hope from one's own self-projection to concern for the other brings to light the more profound question of hope, not only for the Christian tradition but for human seeking generally: the vision of God's concern for the other leads to hope for *his* future.

This concern leads naturally to the second motif in the understanding of the present which is prominent in the sayings source: the emphasis on the community. The community shares the rejection and at the same time the authority of its Lord. It is the present eschatological reality — the rejection of Jesus in the past can be forgiven, but the rejection of the spirit operative in the community cannot be forgiven.[10] Here, at quite an early stage in the history of Christianity, we can see the problem of Catholicism: the

[9] On the question of the place of the golden rule in the message of the Synoptic Gospels, and in ancient ethical teaching generally, see Albrecht Dihle, *Die goldene Regel* (Göttingen: Vandenhoeck und Rupprecht, 1962).
[10] So Tödt, *Son of Man*, pp. 118–20, 274.

problem of the continuing presence of the community of grace.

The forward-looking elements in this community's life constitute the third motif which calls for attention. They can be classified under the headings of *reward* and *participation*. The reward motif is prominent, as it is in every type of synoptic tradition. The Beatitudes are cast in this form. More explicit is the saying about treasure on earth and treasure in heaven (or with God) (Matt. 6:19-21). The close relation of the reward motif to the figure of Christ shown in the saying, fundamental for Q as Tödt has shown: Everyone who acknowledges me before men, the Son of man also will acknowledge before the angels of God (Luke 12:8).[11] We shall not follow this motif of reward further here, except to say that it clearly reveals the understanding that beyond the death of self the believer participates in a reality which is taken up and fulfilled in the final consummation.

This element of fulfillment is even clearer in the other forward-looking element: the motif of participation. God is doing a work. It is God's work, and men cannot force it, but the community is called into the same task as its Lord: "The harvest is plentiful, but the laborers are few; pray therefore the Lord of the harvest to send out laborers into his harvest" (Luke 10:2). "I *send* you," with the word ἀποστέλλω, with its strong connotation of participation (Luke 10:3). "He who hears you hears me" (Luke 10:16). Though it is more characteristic of the Marcan tradition, Q also has the term "follow," which expresses participation (Matt. 10:38). The forward direction of this participation is most strongly expressed in the faith that the community would also take part in the future work of the Son of man: "You will sit upon twelve thrones, judging the twelve tribes of Israel" (Matt. 19:28, cf. I Cor. 6:3). This conviction of being called to participate in the eschatological process, which appears clearly in Q, reaches its height in the New Testament, of course, in Paul with his tremendous sense of

[11] Cf. *ibid.*, pp. 55-60, 64-67.

apostolic vocation.[12] It is not so sharply expressed in Q, no doubt partly because Q expresses the sense of vocation of a community, while in Paul we have a highly individualized self-consciousness. Although the material in Q offers little reflection on this subject, the reward motif and the participation motif reinforce each other in expressing a stance in which it is self-evident that beyond the negation of self there lies a new life in which one already participates, and in which one's goal-directed strivings are not just self-projection, but are part of the process of God's work, and hence take on real significance for the future, being taken up into the eschatological consummation. At the same time, we should not fail to note that these motifs of reward and of fulfillment are matched by an extensive group of sayings about the need to "watch" (Luke 12:39 f., 19:18, etc.) which emphasize the fact that the believing community does not have a secure present possession of the power which is at work in it.

If this analysis of hope in Q will stand up, it reminds us of what a remarkable pattern of early Christian proclamation this was: one which strongly emphasized the death and new life of the believer, but by paralleling this with the humiliation in life of Jesus, followed by his resurrection, with no emphasis on his death; one which powerfully expressed a realized eschatology and a sense of the unique role of the chosen community — motifs that reappear later both in Gnosticism and in Catholicism — and one which still maintained as well a strong sense of the incompleteness and hope-orientation of the life of the believer. We shall in our conclusion try to look at some of the questions which this faith poses for the theological interpreter. Here we can raise only one further question about Q: What if the historical analysis on which this presentation is based is faulty, and there never was such a collection of tradition as we have assumed? Well, in a way that would be embarrassing, and some of the points made above would be rather shaky, to

[12] Cf. William A. Beardslee, *Human Achievement and Divine Vocation in the Message of Paul* (London: SCM Press, 1961).

say the least. But basically the point is that these motifs do occur in very early Christianity. If the historical criticism which uncovers Q is faulty, then these motifs become somewhat subsidiary to a more monolithic main stream of tradition. But they are still there, and at bottom the interpreter of the significance of early Christianity has to deal with much the same range of problems. Before we look further at what these are, we should compare our findings from Q with what appears in the Gospel of Mark.

If we turn to Mark, we find many of the same themes. There is the characteristic difference that Mark is a story; it cannot be transposed into a nonhistorical word as the materials in Q can be. The story focuses emphatically on the element in early Christian tradition that is surprisingly unemphasized in Q: the death of Christ. Correspondingly, the emphasis on newly achieved divine reality — what Dodd called realized eschatology — which is prominent in Q, is present in Mark in more veiled fashion: the "secret" of who Jesus is.[13] In Mark, in other words, the tension of life-through-death is presented more intensely or inexorably: one can scarcely ever, in Mark, look for more than a moment at the side of life and joy without being reminded that it comes only through death and suffering. As in Q, the first word of Mark to the human future of self-projection is a negative one. This is the point of the receptivity of children. They do not have to project themselves. They can accept (Mark 10:15).

Although it is subsidiary to his purpose to present what we would call "unaided human effort," the futility of this, from Mark's point of view, is shown not only by the bungling of someone who tried to resist at Jesus' arrest, and of someone else who had to escape naked (Mark 14:47, 51–52), but also more importantly by the story of Peter's denial (Mark 14:66–72). To all this sort of effort, as well as to the religiously oriented striving of the rich young ruler (Mark 10:17–22), the word of Mark is a sharp "no."

[13] This will be true no matter which interpretation of the "Messianic secret" is followed in detail.

Mark identifies the believing community with Christ, as Q does, in the sense that for the community, as for Jesus during his lifetime, the deliverance from the situation of tension is still future. The believing community, coming after the resurrection, is not thereby exempted from the same trials that fell upon Jesus.

What Mark says about the disciples who were with Jesus applies still to the community for which he was writing, and one important meaning of the projection of the fulfillment into the future is that "historical existence," as James M. Robinson calls it in his *The Meaning of History in Mark*, an existence of struggle, continues for the church as for Jesus.[14] There is not so much concrete illustration of how this community is to exist in Mark as in Q, but the main lines are strikingly similar — drawing at times, of course, on the same Jesus-tradition for material. For the inner relationships of the community we have the striking saying: "Whoever would be great among you must be your servant, and whoever would be first among you must be slave of all" (Mark 10:43–44), where the future as the future of the other is opened by the closing off of one's own projection of himself into the future, just as in a group of Q passages discussed above.

It is not necessary to analyze the present under its negative aspect of persecution, which is so strongly asserted by Mark in chapter 13 and elsewhere. As in all eschatological thought, this present is given meaning by a future orientation, but the striking thing about Mark is how firm he is about not letting the believer off easily, not letting him escape into the not-yet. Thus: "If your foot causes you to sin, cut it off; it is better for to enter life lame than with two feet to be thrown into hell" (Mark 9:45); here the future remains of unquestioned significance, but the thrust is all on the present. Something of the same thrust can be seen in the well-known passage on reward:

[14] James M. Robinson, *The Problem of History in Mark* (London: SCM Press, 1957), pp. 59–60.

Peter began to say to him, "Lo, we have left everything and followed you." Jesus said, "Truly, I say to you, there is no one who has left house or brothers or sisters or mother or father or children or lands, for my sake and the gospel, who will not receive a hundredfold now in this time, houses and brothers and sisters, mothers and children and lands, with persecutions, and in the age to come eternal life. (Mark 10:28–30).

I have always been puzzled by this passage, particularly in connection with question whether the interpreter is to see an element of humor in it. I doubt that the view is right which denies all elements of a light touch, and I think that somewhere along the line of tradition someone must have had a twinkle in his eye, or maybe a kind of Linus' dead-pan expression, when he went on about the "brothers and sisters and children and mothers." At the same time Mark takes the passage seriously, and it points to the present reward for the follower of Christ: here in this present time, in the fellowship of the new community, he gets far, far more than he has given up — with persecutions. But though the emphasis is shifted away from the conclusion "and in the age to come eternal life," it is still there and needs to be there, to give fulfillment to what Mark understood as the essentially temporary character of the situation of historical struggle. The dialectic character of Mark's view of reward comes out even more strongly in the answer to the request for first places made by James and John. Jesus can promise them suffering, but the first place goes to those "for whom it has been prepared" (Mark 10:40), i.e., it cannot be earned by a forward projection of one's own striving. Thus Mark uses a group of traditional passages about reward, and the characteristic emphasis which they receive is that this comes unplanned and, so to speak, unexpected.

The motif of *participation* is also present in Mark, quite as fully as in Q. Jesus calls disciples and sends them out with authority (Mark 6:7). They participate, in fact, in his work, and Mark indicates this by giving them the technical term, *apostle*, authorized delegate, when he recounts their return (Mark 6:30). Their participation includes even their being the vehicles for God's negative judgment — "shake off the dust that is on your feet for a testimony against them" (Mark 6:11). On the other side, "Whoever gives you a cup of water to drink because you bear the name of Christ, will by no means lose his reward" (Mark 9:41). Here, too, compared with Q, it seems that Mark more strongly emphasizes the ambiguity of this participation in the work of God through his Christ. For Mark is continually stressing the imperfectness of the disciples' understanding and obedience — Peter; the disciples who could not cast out the dumb spirit (Mark 9:14–29); their inability to understand about the bread (Mark 8:14–21); other instances could be cited. If these passages are to be interpreted in the sense of the disciples' misunderstanding in the Gospel of John, then this stage is transcended when the exalted Christ is present in his community. But this does not seem to be the intention of Mark. The unflattering portrait of the disciples is not something past, but something which carries forward into the church. Mark would have found it difficult to include a saying like, "You, therefore, must be perfect, as your heavenly Father is perfect" (Matt. 5:48).

None the less, despite their human failings, the disciples are participating in a work of God. "The gospel must first be preached to all nations" (Mark 13:10). Thus, as in Q and in Paul, the disciple is caught up into the eschatological task and participates in the work which leads to the final fulfillment.

We may note in passing that another type of future appears in Mark, though only incidentally: "And truly, I say to you, wherever the gospel is preached in the whole world, what she has done will be told in memory of her" (Mark 14:9). This perpetuation in a human future may be implied in some of the other Marcan sections that at least verge on being personal legends. The explicit appearance of this motif of continuance of an act in the human future is a reminder of how Mark stands at a turning of the ways, and has begun to grapple with the continuing human future as the Church had to do.

To summarize: For Mark, the dialectic, that is, the finding of reality through opposites, is even sharper than in Q. This is shown by his constant reminder to his readers that the struggle is not over, that the human is always failing, that the present moment calls for renunciation. Mark is very firm that Christian existence is not that postponement of life to the future which is often cast as a reproach against Christian faith. Such a stance of faith did exist in early Christianity. It finds clear expression, for instance, in some of the Apocryphal Acts. There are those who find it in Revelation or in Hebrews. But it is not in Mark. Neither does Mark allow his reader to think that the present is already transfigured — a view which could be derived from parts of Q or from John, and which was one of the principal misinterpretations of faith as he understood it that Paul had to contend with. None the less, just as in the case of Q, the phenomenon of faith cannot be adequately represented as expressed in the present for Mark. It reaches powerfully into the future in hope, primarily the hope for the fulfillment of the function of Christ, and into this fulfillment the existence of the believer is drawn, through both the motif of reward and the motif of participation. Though Mark is very anxious to state these motifs in such a way that they will not be misunderstood, it is also inescapably part of his vision of faith that faith participates in and will be drawn into the future which God is creating.

Certainly there is nothing very new in the picture I have painted, except possibly that instead of concentrating, as we usually do, on the figure of Christ or on the Kingdom of God, I have tried to focus on the phenomenon of hope as it is related to the self in two levels to the Synoptic eschatology. It may be argued that it is a mistake to turn away from the distinctive Synoptic formulations about the Christ, the Son of man, or the Kingdom of God, since the picture that emerges when we approach hope in this other way is admittedly a somewhat generalized one. To the early Christians themselves, hope appeared quite concretely, in relation to the resurrected Christ, and not as a structure of their perception of reality in general. Surely early Christianity is a model case of that sort of faith which Eliade describes as the religious awareness of an elite, which cancels out the reality of all other structures of awareness of the ultimate.[15] It is not our intention to dodge this problem, for it has been a perennial one for theology since the eighteenth century and still is — How is the historically unique and "separating" experience of Christ to be understood as a religious universal? But while it is not our intention to dodge this problem, it is our intention to set it aside for the purpose of the present discussion, with only this one comment about it: that from within the structure of this faith itself, the problem is felt and is resolved toward the future. It is the openness of the future for all which enables the community to hold to its historical uniqueness, and the uniqueness of Christ, in the present.

For the time being, however, we must leave this problem aside, since we have intentionally concentrated on the most general forms of hope in the Synoptic strata which we have analyzed. We have tried to deal fairly with the phenomena as they appear. Now we must comment on some of the problems of interpretation, and our basic point is a simple one: that an interpretation which consistently transposes this direction toward the future into the present transforms the structure of faith drastically, far more so than is often realized. It may be that theology will have to go the way sketched out by Schweitzer in our opening quotation, resolutely absorbing the future into the present. Certainly the interpretation of faith toward self-understanding, which has been one of the most characteristic ways of taking eschatology seriously, has this effect. Bultmann has dealt seriously with the theme of hope, and in a most illuminating way. But it is characteristic that for him hope is approximated to faith; "This same thing, that the believer is turned away from

[15] Mircea Eliade, *Cosmos and History* (New York: Harper Torchbooks, 1954), p. 109, n. 6.

himself, is also expressed by the fact that *'faith' is also 'hope'*."[16] We are far from unmindful of the depth of contribution made to our understanding of hope by this approach through radical openness to the future in the present. Nonetheless, it is a different style of faith from that to which we tried to listen in Q and Mark. To illustrate the point with one more quotation, James M. Robinson sums up the message of Jesus as follows in his important book, *A New Quest of the Historical Jesus*:

> Thus the deeper meaning of Jesus' message is: in accepting one's death there is life for others; in suffering, there is glory; in submitting to judgment, one finds grace; in accepting one's finitude resides the only transcendence.[17]

This is a fine statement, but it is typical of the theological milieu in which we work that Robinson cannot find anything to say about the positive side of the future, that for early Christian faith it is victory, not only a victory of God but one in which the life of faith is not lost, but somehow elevated to a higher reality.

There is one aspect of our interpretation of hope which is really subsidiary but which needs to be mentioned at this point. The language of hope in the New Testament is mythological. We can no longer live in the particular mythological world of the New Testament, or at least no longer wholly live in it. Study of the history of the eschatological sayings reveals that there is a tendency to elaborate the pictorial visualization of the future as the community reflects on the tradition of eschatological sayings. Thus the mythological detail tends to be least at the very early stages. We will cite only one example: Tödt tells us that the saying about the disciples sitting on thrones and judging the twelve tribes of Israel does not belong to the earliest level of tradition, and one of his criteria for making this judgment is that this

[16] Rudolf Bultmann, *Theology of the New Testament*, trans. Kendrick Grobel, 2 vols. (New York: Scribners, 1954–55), 1:319.

[17] James M. Robinson, *A New Quest of the Historical Jesus* (London: SCM Press, 1959), p. 123.

picture of the disciples participating in the judgment contains too much apocalyptic detail to go back to Jesus himself.[18] Such a process of elaboration often did take place, no
doubt, but it is an incorrect conclusion that therefore the
"pure" form of the tradition has no concern for fulfillment in
the future. The apocalyptic detail is often secondary, but
the structure of hope which sees the present as taken up
into the future is not secondary, and though we have to
reinterpret it or abandon it, it is a basic part of the style of
faith that we see in the Synoptic strata we have examined.

The basic problem, of course, is that the future in our
world is so problematic. What we have presented from the
Synoptic Gospels we have presented as a phenomenon that
appeared to be real to them. As we become aware of the
structure of movement toward the future in our own world,
it is much more difficult for us to see something of this motif
of fulfillment in it.

In this situation one tendency for Christian theological
interpretation of hope is to take the form of the sort of
restriction of the future to openness toward the future in
the present which has been sketched above. The theological
thrust of this sort of interpretation is Lutheran, in that it
displays a strong animus against anything that could be
labeled a *theologia gloriae*, and strongly upholds the dialectic relation of the present to the future — it is only through
its opposite, humiliation, that glory can be known in the
present. There is much to commend this line of thought,
and we all are in its debt. Its inadequacy, as an interpretation of the New Testament, comes from its discontinuous
view of time: each moment is a separate moment of decision,
and the past is lost once it has gone by.

The other tendency for Christian interpretation of hope
to take is *Heilsgeschichte*, in which the acts of God are
ordered in some kind of sequence and moving toward a goal.
Heilsgeschichte has been severely criticized, because its
overarching pattern, with Hegelian overtones, can be taken
to deprive the parts of meaning in favor of the whole, be-

[18] Tödt, *Son of Man*, p. 64.

cause it tends to make the divine action rationally discernible in history, and because it either sets up an unbridgeable gulf between the channel of sacred history and history at large, or else risks the improbable task of claiming to see a discernible pattern of meaning in history as a whole. These are formidable objections. Perhaps more formidable yet is the basic problem that this way of thinking draws upon a vision of reality that is increasingly of limited access in our culture. It is none the less the case that the *heilsgeschichtlich* interpretations do more adequately represent what is there, so far as the element of fulfillment is concerned: in this view we know that God is the Lord and that whatever is worthy will not be lost, but will be taken up into his final fulfillment. Thus we have one leading interpretation of hope that is one-sided and another that is convincing only to a limited segment of our culture.

In this impasse I make my positive suggestion with real diffidence. In the phrase that used to be circulated here in the Church History Field when I was a student, "I'm a historian: I think in pictures." Besides this, I am a student of the ancient world, and find it somewhat presumptuous to enter into the field of modern theology. Nonetheless: I believe that the problem of hope and of the future is a very serious one in theology, and that it is one which we ought to try to handle more adequately. In order to do this, I think that a new rapprochement between the Biblical Field and the theologians is in order, and in particular, that this problem calls for a new look at the applicability of Whiteheadian thought in theology. You can see why I make this suggestion with real diffidence. Chicago was the center of Whiteheadian theology for a long time, and yet somehow the interchange with the Biblical Field was not as fruitful as it might have been. I do recall a seminar with Professor Rylaarsdam, just about twenty years ago, in which among other things we discussed the comparison between a process view of time and the view of time in Jewish apocalyptic! You can see how long it has taken me to absorb the lessons I was supposed to learn in graduate school. Seriously, however, there were real obstacles to communication between the process theology of Professor Wieman and the biblical scholars. I believe that the versions of process theology which are being developed now are more deeply involved in encounter with the biblical tradition. Of course I am thinking primarily of two Chicago theologians, Professors Ogden and Cobb.

Obviously we enter a very different universe when we move from fulfillment in biblical eschatology to fulfillment in Whiteheadian philosophy. In this latter frame of reference, the locus of fulfillment is the consequent nature of God, which is affected by what happens in the world. As Cobb puts it, "whatever enters into the consequent nature of God remains there forever, but new elements are constantly added."[19] It is precisely the creation of a way of thinking in which it is possible to combine creative advance with the retention of what went before that makes it possible to see a relationship between this Whiteheadian thought and the motifs of reward and participation which we examined in Mark and Q. Indeed, the whole Whiteheadian notion of process, in which "what is given ultimately are actual occasions with real internal relations to past occasions,"[20] is a form which is in many ways highly useful for making intelligible the perception of time in concrete events which we find in the Bible, for this way of thinking combines real relation to the past with real openness to the present. From the turn of our discussion, it is clear that an adequate encounter between biblical categories of time and modern process thought would involve a deeper engagement with the category, "future," than is often the case when process philosophy is developed with all the emphasis on movement out of the past. But my belief is that Whitehead's categories have this potentiality: that they can be used in a framework of thought that is analogous to eschatology in that it is grounded in the future rather than in the past. In a recent

[19] John B. Cobb, Jr., *A Christian Natural Theology* (Philadelphia: Westminster Press, 1965), p. 187.
[20] Cobb, *Theology*, p. 185.

address Wolfhart Pannenberg has seen this same possibility of using Whitehead's thought to explicate a faith that the contingent new becomes present event by taking over the preexisting situation and repeating it insofar as it is not able to renew it.[21]

I am well aware that at best I have sketched a program. To me this program is one of the exciting and genuinely open possibilities in contemporary biblical interpretation. A deeper encounter between the biblical phenomena and a rigorous modern intellectual vision which, while it is of course historically relative like any other form of thought, nonetheless makes it possible for men to think about the whole of reality seems to me a most hopeful prospect. There are, of course, stubborn problems. Whitehead's thought was developed to account for the cosmos, and for man secondarily, and the problem of history has not been central for most of those who have worked with his categories. But it will perhaps be by a concentration on interpretation of how the future comes to expression in the present that the cosmological and the historical can converge. That there is one concrete event full of transcendent meaning, and that there is a final fulfillment — these basic ingredients of Christian eschatological thought are not natural elements of a philosophy of general process. I am not going to undertake here to show how these eschatological elements might be interpreted in process theology, for I started with the more modest task of looking at the structure of faith in fulfillment in eschatological thought, and I believe that this more general structure is susceptible of process interpretation. Attention to the way in which the future becomes present may be the key to a fruitful approach to the convergence of historical-eschatological thought and process theology. In its own mythological way, apocalyptic thought already historicized cosmological speculation, and perhaps a similar task is before us now.[22]

[21] Wolfhart Pannenberg, "Appearance as the Arrival of the Future," *Journal of the American Academy of Religion*, 35 (1967): 118.

[22] Cf. Jürgen Moltmann, *Theologie der Hoffnung* (Munich: Chr. Kaiser Verlag, 1965), pp. 120–24.

One point in conclusion: it may be that the particular line of thinking which I have suggested will not be as fruitful as I hope it might be. But at any rate we are in a period of the interpretation of biblical faith when we have to give renewed attention to the meaning of the future. In my view, as shown above, it will be part of a Christian interpretation of the future that life is not simply receptive toward the future, but that it may be called to participate in work which faith believes will be taken up into the future, as in the eschatological faith which we surveyed. To put it differently, faith moves from a deficiency-oriented, future-oriented achievement orientation, to a present-oriented receptive orientation, and then moves through this to a transfigured achievement orientation, in which the striving of the self is enlisted not for the fulfillment of its deficiencies, but for the other. Our reaction against the rigidities with which this sense of enlistment of the self toward the future has often been expressed in Christian communities should not blind us to this fundamental intention of the act of faith. And one can add that if we cannot make the future meaningful in Christian theology, if we finally agree with Schweitzer that the resolute absorption of the future by the present is the outcome of our interpretation, the future will still be a real issue and men will still find ways of living out of and toward the future — the eschatological heritage is still so deeply built into our culture.[23]

[23] Cf. Ernst Bloch, *Das Prinzip Hoffnung*, 2 vols. (Frankfurt: Suhrkamp, 1959).

# 9

---

*Jesus and Eschatology*

MARTIN RIST

*What Is Eschatology?*

The subject of this paper is a controversial one, in part because there are many definitions of eschatology, as well as of apocalypticism and the Kingdom of God. In order to alleviate some of the difficulties, the major terms used in this paper will be defined — first of all, the term "eschatology." It is said to be fairly recent. Apparently its first appearance was in a book by George Bush entitled *Anastasis*, published in 1845. James Martineau somewhat later used it in a paper, "The Eschatology of the Apocalypse and the Epistles," published in *Studies of Christianity* in 1858. As the titles of the works by both Bush and Martineau indicate, "eschatology" had to do with the doctrine of last things — with resurrection for Bush, and with apocalypticism for Martineau — of life after death and of the future world-age to come. Shailer Mathews clearly defined the word as follows: "Eschatology is that department of theology which is concerned with the 'last things,' with the state of the individual after death, and with the course of human history when the present order of things has been brought to a close." [1]

However, with the passing of Shailer Mathews' generation the term "eschatology" has been broadened to be much more inclusive, and consequently less distinctive, in meaning, so that it is applied to sources that according to the original meaning would not have been considered eschatological. As Jenni has observed in a recent article on Old Testament

[1] Hastings' *Dictionary of the Bible*, 1 vol. (New York: Scribner's, 1909).

eschatology in *The Interpreter's Bible*, according to the original sense of the word there is nothing in the Old Testament that could strictly be considered to be eschatological, save for the references to the resurrection in Isa. 26:19 and Dan. 12:1–4. Accordingly, in order to justify an article on the eschatology of the Old Testament he reinterpreted eschatology as referring "to a future in which the circumstances of history are changed to such an extent that one can speak of a new, entirely different state of things without, in so doing, necessarily leaving the stage of history." Parenthetically, a "new, *entirely* different state of things" would involve the "leaving of the stage of history." Be this as it may, he clearly intended that his definition would deal with what Cadbury terms antemortem, not postmortem, situations, with this present world-age, not with the quite different world-age to come. Consequently, if his broad definition is used, the prophetic proclamations of the Day of Yahweh or its equivalents become eschatological, as well as related concepts such as the Kingdom of God or the Messianic Kingdom. A number of scholars have broadened the definition in this manner so that it might apply to almost any future event. Indeed, A. Wilder practically said so when he wrote that "eschatology" is "that form of myth which represents the unknown future."[2]

However, as a rule the broader and more general a definition becomes the less functional and useful it is. Accordingly, in this paper eschatology will be definitely restricted to postmortem, not antemortem situations, such as the resurrection, eternal life, immortality, the end of this evil world-age and the beginning of the new world-age.

### Jesus as a Synagogue Jew

The disadvantages of attempting to focus our attention upon the eschatological views of Jesus are well known to any New Testament scholar. These are clearly summed up by Cadbury. He states that the thought of Jesus on this sub-

[2] *Eschatology and Ethics in the Teaching of Jesus* (New York: Harper & Brothers, 1939), p. 4.

ject must be recovered behind the reported sayings of Jesus in the gospels, especially the first three. But it is not only the evangelist of a written gospel that must be allowed for. Between a given evangelist and Jesus "oral if not written tradition has been at work, altering and varying his original viewpoint."[3] This pregospel tradition, he continues, "accounts for most of the apparent discrepancies among the Synoptic sayings of Jesus, since the single units of tradition had passed through different media in the process." Although he does not specifically say so, Cadbury accepts the presuppositions of *Formgeschichte*, or better, *Traditionsgeschichte*, which posits a period of oral transmission, and probably some written transmission as well, between the original sayings of Jesus as he spoke them in Aramaic and their ultimate deposit in written Greek gospels. The methodology involves not merely a consideration of form but also of the *Sitz im Leben*, the probable life situation, reflected by the sayings. Basically, it involves the application of accepted historical methodology to any given gospel pericope of tradition.

One important factor in the study of Jesus is to determine, if possible, which of the numerous groups in the Palestine of his day he may be classed with. This determination may be accomplished partly by the process of elimination. It is clearly evident that he was not a Priest, not a Levite, not a Sadducee. Although he may have been mistakenly crucified as a member of the fanatically nationalistic party, the Zealots, this relationship may also be ruled out. Rather obviously he was not a Samaritan. Just as certainly he was not, like Philo, Barnabas, or Paul, a Greek-speaking Jew of the Dispersion. Since the days of Bahrdt in 1782 he has been linked with the Essenes, and more recently with Essene-like Qumran community. Although numerous other Jewish groups are named in the New Testament and other early Christian literature, there is no Christian mention of the Essenes or allusion to them until the days of Hippolytus. Certainly this

[3] "Intimations of Immortality in the Thought of Jesus," *Harvard Theological Review*, 53 (1960): 14.

lack of mention may be cited along with other evidence to disprove any connection of Jesus with the Essenes. It is doubtful that he was affiliated with any dualistic movement. Since for him this world as created by God was good, not evil, it is unlikely that he accepted a proto-Gnostic position, if, indeed, there were any proto-Gnostics in his environment. Further, since he believed that God not only created this world but that God, not Satan, was the ruler of this present world-age, he probably was not connected with any apocalyptic movement. Although he was somewhat lax with respect to some aspects of the observance of the Torah, he is not to be classified with the *Am-ha-aretz*, the sinners whom he had come to save and the lost who ignored and disregarded the Torah and its many precepts. However, the most strict among the Pharisees might have been tempted to call him by this epithet. According to all four of the gospels he had some association with John the Baptist, the prophetic, not apocalyptic, preacher of repentance, righteousness, and the Kingdom of God. Indeed, the attempts in the gospels to gloss over this relationship might be taken to indicate that he was at one time, as some believe, a disciple of John the Baptist, the "greatest born of woman."

Some have thought that Jesus was a Pharisee, for he had much in common with them. Bultmann even went so far as to say that he not only was a Pharisee but a rabbi as well. However, both of these identifications are questionable. By the process of elimination in part, and positively, because Jesus, as was his custom, regularly attended the synagogue on the Sabbath, I have come to describe him as a Jew of the synagogue. This would account in some measure for the similarities of his teachings to the teachings of the Pharisees who, apparently, had a close relationship to the synagogue, so close that with the destruction of the Temple the synagogue under Pharisaic direction became the religious center of Judaism. This designation does not mean that Jesus must at all points be in agreement with the Pharisees; on the contrary, we know that he frequently took issue, at times quite forcibly, with their teachings.

## Jesus and Eschatology

### The Resurrection of the Dead

As stated above, there are but two clear instances of the belief in the resurrection in the Old Testament, Isa. 26:19 and Dan. 12:1–4. Normally, for the Hebrews, the disembodied spirits of the dead, both of the righteous and of the wicked, went to Sheol (the equivalent of the Greek Hades), the dark, dreary, godless pit in the underworld where they merely existed, without any discrimination between the good and the evil. Sheol, like Hades, was at first a place of no return, that is, it was the final destination of the dead. As time went on the basic views of Sheol underwent change, so that it came to be considered as the intermediate abode of the disembodied spirits, first of the righteous only, who would be resurrected as a just reward. It was but equitable that the righteous dead be restored to life in their bodies of flesh and blood so that they might share in God's glorious kingdom here on earth, or in its equivalent, the Messianic Kingdom, or, in keeping with the apocalyptic hope, in the new world-age under God's control. The wicked might remain in Sheol, which might be for them the equivalent of Gehenna or hell, a place of punishment. As a variation there was also the belief that the wicked would also be resurrected so that they might be adequately punished in their flesh for their wickedness. Beliefs in the resurrection in one form or another appeared in some of the so-called intertestamental literature,[4] and in the Pharisaic teachings as well. There apparently is no evidence that the Qumran community taught a belief in the resurrection, one of a number of basic distinctions between Jesus and this group.

Along with the resurrection, as early at least as the date of Dan. 12:1 (cf. 7:10), there developed a concept of an eschatological judgment, not of nations, but of individuals, a postmortem judgment of both the righteous and the wicked. This concept, in contradistinction to the judgments

[4] See M. Rist: "Eschatology of the Apocrypha and Pseudepigrapha," in *The Interpreter's Dictionary of the Bible* (New York: Abington, 1962) 2:133–35.

on the nations in this world-age as predicted in certain of the prophetic books, is definitely eschatological.

It is understandable that Jesus evidently entertained a belief in the resurrection of the dead, for this was taught both by the Pharisees and in the synagogue. The Sadducees, who according to our best knowledge, did not accept the resurrection belief, asked Jesus a reductio ad absurdum question in order to discredit this eschatological hope: If a woman married seven brothers in succession, whose wife would she be in the resurrection? (Mark 12:18–27 and parallels in Matthew and Luke). Jesus, purportedly referring to scripture for authority, but citing no scripture, stated that since the resurrected would be like angels (who are sexless) there would be no marrying in heaven. Next, he cited a proof text to support the doctrine of the resurrection. He might have quoted Isa. 26:19 or Dan. 12:1–4. Instead, he quoted Exod. 3:12, "I am the God of Abraham, and the God of Isaac, and the God of Jacob," and by an ingenious, rabbinic type of interpretation he used this passage as a proof text for the resurrection, for if God *is* the God of Abraham, Isaac, and Jacob, these patriarchs are alive. Actually, there was a Jewish belief that Abraham especially, and Isaac and Jacob as well, were heavenly dwellers. The entire setting is so Jewish in its character that the pericope is usually considered to be authentic.

Again, the strange myth (frequently misnamed a parable) of the rich man and Lazarus, the poor man, is found only in Luke 16:19–31. The pericope does not describe the resurrection, but depicts the fate of men after death, of the wicked in a place of fiery punishment in Hades and the righteous on Abraham's bosom in another compartment of the lower world, possibly Paradise. This Jewish depiction of what happens to persons after death might possibly, but not definitely, be representative of Jesus' views. It may be compared with the reputed promise of Jesus to the repentant criminal on the cross, also in Luke alone: "Truly, I say to you, today you will be with me in Paradise" (Luke 23:43). We may well wonder who heard this promise from the cross and retold it for the gospel record. Also, we may inquire concerning what powers Jesus possessed in order to have this promise fulfilled.

A further feature of Jesus' teaching about the resurrection may be mentioned. Save for predictions attributed to him concerning his own resurrection, which are questionably authentic, he did not stress the resurrection belief. This lack of emphasis may have been due to his ardent expectation that the kingdom which he proclaimed would be established so soon that few if any of his followers would die before its inauguration.

### Immortality

There were a number in the Greek world who came to entertain a belief in immortality, a blessed life of the soul without the body after death. The basic difference between humans and the gods were that humans were mortal and gods immortal. Indeed, some of the gods had been humans, more or less, who had achieved immortality in one way or another. A belief developed that at death the soul of the dead would leave the body permanently. Instead of going to Hades after death, the soul of the wicked person might go to Tartarus for a life of eternal punishment, and the soul of the righteous person would ascend to the heavenly, celestial regions to dwell forever in blessedness with the gods. For some this blessed immortality might be acquired through initiation in the so-called mystery religions, which were increasingly popular. A Hellenistic concept of immortality was taught by Philo, the Hellenistic Jewish philosopher and theologian of Alexandria, and by his contemporary (more or less), the author of the Wisdom of Solomon. According to the latter, when an individual dies he is judged personally. The wicked will be sentenced to eternal punishment, the righteous will be rewarded with an eternity of blessedness and joy with God and his angels in heaven. (Wisdom of Solomon, chapter 5). The martyrological document known as IV Maccabees presents a somewhat similar viewpoint. These sources are, of course, Hellenistic, not Palestinian, in character and give no place to the doctrine of the resurrection of the body.

Unlike the Synoptic Gospels, the basic theme in the Fourth Gospel is not the Kingdom of God, but life, that is, eternal life or immortality. To be sure, Jesus is said to have experienced a physical resurrection from the dead following his crucifixion, but there is also the variant concept that when he was lifted up on the cross he was glorified and went to be with God. In any event, according to this gospel the followers of Jesus are to look forward to eternal life, not to a physical resurrection.

The Kingdom of God is mentioned but twice in this Gospel, and both times in the same passage, John 3:1–7, where it is obviously equated with eternal life. Unless one is born again and from above (apparently by means of the initiatory sacrament of baptism by water and by the Spirit) he cannot attain unto eternal life. Furthermore, he must also participate in the Eucharist, which has sacramental efficacy, for "he who eats my flesh and drinks my blood has eternal life" (John 6:54). That this Hellenistic concept, not unrelated to the promises of the mystery religions, represents an eschatological teaching of Jesus is doubtful.

### Gnosticism

There was still another view of immortality which, for lack of a better name, has been called Gnosticism. For the Gnostic there were two worlds, the world of matter (including flesh and blood), which was irredeemably evil, and the world of the spirit, which was eternally and perfectly good. The first was terrestrial, the second celestial. Through some mischance or other a human soul, which originated in the heavenly region of the spirit, had become incarnate in a body of flesh and blood. This body was its tomb, its prison. Through mystic initiations, through certain ascetic observances of some groups, and usually through the impartation of a saving secret gnosis the soul of an individual might be freed from the body in this life, and at death be enabled to return to its heavenly home. In some instances, as with the Carpocratians, there was to be a series of reincarnations until the soul was eternally freed. Jesus Christ, who had come from heaven in a seeming body (not incarnate) and had returned was the Gnostic redeemer who would impart the saving gnosis and would be one to show the way back to the celestial region of the spirit: "I am the way, the truth, and the life" (John 14:6).

It might possibly be that the saving gnosis for the fourth evangelist was the gospel itself (chapters 1–20). This possibility is suggested by the brief preface to the quasi-Gnostic Gospel of Thomas: "These are the secret words which Jesus the living spoke and which Didymus Judas Thomas wrote. And he said, He who will find the interpretation of these words will not taste death." It seems to be obvious that the teachings of Jesus in this Gospel of Thomas are presented as the saving gnosis. Similarly, John 20:31, which may have been the original ending of this gospel, states that this gospel (which contains the deeds and words of Jesus) was written "that you may believe that Jesus is the Christ, the son of God, and that believing you may have life." Could the author have intended his words to mean "that you may *know* that Jesus is the Christ, the son of God, and that by *knowing* you may have *eternal life*?" In other words, was the Fourth Gospel, like the Gospel of Thomas, intended to be a kind of saving or redeeming gnosis necessary for attaining eternal life?

Some time ago I suggested that Matthew 11:25–30 (partially paralleled in Luke 10:21–23) was a primitive Christian baptismal hymn with Johannine, if not, indeed, Gnostic overtones,[5] which had been ascribed to Jesus. It begins with the statement that the Father, the Lord of heaven, had hidden all things from the wise, and had revealed them to babes (the newly baptized?). All things, Jesus is made to say, had been delivered to him by his Father, and no one *knows* the Son save the Father and no one *knows* the Father save the Son, and he to whom the Son wills to reveal the Father. Accordingly, Jesus summons those who are burdened with sin

[5] "Is Matt. 11:25–30 a Primitive Baptismal Hymn?" *Journal of Religion*, 15 (1935): 64–77; cf. Thomas Arvedson, *Das Mysterium Christi: Eine Studie zu Mt. 11:25–30* (Leipzig, 1937). Arvedson presents similar views, save that he relates the hymn to the eucharist rather than to baptism.

to come to him, to take his yoke upon them, whereupon he will give rest (immortality) to them. Could this quasi-Gnostic "hymn" have been an authentic teaching of Jesus?

*Apocalypticism*

The apocalyptic hope[6] has been and is an important eschatological concept. Very recently, for instance, Billy Graham exhorted his millions of hearers to be prepared for the immediate coming of the end. He cautiously neglected, however, to give the exact day and hour. Some scholars have stated that apocalypticism is an outgrowth of Old Testament prophetism, of the concept of the Day of Yahweh, and that it is closely related to the belief in the Kingdom of God. This, I suggest, is a mistaken identification. More probably, I believe, it came into Judaism from the dualistic eschatology of Zoroastrianism. As is true of the word "eschatology," the term "apocalypticism" has been defined so broadly and loosely, if indeed defined at all, that it has been applied to a wide variety of sources. Thus, books or portions of books as diverse as Amos, Zechariah, Joel, Ezekiel, Isaiah 24–27, Daniel, Jubilees, the Testaments of the Twelve Patriarchs, II Baruch, I Enoch, the Psalms of Solomon, II Esdras, Mark 13, the Ascension of Isaiah, the War of the Sons of Light against the Sons of Darkness, Revelation, Hermas, the Apocalypse of Paul, the Apocalypse of Peter, the Vision of Er (from Plato's *Republic*), and still many others, have been termed apocalyptic by one writer or another. This all leads to unnecessary confusion.

Some time ago,[7] in an effort to produce some order out of the manifest confusion, I attempted to formulate a definition of apocalypticism which would be descriptive of a certain definite pattern of thinking. First of all I collected and compared a variety of definitions and descriptions. Secondly, I studied every source, Persian, Jewish, Egyptian, Greek, Christian, Mohammedan, that was generally considered by

[6] Cf. my Introduction to Revelation in Vol. 12 of *The Interpreter's Bible*, also my article "Apocalypticism" in *The Interpreter's Dictionary of the Bible*.
[7] "The Apocalyptic Pattern," *The Iliff Review*, 1 (1944): 15–21.

scholars to be apocalyptic. As a result of this preliminary study I readily discarded a number of sources as being too unlike the rest in their fundamental characteristics to warrant inclusion. Then I proceeded to discover a common denominator of features in the remaining sources. These I termed the primary features, which when combined together formed the basic apocalyptic pattern. Other features, found in some sources but missing from others, I termed secondary features. No feature, primary or secondary, is in and of itself apocalyptic. It is only when the primary features are combined that a source may be termed apocalyptic. The secondary features add color and interest to the basic pattern, but they are not an essential part of it. Their presence or absence from a source has no bearing upon the apocalyptic concept itself.

What then are the primary features? First of all, an apocalypse is eschatological, according to the definition given above, because it deals with last things, with the last times, with life after death. Secondly, it is dualistic. One aspect of its dualism is the presence of two opposing cosmic forces, Satan, or his equivalent, as the force of evil, and God as the power of good. Likewise, there is the dualism of two distinct world-ages. The first, the present world-age, is under the control of Satan. Consequently it is thoroughly evil, irredeemably so, and is temporal. The second, the future world-age, will be perfectly good and eternal, for it will be under the direct control of God himself.

Accordingly, an apocalypse may be defined somewhat as follows: It is the eschatological, dualistic belief in two opposing cosmic powers, God and Satan (or his equivalent), and in two distinct world-ages — the present temporal and irretrievably evil age under Satan's control, who oppresses the righteous but who will soon be overthrown by God, and the future, perfect, and eternal world-age under God's control, when the righteous from among the living and the dead will be rewarded and blessed forevoer.

This is a limiting definition that describes a very distinctive type of eschatological thinking. It may be contended that a definition if it is to be of value should be somewhat restricted and distinctive in character. This definition meets this criterion. Remove one primary feature, and the pattern is broken; add one or more of the secondary features, and the pattern remains unchanged.

There are a number of secondary features; most of them are to be found in Revelation but this does not make them apocalyptic per se. None of them is basically apocalyptic. Some are derived from the Old Testament prophetic books, but this does not make these writings apocalyptic. Among these secondary features are purported visions (this accounts for the word "apocalypse" itself); pseudonymity; numerology; animal symbolism; angelology; demonology; heavenly books; a heavenly city; astralism; a judgment scene; the so-called apocalyptic woes; a messiah; an antimessiah; a messianic interval. To be sure, in the light of the Christology that developed, the Christian apocalypses perforce included a messiah (Jesus Christ), a messianic reign, and at times an anti-Christ, but these are additions to the basic pattern. Even in Revelation it is obvious that the heavenly Christ with his millennium is an added feature, a somewhat unnecessary increment.

It will be noted that apocalypticism provides a dramatic explanation for oppression and persecution of the righteous followers of God, and at the same time presents a solution for these evils. God, usually for no apparent reason, has abdicated this present world-age to Satan; this explains why the righteous suffer and are oppressed. Since Satan is quite powerful, they cannot improve the situation, instead, they await the intervention of God, either directly or indirectly, who will overthrow Satan, destroy his power, bring his evil world-age to an end, and inaugurate his own new and perfectly good and eternal world-age for the enjoyment of his righteous followers. Down through the centuries the apocalyptic hope has been most acceptable to untold millions of Christians. Indeed, it was a very important belief among the early Christians, and no doubt was an important factor in the spread and survival of Christianity despite its basic pessimism and defeatism insofar as this present world-age was concerned.

Our earliest documentary evidence for this pattern in Christianity is provided by Paul. In verses 20–28 of the eschatological fifteenth chapter of I Corinthians, he succinctly sums up the basic pattern without any secondary features, save, perhaps, astralism. Paul was a dualist in that he believed in two distinct world-ages, the first and present one under the control of Satan and other evil forces, including the stoicheia (angelic astral spirits), the personified heavenly powers and principalities, and Sin and Death, also personified. The end of this present world-age will be brought about by the second coming of Christ. At his coming there will be a resurrection of his followers, who, along with the living who belong to Christ will share in Christ's reign, which will be of indefinite duration. It will conclude when Christ has defeated all of the evil forces who are his enemies. The last of these is Death. Whereupon he will give over his control to God, who in the new world-age will be everything to everyone. This is basically the pattern of Revelation. Revelation, however, has two resurrections — the first of the very righteous, the martyrs, and the second of all of the rest of mankind. Save for this minor variation, Paul and the author of Revelation have followed the same apocalyptic tradition. It should be noted that whereas this same pattern is found in Jewish apocalypses (two, at least: II Esdras and Elijah with a messianic interim), I have never been able to identify it in any of the extant rabbinic sources. It was obviously a common and somewhat popular belief, transmitted quite likely in both oral and written traditions. Since a messianic kingdom came to be included in some Jewish and in all Christian apocalypses, it is understandable why messianism came to be considered to be apocalyptic in its nature.

### Kingdom of God

The familiar phrase, the Kingdom of God (or of Heaven, a euphemism for God) should actually be rendered as the reign or the sovereignty of God. Although frequently used in the Synoptic Gospels, usually in a teaching of Jesus, and subsumed in the kingdom parables, it is never clearly defined. It was, as we know, basically a Jewish concept which was current in Jesus' day, so current, in fact, that he may have felt no compulsion to define it. In fact, quite understandably, he may have assumed that his listeners knew exactly what he was talking about.

The concept of the Kingdom or Sovereignty of God is closely related to, if not derived from, the Shema, the ancient Hebrew creedal statement which was recited in the morning and in the evening each day by every pious Jew, and was a basic element of the synagogue service: "Hear, O Israel, the Lord our God is one Lord, and you shall love the Lord your God with all your heart, with all your soul, and with all your might" (Deut. 6:4-6). According to Shechter "the Shema not only contains a metaphysical statement (about the unity of God), but expresses a hope and belief — for everything connected with this verse has a certain dogmatic value — in the universal kingdom of God."[8] To love God meant not only to worship him, and him alone, but also to obey him completely. Obeying God involved knowing his will for man, as revealed in his Torah, both written and oral. Accordingly, the righteous man who is depicted in Psalm 1 has "his delight in the Law of the Lord, and on his Law does he meditate day and night." Consequently, when a person knows and obeys God's law, God's will, then God's sovereignty has been established over him. This is what some of the rabbis understood the "yoke of the law" to mean. Furthermore, when more and more worshipers of God knew and obeyed his law, the sovereignty of God would be further extended. This idea was related to the national hope that in time the rule of pagan conquerors would be brought to a decisive end either directly by God himself in his own way and at the time of his choosing or by a messiah acting as

[8] Solomon Schechter, *Some Aspects of Rabbinic Theology* (New York: Macmillan, 1909, reissued 1923), p. 64. His discussion of the Kingdom in chapters 5 and 6 is very instructive.

his agent. Then God's rule, his reign, would be established over Israel, and his theocracy would come into being. For some his sovereignty would also be extended over the nations as well.

This expectation is implied or stated in a number of sources. The conclusion of the Song of Moses states: "The Lord will reign forever and ever" (Exod. 15:18). Psalm 145 begins with the words: "I will extol thee, my God and King, and bless thy name forever and ever." We read in the Psalms of Solomon, definitely a nonapocalyptic source. "O Lord, thou art our King forever and ever, for in thee, O God, our soul does glory. . . . But we hope in God our deliverer, for the might of the Lord is forever with mercy, and the kingdom of our God is forever over the nations in judgment" (Pss. Sol. 17:1–4). Similarly, there are two passages in the messianic, nonapocalyptic War of the Sons of Light against the Sons of Darkness: "And to the God of Israel shall be the Kingdom and among his people will he display might," and "Thou, O God, resplendent in the glory of thy Kingdom and the congregation of the Holy Ones are in our midst as a perpetual help."

Save for the Shema and the other Old Testament references, Jesus probably was not acquainted with the passages cited, but as a worshiper in the synagogue he must have known the Kaddish very well. The Kaddish was a kind of benediction used at the conclusion of a service, a homily, a lecture: "Magnified and hallowed be his great name in the world which he created according to his will, and may he make his Kingdom sovereign in your lifetime and in your days." The resemblance to the Lord's Prayer is striking. Furthermore, there is a similarity to the eleventh of the Shemoneh Esreh, the Eighteen Benedictions which were recited three times a day by every pious Jew in his personal devotions. It was also used in the synagogue ritual. It beseeches God to: "Restore our judges as in former days, and our counselors as at the beginning, and be thou alone Ruler over us." This petition would be doubly meaningful at a time when a foreign power, such as the Romans, was the

ruler of the Jewish nation. It should be noted that the Kingdom of God and the messianic kingdom represented virtually the same hope, except that in the latter expectation
the messiah would play a role of greater or less significance
as an agent of God's.

It will be seen that the Kingdom of God concept is basically monotheistic, indeed, monistic, not dualistic. It presupposes that God, not Satan, is in control of this present
world-age. The current situation may be evil, indeed, the
Jews might be a conquered nation, but this is by reason of
Israel's disobedience, not through the machinations of Satan. This present world-age is not irredeemable. On the
contrary, thorough repentance, the knowing and doing of
God's law, God will establish his own reign not alone over
individuals but over Israel. In one way or another the conquerors will be removed, perhaps through a victorious war
led by a messiah or in some unexplained manner. This view
is not pessimistic, is not defeatist, with reference to the present world-age. Quite on the contrary, it is quite optimistic,
and man has a part to play in its change for the better.

In some instances an eschatological element, the resurrection, was added to the concept of the kingdom. This,
seemingly, was to provide a suitable reward for the righteous dead and a punishment for the wicked. According to
Psalms of Solomon 13, when God visits the earth, i.e., when
his kingdom is established, there will be a day of redemption for the righteous and retribution for the wicked. The
righteous will rise to life and joy and the wicked to destruction. Similarly, the second of the ancient Eighteen Benedictions states: "Thou art mighty forever, thou sustainest the
living and give life to the dead." Likewise, the misnamed
Apocalypse of Baruch (II or Syriac Baruch) represents God,
not Satan, as being in control of this present world-age
which will show improvement and culminate in a kingdom
(with or without a messiah) accompanied by a resurrection
and a judgment. Further, in the Testament of Benjamin
10:6–8 where the future kingdom is to be here on earth in
this world-age there will be a resurrection, first of the Old

Testament heroes and patriarchs, next of the rest of the righteous and of the wicked. Consequently, eschatology intrudes into the kingdom, but this does not make the kingdom itself eschatological.

In the development of the apocalyptic pattern a merger of the belief in a messianic kingdom with apocalypticism was brought about by inserting a messianic reign of limited duration between this world-age of Satan's and God's future world-age. In II Esd. 7:27–28 the duration is four hundred years, in the neo-Hebraic Apocalypse of Elijah, forty years, in Revelation, one thousand years, and in I Cor. 15:24–26, until Christ destroys Death.

Accordingly, the Kingdom or Reign of God was to be a divine theocracy, with all that this implies. It would be a period of righteousness, when God's will will be known and obeyed, it would be a time when he, and he alone, would rule. This was the basis of Jesus' own mission and teaching. F. C. Grant has stated this very well: "It was this idea which Jesus made his own, the vehicle of all his teaching, which he elaborated, deepened, and surrounded with ethical and spiritual sanctions and conditions, which he identified with the purpose of God in his own time, and adopted as his own prophetic or messianic mission; he was, or was to be, God's agent in the final establishment (or reestablishment) of the divine Being in this world." [9]

According to our earliest gospel, Jesus began his mission by proclaiming: "The time is fulfilled, and the kingdom of God is at hand; repent and believe in the gospel." (Mark 1:15; Matt. 4:17). Jesus not only agreed that the Shema was the greatest of the commandments, but also that those who obeyed it were "not far from the kingdom of God," i.e., were very close to the kingdom (Mark 12:34, omitted by Matthew). In a parallel passage in Luke 10:25–28 based upon a source other than Mark's, observance of the Shema will bring about eternal life (i.e., the kingdom). Similarly, the Ten Commandments are cited by Jesus as being important in acquiring eternal life, that is, the kingdom. (Mark 10:17–

[9] *The Gospel of the Kingdom* (New York: Macmillan, 1940), p. 116.

22). According to Matt. 5:19 he who teaches the precepts of the commandments (the Law), will be called great in the kingdom of Heaven. Similarly, according to Matthew 23:2, his followers are to observe what the scribes and the Pharisees, who sit in Moses' seat, teach, namely, the law. The closest that Jesus comes to defining the kingdom is in the Lord's Prayer in Matthew (paralleled in the Didache): "Thy Kingdom come, thy will be done." The two petitions are all but synonymous; when the kingdom comes, God's will or law will be done; and when God's will or law is done, his Kingdom will arrive. This, I am convinced, together with repentance and forgiveness of sins ("and forgive us our debts") characterized Jesus' mission. He was like John the Baptist, who, in turn, was thought to have been the fulfillment of the prophecy in Malachi 4:5: "Behold, I will send you Elijah the prophet before the great day and terrible day of the Lord comes." Indeed, it is possible that Jesus looked upon himself as being another Elijah, instead of a messiah. The episode at Caesarea Philippi may reflect an authentic tradition, since it is against the evangelist's view that Jesus was the messiah: "Who do men say that I am?" And they told him "Some say John the Baptist, and others Elijah, and others one of the prophets." The situation was saved for the later Christological belief by Peter who reputedly but not certainly said, "You are the Christ," i.e., Messiah.

The kingdom of God had political connotations, for when it would be established the pagan conquerors of Israel would in some way or other be displaced by God or by his messiah. Jesus obviously deemphasized the political implications, but even so when the kingdom he proclaimed would be established there logically would be no place for Caesar and for Roman sovereignty. The political overtones of his proclamation very possibly led to his arrest and execution by the Roman procurator, Pontius Pilate, who could admit of no other ruler than Caesar. By including at times the resurrection in his teachings, Jesus introduced an eschatological factor into the concept of the kingdom, but without making it an apocalyptic expectation. This and other developments were the product of Christian speculation. Again, to quote Grant:

> The New Testament shows evidence, therefore, of a steady movement away from a this worldly conception of the Kingdom which might possibly be misunderstood in a political sense, in the direction of a purely transcendent, other worldly conception, and resulting eventually in a diametrically opposite idea to that reflected as the popular hope, shared by many of Jesus' followers, in the Synoptic gospels." [10]

## The Messiah

Various views concerning the Lord's anointed, the messiah, were entertained by the Jews, although, to be sure, many of the Jews had no messianic expectations. The messiah might be a human being, usually a Jew of Davidic or of Levitic descent, but he might also be a non-Jew, as was King Cyrus of the Persians. (Isa. 45:1, cf. Dan. 9:25). Also, in a few instances, as in the Qumran texts and the neo-Hebraic Apocalypse of Elijah, there are two messiahs. Another type of messiah was nonhuman, a supramundane, angelic kind of personage, called the Son of man. This phrase was used in Ezekiel to designate the prophet; it also might be used generically to mean mankind. Perhaps in some cases when used by a person concerning himself it might be the equivalent of the first personal pronoun "I." The rabbis used it as an equivalent for our indefinite phrase "a certain man." In Dan. 7:13 one "like a son of man" is possibly symbolic of the faithful saints of Israel in contrast to the beasts that symbolized the foreign nations. In any event, he was not the messiah. In I Enoch 46–48 and 62–71, "Son of man" is a designation of a preexistent angelic being who, as God's agent, will appear at the close of this world-age to remove the kings and mighty from their seats, to judge at the final judgment. The "man" in II Esdras who was a warrior messiah was also of heavenly origin.

[10] *Ibid.*, p. 123.

Regardless of the messiah's origin and nature he usually performed one or more of the following functions as an agent of God; purging Israel of the heathen conquerors; destroying the heathen; judging; restoring Israel; introducing the Kingdom of God or an era of blessed peace. He might have a forerunner in the person of Elijah or Enoch. A messiah who suffered and died for the sins of the people was unknown in Judaism.

Jesus is credited with using the phrase "Son of man" rather frequently. At times this may be a periphrasis for "I," in at least one place it means "mankind." In other places it designates a transcendent, heavenly messiah who has suffered and died, gone to heaven, and then will soon return in power and glory to establish God's reign. Some urge that Jesus identified himself with this Son of man. Others suggest that he was referring to someone other than himself. But still others believe that this combination of a suffering and conquering Son of man was the product of early Christian thinking with reference to the death of Jesus upon the cross, his resurrection and ascension, and his expected return in glory and power from heaven. In the event that Jesus did identify himself with this son of man, who was to return soon, he was proven to have been quite mistaken, for there was no such return. Moreover, the belief is based upon a mistaken world view in which a person might ascend to heaven where God supposedly dwells and then return to earth from above.

The phrase is found, among other places, in Mark 13:26, "And then they will see the Son of man coming in clouds with great glory and power." This is imbedded in the so-called Little Apocalypse; I say so-called because this chapter falls short of complying with the definition of apocalypse which has been given. There is no marked dualism in this passage either of two opposing cosmic forces or of two distinct ages. Furthermore, it is not eschatological, inasmuch as no resurrection is predicted. At best it is messianic.

There is a strange teaching, insofar as the Gospel of John is concerned, in John 5:24–29. As it stands it lacks some of the dualistic elements of apocalypticism, but it may be a residuum of an apocalyptic teaching attributed to Jesus. Verses 28–29 read as follows: "Do not marvel at this; for the hour is coming when all who are in the tombs will hear his (i.e., the Son of man's) voice, and come forth, those who have done good, to the resurrection of life, and those who have done evil, to the resurrection of judgment." This eschatological passage is quite alien to the rest of the Gospel of John. We shall never know its origin, nor how it came to be included in this gospel. However, it is probably not an authentic teaching of Jesus.

It is difficult to believe that Jesus' message was apocalyptic in character, for apocalypticism posited a dualism that apparently was alien to his own basic views. If, as we have supposed, he was a Jew of the synagogue, and as such was influenced by Pharisaic views, and hence would be receptive to the concept of the Kingdom of God, he would easily see the fundamental dualism of apocalypticism. To repeat what has been stated above, the apocalyptic thinker believed that Satan, not God, was in control of this world-age, of this world, or of mankind. God had temporarily abdicated his authority, his sovereignty was transcendent in heaven, not immanent on earth. According to the concept of the Kingdom of God there was no thought of this kind of dualism. Satan, to be sure, was in existence, and was a foe of both God and man, but he was not in control of this present age, or of the world. I, at least, want to believe that Jesus was in accord with the Psalmist who wrote: "The earth is the Lord's and the fullness thereof; the world and those who dwell therein." (Ps. 24:1). Indeed, the evidence in the Synoptic Gospels is that for Jesus, God was immanent as well as transcendent. Furthermore, it is my belief that Jesus was optimistic, not pessimistic, concerning this present world-age, indeed the only world-age that he was aware of. That is, he believed that it was capable of great improvement. Indeed, this was what he based his life, his career upon. Why preach repentance and obedience to God's will if this would be of no avail? Furthermore, in keeping with his opti-

213

mism, I believe that he was anything but a defeatist. Mankind was not hopelessly helpless in overcoming evil. Quite on the contrary, I am of the opinion that for him man had both the duty and opportunity to assist in bringing the Kingdom of God into existence.

Another matter is the concept of realized eschatology. This, on the basis of the original definition of eschatology, is a paradox. In any event, if, save for the resurrection of some or all of the dead, the concept of the kingdom is noneschatological and is this-worldly rather than other-worldly, then there is no place for the concept of realized eschatology. To be sure, for Jesus the advent of the kingdom was at hand, if only men would repent and do God's will. But this is not an eschatological advent.

Furthermore, the idea of an interim ethic is, I believe, foreign to Jesus' expectations. His ethical teachings were to be considered as God's will for man, in keeping with the teachings of the Law and the Prophets which Jesus had no desire to annul and with certain features of the oral Torah, the traditions of the fathers as taught by the Pharisees and in the synagogues as well. It was by repenting and doing the will of God, as Jesus interpreted this will on the basis of the written and oral Torah, that the kingdom would be ushered in. Insofar as the teachings were ethical, this was no interim ethic, but it was the ethic that not only preceded the inauguration of the kingdom but also the ethic that would characterize life in the kingdom.

What I have concluded may well be an idealistic rationalization, an attempt, perhaps, to look upon Jesus as something more than an apocalyptical preacher and teacher whose eschatological expectations were incapable of fulfillment in this world-age. This conclusion, however, is compatible with that reached by F. C. Grant some years ago in his book, *The Gospel of the Kingdom*. To be sure, it is possible that Jesus held to both the monotheistic, nondualistic, noneschatological, nonpessimistic, nondefeatist concept of the Kingdom of God while at the same time inconsistently maintaining the dualistic, eschatological, pessimistic, defeatist apocalyptic hope. John Knox in reviewing Grant's book said as much: "Elements of both prophetism and apocalypticism — perhaps quite incompatible elements — were almost certainly present. We must avoid the error of attributing absolute consistency to Jesus, whether in acceptance of apocalypticism, or in his independence or repudiation of it."[11]

This may be true. However, we are not asking "absolute" consistency of Jesus, just a reasonable consistency such as that exhibited by the rabbis who did not intermix apocalypticism with the hope of the kingdom. The assumption has been that Jesus as a synagogue Jew would be favorable to the concept of the Kingdom of God with a receptiveness that may well have been increased by his association with John the Baptist, but not well-disposed toward the apocalyptic hope.

[11] *Journal of Biblical Literature* 60 (1941): 75.

# 10

## Recent Trends in Research
## in the Christology of the New Testament
### NORMAN PERRIN

The occasion for which these essays are prepared makes it appropriate for me to reflect on the current state of things in a particular aspect of our discipline: the study of the Christology of the earliest Church as this is reflected in the New Testament. In this area some considerations have recently come to the fore which seem to me to be of great importance and to have far reaching consequences for our work, and it is my wish to call your attention to them.

In the first place we have an ever wider-spreading acceptance of the fact that sayings found in the Synoptic Gospels have a previous history in the tradition of the Church. This is not, of course, new — Bultmann argued it and traced the history of many sayings in the tradition in his *Geschichte der synoptischen Tradition*, first published in 1921 — but its widespread acceptance is new. Today, for example, Roman Catholic scholars talk about the three possible *Sitze* of a synoptic saying: the *Sitz im Evangelium* (setting in the purpose of the evangelist), the *Sitz im Leben Ecclesiae* (setting in the life and work of the Church), and the *Sitz im Leben Jesu* (setting in the life of Jesus). In Protestant biblical scholarship such a viewpoint is now almost universally accepted. Many who would resist Bultmann find themselves inveigled into acceptance of the approach by Jeremias' history of tradition work upon the parables,[1] and the recent

[1] J. Jeremias, *The Parables of Jesus* (English translation by S. H. Hooke of *Die Gliechnisse Jesu*, 6th ed., 1962) (New York: Scribner's, 1963).

upsurge of work on the theology of the synoptic evangelists which the approach has made possible is itself major testimony in its favor.[2]

The acceptance of the fact that synoptic sayings have a history in the tradition makes a great deal of difference to the study of Christology, especially in connection with the beginnings of Christology, because it raises serious questions with regard to sayings which have hitherto been held to tell us something about Jesus' understanding of himself and in this way to mark the beginning of Christology. Let us take as an example Mark 14:62.

> And Jesus said, "I am; and you will see the Son of man sitting at the right hand of Power, and coming with the clouds of heaven."

If this may be regarded as an authentic saying of Jesus then we can follow O. Cullmann: "He [Jesus] says in effect that his messiahship is not that of an earthly Messiah . . . but that he is the heavenly Son of Man and the heavenly High Priest,"[3] and go on from there to draw from this serious considerations with regard to the origin and early development of New Testament Christology. But if this saying has a previous history in the tradition then all this suddenly becomes inadmissible; the saying in its form in Mark is evidence for an aspect of Mark's Christology and earlier forms of the saying become evidence for stages of christological development in the Church before Mark. Only the earliest form of the saying could tell us anything about Jesus' understanding of himself, and even that would only be the case after we had faced the question whether that earliest form is more likely to have come from Jesus or from the early Church. In the case of Mark 14:62 the history of the saying in the tradition is in fact extraordinarily complex and the ultimate origins of its disparate parts turn out to be Chris-

[2] On this see N. Perrin, "The Wredestrasse becomes the Hauptstrasse," *Journal of Religion*, 46 (1966): 296–300.

[3] O. Cullmann, *The Christology of the New Testament* (English translation by S. C. Guthrie and C. A. M. Hall of *Die Christologie des Neuen Testaments*, 1957) (London: SCM Press, 1959), p. 89.

tian reflection on the resurrection of Jesus on the one hand, and Christian passion apologetic on the other.[4] But it is not so much my purpose now to argue the details of the origin(s) and history in the tradition of Mark 14:62 as to point out that the acceptance of the fact that a saying, any saying, has or can have a history in the tradition changes everything with regard to the way we approach it, and the use we are able to make of it, in connection with the study of the beginnings of Christology.

A second consideration to call to your attention follows from this first one and indeed has already been stated in connection with it. If a saying has a history in the tradition then its various forms are evidence for the theological emphases at work in the tradition and its final form in a gospel is evidence for the theology of the evangelist concerned. In the study of New Testament Christology it was Bousset who first argued systematically that sayings attributed to Jesus in the synoptic tradition were to be treated as evidence for the theology of the early Church. For example, in connection with Son of man sayings — and Son of man sayings would be generally accepted as the most important "christological" sayings in this context — he argues: "In all our considerations we have no wish to deny the possibility that an individual Son of man saying could have come from the lips of Jesus. But one cannot escape the impression that in the majority of these sayings we have before us the product of the theology of the early Church. That is the sure starting point for our work."[5] The work that has been done since then has validated Bousset's argument a hundred times over. We might consider, for example, much the most important recent book on the Son of man sayings, H. E. Tödt's *The Son of Man in the Synoptic Tradition.*[6] Over and over again

[4] N. Perrin, "Mark xiv.62: The End Product of a Christian Pesher Tradition?" *New Testament Studies,* 12 (1965–66): 150–55.

[5] W. Bousset, *Kyrios Christos,* 5th ed. (Göttingen: Vandenhoeck & Ruprecht, 1965), p. 10. The translations of Bousset within this essay are by the present writer.

[6] English translation by D. M. Barton of *Der Menschensohn in der synoptischen Überlieferung* (2d ed., 1963). (Philadelphia: Westminster Press, 1965.)

Tödt is able to illuminate the theology of the evangelists, the theology of the sayings source and theological emphases at work in various aspects of the tradition by a systematic treatment of these sayings from this perspective. The way in which the tradition comes alive under this kind of treatment is quite remarkable and wholly convincing — at any rate to me! Let me give you just one instance, Matt. 12:32 = Luke 12:10: [7]

> "And whoever says a word against the Son of man will be forgiven; but whoever speaks [Luke: blasphemes] against the Holy Spirit will not be forgiven [Matthew adds: either in this age or in the age to come]."

This saying represents "la formule concise et succincte d'une importante maxime missionaire de l'église primitive" (Fridrichsen) and it tells us a great deal about the theology of the Church from which it comes. First, this Church has begun to think of Jesus as the one who is to come in glory and authority as the Son of man and then to go on from this to meditate upon his earthly ministry as already having reflected something of this authority. Then, secondly, the saying reflects the Church's eschatological consciousness of herself as the community of the end time, already possessing the Holy Spirit, the coming of which was to be a feature of that end time, according to Jewish expectation. Further, the saying shows the Church reflecting upon the Jewish rejection of Jesus, who as Son of man is also, of course, Messiah, and from both this rejection and her eschatological self-consciousness, deriving an impulse toward the Jewish mission. Finally, the saying echoes the beginning of a consciousness of the problem that was to haunt the Church for decades, the problem of the comparative failure of the Jewish mission. All of this is clearly within this saying, and every aspect of it is abundantly attested elsewhere in the New

[7] In what follows I am developing in my own words insights ultimately derived from Tödt, Son of Man, pp. 114–25, especially p. 119, and from A. Fridrichsen, "Le Péché contre le Saint-Esprit," Revue d'Histoire et de Philosophie religieuses, 3 (1923): 367–72, especially p. 369, an essay not used by Tödt.

Testament as a theological concern of the early Church. The conclusion is irresistible: the saying is a product of, and evidence for, a stage in the developing theology of the early Church.

What is true of this particular saying is shown to Tödt to be true of the vast majority of the Son of man sayings altogether, as Bousset had argued. I would myself go even further than Tödt and Bousset, for I am of the considered opinion that every single Son of man saying is a product of the theologizing of the early Church.[8] Whether one accepts my radicalization of Tödt's position or stays with his comparative conservatism is, moreover, the choice that confronts one today. The kind of work that Tödt represents has been so successful that there is no turning back from its consequence: if not all, then at least the majority of the Son of man sayings represent the theology of the early Church. But Son of man sayings are by all odds the "christological" sayings that have the strongest claim to go back to Jesus; if this is true of them how much more must it not be true of sayings using Son of God or Son of David? Today the burden of proof must be held to lie very heavily upon anyone who wants to claim that a saying expressing a definite Christology, or using an explicit christological designation, goes back to Jesus himself.

A third consideration playing a significant part in contemporary developments in the study of New Testament Christology is a concern for factors in the life of the early Church to which developments in Christology may be related. Here again Bousset was the pioneer and we may refer once more to his work on Son of man. He argued that the development of a Son of man Christology was the way in which the disciples came to terms with the terrible problem posed for them by the crucifixion. "They came to recognize that suffering and death was the only possible way in which Jesus of Nazareth could attain the exalted status of Son of man. The cross was the means of bridging the gulf

[8] For the details see N. Perrin, *Rediscovering the Teaching of Jesus* (New York: Harper & Row, 1967), pp. 164–99.

between the lowliness of Jesus of Nazareth and the heavenly glory of the Son of man."[9] The linking of christological developments with factors at work in the life and experience of early Christianity in this kind of way has come to be a major emphasis in recent work. A very good example can be quoted from R. H. Fuller's recent and important book, *The Foundations of New Testament Christology*.[10] Fuller calls attention to a fundamental change in christological emphasis which has taken place between the stage of development represented by Acts 3:20 f.:

". . . the Christ appointed for you, Jesus, whom heaven must receive until the time for establishing all that God spoke by the mouth of his holy prophets from of old;"

and that represented by Acts 2:36:

". . . God has made him both Lord and Christ, this Jesus whom you crucified."

In the first of these texts Jesus is the one who at his resurrection/ascension was predestined to appear as the Christ at the parousia. In the second text the resurrection/ascension is Jesus' exaltation and he has already been appointed both Lord and Christ and is already actively reigning. Clearly a far-reaching shift of perspective is involved in the difference between these texts, and Fuller faces squarely the questions as to how, when, and why it came about. It is his answer to the last of these questions that concerns us: "Third, why? The answer must surely be, the delay of the parousia, and the increasing experience of the Spirit's working in the church."[11] This is characteristic of contemporary work on our subject; one of the most radical changes observable in the development of New Testament Christology is firmly and satisfactorily explained on the basis of factors

[9] Bousset, *Kyrios Christos*, p. 16.
[10] New York: Scribner's, 1965. On this book see N. Perrin, "New Beginnings in Christology," *Journal of Religion*, 46 (1966): 491–96.
[11] Fuller, *Foundations*, p. 186.

at work in what may loosely be called the "experience" of New Testament Christianity.

Observations of this kind have a most significant consequence for the study of the Christology of the early Church, for they mark a shift in the focus of concern. Christology is now seen not so much as a product of reflection upon the past event of Jesus as upon the present "experience" of Christians. The Church's developing convictions with regard to the resurrection, her consciousness of herself as the eschatological community, the necessity for an apologetic to Judaism, the delay of the parousia, the physical facts of movement from Palestine to the wider world and from a Jewish to a predominantly Gentile environment — these are now the kinds of things upon which we must focus our attention as we seek to delineate and to understand the origins and developments of the varying christological patterns reflected in the New Testament texts.

A fourth factor at work in the contemporary study of New Testament Christology is the impact of recent discoveries, especially those of the texts from Qumran and from Nag Hammadi. It has always been the case that scholars have concerned themselves with the "raw materials" of Christology, the materials available in Judaism and Hellenism which may have been used in the process of formulating Christology. The work of Bousset is here, again, epoch-making; he brought to his study of Christology "from the beginnings of Christianity to Irenaeus" the results of his own very considerable work, *Die Religion des Judentums*, and those of the immense labors of the history of religions school on Hellenism, and New Testament Christology was never to be the same again. Here in America his example was followed by Foakes Jackson and K. Lake, whose very important essay "Christology," published in 1920,[12] follows the pattern of focusing attention upon "the technical terms" (Messiah, Son of man, etc.) in turn and begins the discussion of each one with a study of its use in Judaism/Hellen-

[12] Foakes Jackson and Kirsopp Lake, eds., *The Beginnings of Christianity* (New York: Macmillan, 1920) 1:345–418.

ism. This has been the pattern followed right down to the present and it is here that Qumran and Nag Hammadi play their part, for they offer us a great deal of new information about the immediate environment of early Christianity in Judaism and Hellenism respectively, and this information will inevitably influence our christological studies. I have worked with the Qumran texts in a way that I have not with those from Nag Hammadi, so I will illustrate my point from these texts.

The Qumran texts, in my view, raise the question whether we have not been too quick to think of titular conceptions in Judaism, i.e., of definite ideas and expectations bound together by a given titular expression which could be used by itself and would carry the ideas and expectations with it. Qumran introduced us to a new kind of literature, the *pesher*, and taught us how far and in what ways Jews could use Old Testament texts in the formulation of their expectations. This led me to question, for example, whether "Son of man" exists as a titular conception in ancient Judaism and whether we should not rather think of a constant use and reuse of Dan. 7:13, 14 as seers and scribes of different groups formulated their expectations.[13] If this should be the case then Jesus could never have referred to a coming Son of man; the Son of man expectation in early Christianity would begin with an interpretation of Jesus' resurrection in light of Ps. 110:1 and Dan. 7:13. I propose to investigate "Son of God" from this perspective also for, as is well known, this has never been found as a messianic title in Judaism. But it does turn up in Qumran in such a way as to lead R. H. Fuller to claim that "Son of God was just coming into use as a messianic title in pre-Christian Judaism."[14] But the context in Qumran is that of a *pesher* on II Samuel 7, i.e., a document in which a scribe is using that scriptural passage (with others) in the formulation of particular eschatological expectations, which leads me to question the use of "messianic

[13] See N. Perrin, "The Son of Man in Ancient Judaism and Primitive Christianity: A Suggestion," *Biblical Research*, 11 (1966): 17–28; *idem*, *Rediscovering the Teaching of Jesus*, pp. 164–85.

[14] Fuller, *Foundations*, p. 32.

title" here and to ask whether we must not seek a *pesher*-type use of II Samuel 7 (and related texts) in early Christianity as the basis for the formation of a Son of God Christology.

Thus far this chapter has been concerned with particular factors which I would claim are coming to the fore today in the study of the Christology of the New Testament and with something of their immediate significance for this discipline. Now let me offer you a change of perspective, and instead of thinking of factors at work let us think of trends which seem to be establishing themselves. This may only be to look at the same material from a different angle, but it will offer us a different view of it.

Perhaps the most spectacular of these trends which seems to be establishing itself in our context is what could be described as the movement from a concern for the messianic consciousness of Jesus to a consideration of a Christology which may be implicit in his message. Let me illustrate the change that has taken place here by adducing the testimony of two English scholars. The first is A. S. Peake, who in 1924 asks: ". . . is it not clear from the records themselves that Jesus believed himself to be the Messiah, the Son of David, the Son of Man, the Son of God?" He speaks of Jesus' consciousness of divine sonship attained at his baptism and argues that the motif of the messianic secret is due to the difference between Jesus' understanding of messiahship and the disciples': ". . . it was far better that Jesus should lead them through intimate familiarity with Him, through watching His actions and listening to His words to form their own judgment of Him, rather than by premature disclosure to force the truth upon them before they were ready for it, and when they would inevitably have misunderstood it." [15] That was A. S. Peake in 1924 and he was, of course, typical of his day. Today a typical voice would be R. H. Fuller's:

An examination of Jesus' words — his proclamation of the reign of God, and his call for decision, his enuncia-

[15] A. S. Peake, "The Messiah and the Son of Man," *Bulletin of the John Rylands Library*, 8 (1924): 3–32.

tion of God's demand, and his teaching about the nearness of God — and of his conduct — his calling men to
follow him and his healings, his eating with publicans
and sinners — forces upon us the conclusion that underlying his word and work is an implicit Christology. In
Jesus as he understood himself, there is an immediate
confrontation with "God's presence and his very self,"
offering judgment and salvation.[16]

One can see immediately that a very great change has
taken place, a change for which there are a number of
pertinent reasons. One of these is that a view such as Peake's
necessitates a great deal of psychologizing about Jesus. One
has to speculate about his psychological and spiritual experiences at the baptism and temptation, about his motivation
and intention in connection with the disciples and the High
Priest, and so on. But such psychologizing and speculation
are absolutely foreign to the sources themselves, for the
gospels never concern themselves with these things. Moreover, to fill in the gaps we have to supply material by analogy from the experience of other human beings, especially,
of course, from what we can imagine on the basis of our
knowledge of our own experience. The result is that we tend
to end up either with a picture of a Jesus who looks curiously
like ourselves — or as we would like to look — or with a picture of a man who seems to be suffering from delusions of
grandeur. Which of these it is depends upon whether we
accept or reject as authentic the more explicit claims to be
found on the lips of the Jesus of the gospel tradition. The fact
is that psychologizing about Jesus leads one into a morass,
and this is a lesson that contemporary critical scholarship
has learned well, so that today a view which involves this
kind of thing would be generally rejected.

Another reason for the change is that critical scholarship
now almost uniformly accepts the more explicitly christological sayings as coming from the early Church. This is part of
the general tendency to regard the synoptic sayings as

[16] Fuller, *Foundations*, p. 106.

reflecting the theology of the early Church, to which I called your attention earlier. But the rejection of these christological sayings is not due to the acceptance of any vaguely defined general principle, of which it might be held that the opposite could equally be true; it is due to the fact that we can demonstrate that these sayings and their contexts reflect the characteristic concerns and theology of the early Church, and that they are couched in terms characteristic of the liturgical and confessional formulas of that Church.

There is today no going back from the basic change of emphasis and focus indicated by the difference between Peake and Fuller, and this is the more so for me because my own work on the teaching of Jesus has led me to a position like Fuller's, although perhaps slightly more radical. Let me therefore pursue for a while Fuller's concern, but in my own words and my own way. I have spent the last ten years of my life in *Leben-Jesu-Forschung*, for in the autumn of 1957 I began the work that eventually resulted in a book *The Kingdom of God in the Teaching of Jesus* [17] and as soon as I had finished that, I broadened my concern to do the work which has resulted in *Rediscovering the Teaching of Jesus*, published by Harper & Row in 1967, the scope of which can be gathered from its subtitle, *The Reconstruction and Interpretation of the Teaching of Jesus*. How well or how badly I have worked in these years is not for me to say, but I can say that they have convinced me of the very real limits set to our knowledge of the teaching of Jesus. At the same time, however, our current knowledge of the historical Jesus and his teaching, for all its limitations in extent, is very firm knowledge indeed, and extremely unlikely to be shaken in any foreseeable future. We have sure knowledge of his teaching in parables, and of the general context in his ministry against the background of which these parables are to be understood. We know and can understand historically his proclamation of the Kingdom of God, although there remains the very real problem of how we are to interpret it, so to speak, existentially. We can reconstruct the

[17] Philadelphia: Westminster Press, 1963.

prayer he taught his disciples, and appreciate the real force of the differences between that prayer and those of the Judaism of that day. I would claim that we can also understand the tremendous significance of his concern for, and table fellowship with, "the tax collectors and sinners," a group designation I would translate "tax collectors and other Jews who had made themselves as Gentiles." We can add to this list certain aspects of his challenge to discipleship, especially such as arise naturally out of the context of the Kingdom proclamation. But when we have done that we have reached the end of our catalog. I am personally unconvinced at the moment, that we know anything about his interpretation of the Jewish law or that we can say how he understood his own death.

You can see that I meant what I said about the limitations set to our knowledge of the historical Jesus. Yet I want to call your attention to what is surely to be regarded as a most significant thing: each of the major elements of teaching I cataloged above contains a surprising aspect of uniqueness, of boldness, of audacity. The parables include, for example, the parable of the Prodigal Son, which has to be understood as a parable designed by Jesus to defend his acceptance of penitent "tax collectors and sinners" in the name of the Kingdom of God. But if he did this, then he is defending an aspect of his own conduct by reference to the essential nature of the forgiveness of God. He is acting, and implicitly claiming to act, as I once heard Ernst Fuchs express it in a class at the "Kirchliche Hochschule" in Berlin, "Als ob er an die Stelle Gottes stünde" (as if he stood in the very place of God himself). The proclamation of the Kingdom of God certainly included the claim that aspects of the ministry of Jesus were the fulfillment of the age-old hope of the Jewish people: "From the days of John the Baptist until now, the Kingdom of God suffers violence and violent men plunder it" (as I would translate and interpret Matt. 12:32) is an authentic saying of Jesus and certainly implies that the kingdom is present in his ministry. The Lord's Prayer includes the remarkable mode of address to God,

Abba (Father). Jeremias has shown that this is unique in ancient Judaism, that here Jesus is deliberately shattering all precedent, and teaching his disciples to do so.[18]

In all of this we can see one thing clearly: Jesus is *implying* a tremendous claim for himself and his ministry. This is the element to which Fuller quite correctly calls our attention. But there is a further element here to which attention must also be called: Jesus' words and deeds may imply something about the person of Jesus, but their actual authority, historically speaking, derived from the Kingdom of God. Jesus' authority was derived from the kingdom he proclaimed. Let me illustrate what I mean here by reference to the remarkable feature of the ministry of Jesus pointed out by Jeremias: the way in which Jesus addressed God as Abba and taught his disciples to do so. It can be argued that this usage reflects Jesus' consciousness of a unique relationship with God and his authority to bring his followers to share that relationship. But although this would be true up to a point it would be to put the emphasis in the wrong place and to miss the crux of the whole matter so far as the followers are concerned. In fairly extensive discussions of the Lord's Prayer in the context of the total message and ministry of Jesus[19] I believe I have been able to show that what the prayer reflects, and what makes the prayer possible, is the way in which the follower of Jesus had come to know God acting as king in his own experience, to enjoy the blessings of that activity as he responded appropriately to it, to find himself able to enter into a new relationship with God and his fellowmen because of what he believed God had done and was doing. In other words, the immediate reason for the follower's newfound ability to address God as Abba is not

[18] J. Jeremias, *Abba* (Göttingen: Vandenhoeck & Ruprecht, 1966), pp. 15–67; idem, *Central Message of the New Testament* (New York; Scribner's, 1965), pp. 9–30. The argument so far as the address to God is concerned assumes the comparative originality of the Lucan version of the prayer as against the Matthaean, a point Jeremias makes convincingly.

[19] N. Perrin, *The Kingdom of God in the Teaching of Jesus*, pp. 191–98; idem, *Rediscovering the Teaching of Jesus, passim.*

Jesus' consciousness of a special relationship with God but the follower's own experience of the kingdom.

What is true of the address to God is true of the totality of the message of Jesus: it implies a claim for his person and it reflects his authority. But if we concentrate our attention upon that implication and build greatly upon that authority then we are doing violence to the message itself. The authority of that message was derived from the reality of the kingdom it proclaimed, not from the person of the proclaimer. However true it may be to say that the person cannot be separated from his words, it is also true that the authority of the historical Jesus was the authority of the proclamation, not that of the proclaimer. True, as Bultmann is so fond of saying, in the early Church the proclaimer becomes the proclaimed, and this shift soon had its natural consequences in a view of the ministry of Jesus in which the authority is that of the proclaimer, not of the proclamation. But this is the early Church and we do well to be wary of this view in our consideration of the historical Jesus.

I feel it is necessary to sound this note of caution about the Christology implicit in the words and deeds of Jesus, but having done this I want to reiterate the fact that I share the shift of emphasis from the messianic consciousness of Jesus to a Christology implicit in his ministry and message. This is a trend which is firmly establishing itself in our discussion.

There is a second trend which I believe is also establishing itself, and to which I would call your attention: a tendency to locate the beginnings of Christology in the early Church, not in the ministry of Jesus. Of course, this is simply the reverse of the coin of which the first trend is the obverse, but it is also sufficiently important to warrant a moment's consideration in its own right. Those of us who were brought up in a comparatively conservative Anglo-American theological tradition can probably all recall with what a sense of shock we first read the opening sentence of Bultmann's *Theologie des Neuen Testaments*: "The *message of Jesus* is a presupposition for the theology of the New Testament rather than a part of that theology itself." Certain it came as a shock to me, a pupil of T. W. Manson; indeed, a good deal of my academic pilgrimage in these past ten years might be described as a coming to terms with that statement. Today, however, I have come to terms with it and can in fact join with Bultmann in his radical distinction between the message of the historical Jesus and the theology of the early Church, as will have become evident to you in the course of this paper. Certainly I can echo it so far as Christology is concerned; the starting point for New Testament Christology is not the message of the historical Jesus – not even the implicit Christology of that message – but the theologizing of early Christianity.

This can be seen most clearly in the case of the Son of man Christology, and here I must pick up again some of the earlier threads of this paper. There can be no doubt but that the earliest Christology of Palestinian Christianity was one which identified Jesus as the coming Son of man. H. E. Tödt has shown how pervasive the theology associated with the apocalyptic Son of man sayings is in the earliest Christian source we possess, the sayings source Q, itself certainly Palestinian,[20] and R. H. Fuller describes the first step taken by the Church in her theologizing as follows:

> Jesus had declared that his own eschatological word and deed would be vindicated by the Son of man at the end. Now his word and deed had received preliminary yet certain vindication by the act of God in the resurrection. The earliest church expressed this newborn conviction by identifying Jesus with the Son of man who was to come.[21]

The only question I have in this connection, as I indicated earlier, is whether this first step was an identification of Jesus with a Son of man whose coming Jesus had proclaimed or

[20] Tödt, *Son of Man*, pp. 232–75.
[21] Fuller, *Foundations*, pp. 143 f.

whether the Christian Son of man conception in its totality does not have its origin in an interpretation of the resurrection of Jesus in light of Ps. 110:1 and Dan. 7:13. But in the matter with which we are concerned at the moment this is clearly irrelevant: whether the first step is identification or interpretation, its impulse is Christian conviction concerning the resurrection. In other words, the first step in Christology is a post-Easter step taken in response to a factor at work in earliest Christianity. It is not directly a response to the message or ministry of the historical Jesus, for these only took on christological significance when they were interpreted in light of the resurrection and when christological emphases which had developed in early Christianity were read back into them. What is true of the Son of man Christology is certainly going to be true of the other christological patterns, those using Son of God, Son of David, Christ, Lord, and so on, for none of these has anything like the secure place in earliest Christianity that Son of man has. True, the prayer *Maranatha* indicates that a use of the term "Lord" of Jesus is also early, but then this is almost certainly due to the use of Ps. 110:1 in connection with the resurrection and the creative impulse, for it is therefore equally to be located in early Christianity. It might be argued from Jesus' use of Abba that he used Son of God of himself in a technical sense,[22] but such an argument would have to be able to show: (1) that Jesus' use of Abba sprang from convictions concerning himself and his person and not from convictions concerning the Kingdom of God; (2) that the use in early Christianity is due to something Jesus said of himself and not due to an interpretation of Jesus in light of II Samuel 7 (and related passages); and (3) that a saying such as Matt. 11:25–27=Luke 10:21–22 is authentic, something that is quite impossible while the burden of proof lies upon the claim to authenticity, as it must be held to do today. So I believe that I am fully justified in claiming that the location of the beginnings of Christology in the early Church rather than in the ministry of Jesus is

[22] As it has been recently by I. Howard Marshall, "The Divine Sonship of Jesus," *Interpretation*, 21 (1967): 87–103.

a trend that is establishing itself in our work, and that there is good reason for this being the case.

If these two trends of which I have spoken are indeed establishing themselves then it is clear that future books on the Christology of the New Testament are going to look rather different from those popular in the immediate past. But then this, I would argue, should be the case.

# 11

## The Place of the Areopagus Speech in the Composition of Acts

### PAUL SCHUBERT

One of the most obvious and important clues for the structure and composition of the book of Acts is the numerous speeches which extend from chapter 1 to chapter 28. Many of them have long occupied the special attention of scholars. Thus the so-called missionary speeches of chapters 2, 3, 10, and 13 have been studied with a view to recovering from them the specific content of the earliest Christian teaching[1] — a legitimate undertaking, but as yet quite inconclusive. To Stephen's speech of 7:2–53 with his preceding trial (6:1–7:1) and subsequent martyr death (7:54–8:3) many monographs and articles have been devoted,[2] but no persuasive picture of the underlying historical events has as yet emerged. No single speech has received more attention than Paul's speech on the Areopagus at Athens. Was it actually given by Paul himself and more or less accurately reported by Luke, or was it really composed by Luke himself, who put it into the mouth of Paul?[3] In either case the Areopagus speech with its colorful setting (17:15–18:1) and dramatic content (17:22–31) seemed to stand apart from the tone and content of the other speeches, from those which preceded

[1] See, e.g., C. H. Dodd, *The Apostolic Preaching and its Developments* (Chicago: Willett, Clark & Co., 1937).

[2] See Marcel Simon, *St. Stephen and the Hellenists in the Primitive Church* (London: Longmans, Green, 1958); for the older literature see p. 117, n. 1–4.

[3] The first alternative is B. Gärtner's answer in *The Areopagus Speech and Natural Revelation*, trans. C. H. King (Uppsala: Gleerup, 1955); the second alternative is Dibelius' answer throughout his *Studies in the Acts of the Apostles*, ed. H. Greeven, (New York: Scribner's, 1956).

it (chaps. 1–15) and from those which followed it (chaps. 20–28).

In view of such disparate methods and results it is advisable to follow up a suggestion made by H. J. Cadbury,[4] namely, to analyze carefully the form and function of all the speeches of Acts and to observe the extent and the kind of interrelationship that exists between them. Cadbury has done much to bring about the present consensus that the speeches have "their common origin in the mind of the editor." "Even those persons who incline to consider the speeches in Acts close approximations to addresses actually given by Peter, Stephen, and Paul will probably admit that the voice is the voice of Luke. . . . Besides the characteristics which the speeches share with the vocabulary of Luke and Acts, they share with each other some elements of likeness that go beyond mere style and vocabulary into the subject matter itself."[5] "Though each speech deserves and rewards independent study it is worthwhile to inquire collectively about them."[6] I believe that these two tasks must be pursued simultaneously, each working as a check upon the other.

Thus we gain our outline. First, we try to determine in a preliminary way the most important intentions which Luke pursued in conceiving and executing his two-volume work (I). Next we analyze the speeches from chapters 1–15, and observe their interrelations (II); next comes the analysis of the theme and content of the speech itself (17:22b–31) (III); then we ask what are the specific theologoumena of the Areopagus speech already dealt with in the preceding speeches of chapters 2–15 (IV); finally, we ask what light the farewell speech (Acts 20:18–35) sheds on the Areopagus speech (V). Only this total analysis itself and its results can show the adequacy of this procedure. In any case this analysis will shed some light on the place which the Areopagus speech occupied in the intentions of the author of the book of Acts.

[4] In *The Beginnings of Christianity*, ed. Foakes Jackson and K. Lake (New York: R. R. Smith, 1931), "The Speeches of Acts," 5:402–27.
[5] *Ibid.*, p. 407.
[6] *Ibid.*, p. 404.

## The Place of the Areopagus Speech

### I. The Literary Intentions behind the Two-Volume Work

For many centuries the Acts of the Apostles have been read, admired and criticized as the oldest history of Christianity [7] from first post-Easter beginnings in Jerusalem to the strangely triumphant entrance of Paul in Rome, the capital of the Roman Empire. This is no serious misunderstanding of Acts, but we may now say, more precisely, that the whole of the two-volume work Luke-Acts, coming to us from the end of the first century A.D., is a narrative about the proclamation of the Word of God which begins with the teaching of Jesus himself and leads in rapid strides irresistibly (ἀκωλύτως) to the open and unhindered proclamation through Paul in Rome.[8] This is already an indication that Luke, the author, must still be regarded as a historian, but also as a resourceful and gifted literary author and as a theologian of some size. He remains a historian, since the course of this proclamation runs from Jerusalem and Syrian Antioch, via Asia Minor, Macedonia, and Greece, to Rome. Luke describes this course planfully in a relatively unified perspective and with due regard to the facts he knew. This corresponds very well to his presentation of the words and deeds of Jesus (Luke 24:19; Acts 1:1; 10:37–39; 28:31) more historically conceived by him than by either Matthew or Mark.

The unprejudiced and attentive reader — a rare animal — of the first chapters of Acts may well expect that the whole of Acts will deal with Peter and the college of the twelve apostles and with their world-mission (see 1:8b). It is undoubtedly the knowledge of and the respect for facts (both of which the authors of the numerous apocryphal Acts lacked) which force Luke to shape the course of events quite differently. Although Luke-Acts ascribes to the twelve apostles

[7] In Acts 11:26 and 26:28 and in I Pet. 4:16 the disciples of Jesus are for the first time called χριστιανοί.

[8] The phrase "Word of God" is one of the most massive and characteristic key-terms. It occurs twenty-five times in Acts, as against six occurrences in the genuine Pauline epistles. Even in the Gospel of Luke it is used in four thematic passages (5:1; 8:11.19; 11:28). Note also the related term ῥῆμα θεοῦ in the Lucan infancy-stories (Luke 1:37 f., 65; 2:15–19, 29, 50 f.) and in 3:2.

a greater significance than any other New Testament book does, Paul is soon introduced at the death of Stephen (7:58); his so-called conversion is dramatically told in 9:1–30; he takes the front of the stage in 13:1 ff. and is the sole agent after chapter 15, "a chosen instrument of mine to carry my name before the Gentiles and kings and the sons of Israel; for I will show him how much he must suffer for the sake of my name" (9:15–16). This is indeed the topic-sentence of the larger second half of Acts. Peter and the Twelve quietly and surprisingly disappear entirely from the scene after the apostolic council of chapter 15, without a farewell scene or a tear shed.

These elementary and basic observations point clearly to Luke's second intention in the structure of Acts: the authority of Paul, at least equal to that of Peter and the Twelve, is secured by three elaborate accounts of his Damascus experience (chaps. 9, 22, and 26; see also Gal. 1:17b). It is his commission by the Lord Jesus to be his "chosen instrument," just as the twelve apostles were chosen by Jesus at the beginning of his earthly ministry (Luke 6:12–16) as eyewitnesses to it. Thus Luke succeeded in his intention to secure for Paul a place of high authority with due regard to the still ascertainable facts and to the sensibilities of Jewish Christians who were suspicious of Paul and of enthusiastic Paulinists.

To this concern with creating a balance between Peter and Paul, Luke understandably gave so much emphasis throughout Acts, in so many ways, because as a Christian, as a historian and as a theologian he saw the situation of the church at the end of the first century in such a way that he endeavored to make available to the church as a whole the heritage of Peter and the Twelve as well as the heritage of Paul. Though we may and should criticize Luke's effort at many points, we may still admire his effort on two counts, first for the caution (and not just superficiality) with which he achieved this balance, and second, for the historian's respect for facts, since Peter and Paul no doubt were regarded in wide sections of the late first century church as the outstanding and to some extent rival leaders of the early apostolic period.

## II. The Speeches of Chapters 1–15

In an older essay[9] I have tried to show that the basic elements of Luke's theology are already present in his gospel. They are like a red thread running throughout the gospel from the infancy stories and the programmatic speech of Jesus at the synagogue in Nazareth to the appearance stories of Luke 24. In the speeches of Acts 1–15 they are planfully articulated and developed. They are repeated with significant variations, condensed, or expanded in the individual speeches. They can be profitably stated in two characteristic Lucan phrases. The theology of Luke is the proclamation of the ὡρισμένη βουλὴ τοῦ θεοῦ, of the firm, original and all-comprehending plan of God with all men. This plan God made known to the prophets beforehand and fulfilled in Jesus Christ. The twelve apostles are eyewitnesses to this plan. It culminates in the call to repentance, or conversion (μετάνοια), in order to receive forgiveness of sins and the Holy Spirit.

We are now ready to analyze the individual speeches of chapters 1–15 and to appraise their interrelations.

1) Peter's speech at the election of Matthias (1:16–22). This first formal speech in Acts plays an important part in the theology of Luke. The necessity of the election is shown by an Old Testament prophecy (Ps. 109:8); and Peter here defines the eyewitness character of the witness of the college of the Twelve clearly, so as to match fully the other clear statement of 10:39–42. "One of the men who have accompanied us during all the time that the Lord Jesus went in and out among us, beginning from the baptism of John until the day when he was taken up from us — one of these men must become with us a witness to the resurrection" (1:21–22). This speech states clearly the nature of the special status of the Twelve, which had been carefully prepared for in the

---

[9] "The Structure and Significance of Luke 24" in *Neutestamentliche Studien für Rudolf Bultmann* (Berlin: A. Töpelmann, 1954), pp. 165–86; see especially pp. 178–86.

gospel of Luke, and is impressively repeated and varied in subsequent speeches.

2) Peter's speech at Pentecost (2:14–36, 38–40) is programmatic of all subsequent speeches. It begins with a long quotation (Joel 2:28–32) which shows that the outpouring of the Holy Spirit which the hearers have just witnessed is also the fulfillment of an Old Testament promise (vss. 14–21). God's action through Jesus' deeds, death and resurrection (vss. 22–24), ascension and exaltation to the right hand of God (vss. 33a and 36), the outpouring of Holy Spirit (vs. 33b), the call to repentance and to baptism in order to receive forgiveness of sins and the Holy Spirit — all these events are told in barely six verses. Nineteen verses are devoted to the quotation and interpretation of special prophecies and promises which have found their fulfillment in the christological events just listed. The speech closes (vs. 39a) with the assurance that "the promise is to you and to your children," i.e., to the people of Israel, but this is followed (vs. 39b) by a clear and significant hint "and to all that are afar off, everyone whom the Lord our God calls to him," i.e., to the Gentiles.

All these events of promise and fulfillment are in this speech subsumed under the comprehensive ὡρισμένη βουλὴ τοῦ θεοῦ (vs. 23). This basic theme and thesis of Lucan theology is dominant in all the speeches, even where the term does not explicitly occur. For its occurrence see especially Isa. 46:8–10; 55:7–11 (LXX). Both these passages show, as do many others, how much Luke's theology owes to Second Isaiah.

3) Peter's speech in the Portico of Solomon (3:12–26). It starts with a short summary of the Pentecost speech (vss. 13–15), but new in these short verses are the christological titles servant (παῖς; from Second Isaiah), the Holy and Righteous One, the Author of Life.

New and important to Luke is the thesis that Israel and its leaders killed Jesus out of ignorance (ἄγνοια), but just so they fulfilled the plan of God (vss. 17 f.). To this is joined the call to repentance for the forgiveness of sin (vs. 19). New is, further, the eschatological-apocalyptical affirmation that "the Lord may grant you a time of recovery and send you . . . Jesus. He must be received into heaven until the time of universal restoration comes, of which God spoke by his holy prophets." (*NEB*, vss. 20–21).

Only one specific Old Testament passage is quoted and is interpreted christologically (Deut. 18:15–16: "Moses said: 'The Lord God will raise for you a prophet, as he raised me up,'" etc., vss. 22–23), but enough examples were given in chapter 2, so that in chapter 3 there is a threefold repetition of the generalized statement that "what God has foretold by all the prophets is now fulfilled" (vss. 18, 21*b*, 24). The "proof-from-prophecy" has been firmly established.

It is clear that the speech in the Portico of Solomon abounds in summaries, elaborations, and variations. The second speech reinforces the first. Both have the ὡρισμένη βουλὴ τοῦ θεοῦ as their theme. These two major speeches are separated only by a short summary (2:41–47), for the healing by Peter of the lame man (3:1–10) introduces the second speech and holds the whole section from 3:1 to at least 4:22 together. One more observation must be made on the Portico speech. It contains no fewer than three separate and significant pointers to the next great speech, that of Stephen (7:2–53). (1) At the beginning of the speech God is called "the God of Abraham, Isaac, and Jacob" (3:13), and (2) at the end (vss. 24 f.) the hearers are addressed as the sons of the prophets and of the covenant with Abraham. In the speech of Stephen this God of Abraham, Isaac, and Jacob is *the* theme, especially in vss. 2–16. (3) The Deuteronomy prophecy (3:22–23; Deut. 18:15) shapes the whole section 7:17–44. The prophecy as quoted in Acts 3:22–23 is interpreted in great detail in 7:35–40 as the epexegetical, demonstrative, and relative pronouns of the section indicate: τὸν Μωϋσῆν ὅν . . . ; τοῦτον ὁ θεὸς ἀπέσταλκεν; οὗτος ἐξήγαγεν; οὗτός ἐστιν ὁ Μωϋσῆς (here Deut. 18:15 is repeated, vs. 37); οὗτος; ᾧ; ὁ γὰρ Μωϋσῆς οὗτος, ὅς; all these pronouns are to remind the hearer of 3:22–23.

The speech of Stephen has its special characteristics in that it marks God's action with Israel throughout her whole history as a series of promises or threats and fulfillments. This was a major concern for Luke, for he had to help his Hellenistic Christian readers achieve the same familiarity with the Septuagint (his Bible), which he himself possessed, and without which his theology is not intelligible. Here is massive proof indeed that from Luke's point of view the speech of Stephen is as much a part of Luke's theology as are the so-called missionary speeches of chapters 2 and 3. From the point of view of Luke's literary intentions the speeches of chapters 2, 3, and 7 are addressed to the same readers, as are all the speeches of the succeeding chapters 10–28. They are the readers of the two-volume work, the Greek-speaking Christian communities of Mediterranean coastlands at the end of the first century A.D. Luke is very reader-conscious. This is an outstanding aspect of his literary skill and artistry.

4) Chapters 4 and 5 contain a number of pithy and bold sayings of Peter's in the course of two separate arrests. It may be said that Peter's replies to the threats and cajoling of the High Council are the most lively parts of the chapters, such as 4:10–12, 19 f. These winged words are indications of the mood of boldness and joy which prevails among apostles and disciples under the threat of difficulties from the High Council. But two passages of significance must be mentioned. One is not, strictly speaking, a speech, but a prayer of the friends of Peter after the latter's release from the first arrest (4:24–30). It begins with the invocation "Sovereign Lord, who didst make the heavens and the earth and the sea and everything in them" (vs. 24). We shall see that this theme of God the creator is indeed very typical of several subsequent speeches. Here it is linked significantly with God's mighty plan ( ὅσα ἡ χείρ σου καὶ ἡ βουλή σου προώρισεν ) which bends the plans and actions of the nations to it. A typically Lucan theme.

A similar thought is expressed by Gamaliel, who warns the Council that "if this plan is of God, you will not overthrow it" (5:38–39).

All the "miniature" speeches of chapters 4 and 5 are united in underlining the speeches of chapters 2 and 3, and bringing them to a well-rounded conclusion, so that all the speeches of chapters 1–5 may be regarded as the first cycle of speeches. It remains for the second cycle (6:1–21:38) to bring some secondary modifications and new facts to lead to a primary clarification of the meaning of Luke's theology.

5) The speech of Stephen (7:2–53, 53*b*, 59*b*) — by far the longest in Acts — we have already dealt with in connection with the analysis of Peter's speech in the Portico of Solomon. That its theme is clearly and elaborately set already in chapter 3 proves the central significance it has for the theology of Luke. That he uses a leading Hellenist (Acts 6:5, 8–10) as the mouthpiece of this speech on God's acting with the people of Israel throughout her history in promises and fulfillments shows the significance which Luke attaches to the Old Testament for Hellenistic Christians. The speech appropriately begins the second cycle of speeches whose purposes is to work out, in several directions, the implications and the meaning of Luke's theology.

6) The speech of Peter in Caesarea Palestine to Cornelius and his household (10:34–43). Dibelius has convincingly shown the decisive role which the whole Cornelius-Peter episode (10:1–11:18) plays in Acts,[10] but the speech is not primarily addressed to Cornelius, but to the readers of Acts, in fact to the readers of the whole two-volume work, for it is in substance a remarkably apt summary of the gospel of Luke. Only the initial verses 34–35 allude to the Cornelius-situation. In the following verses a clear distinction is made between Jesus' ministry in Judea and Jerusalem (vss. 36–39*a*) and his final fate, his ἔξοδος, Luke 9:31 [11] (vss. 39*b*–42). Entirely new is verse 42, "and he commanded us to preach (κηρῦξαι) to the people. . . , that he is the one ordained by God to be the judge of the living and the dead" (ὁ ὡρισμένος . . . κριτὴς ζώντων καὶ νεκρῶν). The witness of the Twelve is first

[10] See Dibelius, *Studies*, pp. 109–22, 161–65 for his brilliant analysis of the Cornelius episode.

[11] On the relationship of ἔξοδος, in Luke's account of the transfiguration scene (Luke 9:31) to the pivotal beginning of Luke's so-called central section (9:51) see my essay cited above in n. 9, pp. 181–85.

emphasized as that to Jesus' ministry (vs. 39), then to his death, resurrection and appearances (vs. 41).

The speech reaches its full conclusion (vs. 43) in truly Lucan fashion with a reference to the witness of the prophets, so that "everyone who believes in him (Jesus) receives forgiveness of sins through his name."

All this (vss. 36–43) has little to do with the Cornelius-situation, but it has much to do with the subsequent speeches of Paul in chapters 13 and 17. In this last major speech of Peter's the carefully and elaborately planned balance between Peter and Paul is clearly formulated, to be worked out in chapters 13 and 17. Paul has no claim at all on direct contact with the earthly Jesus, and the Twelve are the eyewitnesses *par excellence*, by the plan of God. Luke never designates Paul as a witness to the resurrection of Jesus, in contrast to Paul's own claim in I Cor. 15:8. Even for Luke his deliberate effort to create a balance between Peter and Paul has its limits; the phrase πᾶς ὁ πιστεύων εἰς αὐτόν (vs. 43) for example, has several Pauline parallels and no others. See for (πᾶς) ὁ πιστεύων Rom. 1:16; 3:2; 4:11; 10:4; I Thess. 1:7; for πιστεύων εἰς Χριστόν see Rom. 10:14; Gal. 2:16 and Phil. 1:29.

7) The first major speech of Paul in Pisidian Antioch (13:16–41)[12] is the only major speech in Acts that has no elaborate setting, though it has important consequences described in verses 42–52. In the main the speech is an effort, carried out consistently, to bring the theology of Paul in line with that of the preceding Petrine speeches, especially with the formulations of 10:34–43.

This is the only speech in Acts which *expressis verbis* is in a Jewish synagogue addressed to Jews and God-fearers

[12] I do not wish to overemphasize the significance of the merely statistical word count of the speeches assigned to Peter and to Paul. Peter's speech at Pentecost consists of 497 words, while Paul's at Pisidian Antioch has 511 words; Peter's speech to Cornelius has 171 words, while Paul's Areopagus speech has 192 words. The total balance of all speeches of Peter's and of Paul's in the whole of Acts is equally close. Nevertheless these statistics may be validly regarded as an indication of the instinctive as well as trained literary sense of proportion which Luke possessed.

(vss. 16*b*, 26, 38). Similarly Cornelius and his household are introduced to the reader as God-fearers (10:2, 22, 35). The first part of the speech is clearly verses 17–25. Verses 17–19*a* are equally clearly a short and apt summary of the main part of the Stephen speech (7:12–45). So Luke once more, looking back on it now, aligns that speech with the others. In verses 19*b*–22 Paul is made to carry forward God's action with Israel to David, of whom it is said, quoting Isa. 44:28, that he "will do all my will" ($\pi o\iota\acute{\eta}\sigma\epsilon\iota$ $\pi\acute{a}\nu\tau a$ $\tau\grave{a}$ $\theta\epsilon\lambda\acute{\eta}\mu a\tau a$ $\mu o\upsilon = \pi\hat{a}\sigma a\nu$ $\tau\grave{\eta}\nu$ $\beta o\upsilon\lambda\acute{\eta}\nu$ $\mu o\upsilon$). From here on (vss. 23–37) Paul, in truly Lucan fashion, interprets David christologically with elaborate examples of the proof-from-prophecy (Ps. 2:7; Isa. 55:3; Ps. 16:10 in vss. 33–36), just as the Pentecost speech does where also Psalm 16 is used. Also the peroration (vss. 28–31) is partly 2:36–39 and partly contains a clear but crude "Paulinism": "Let it be known to you therefore, brethren, that through this man forgiveness of sins is proclaimed (see Luke 24:47) to you, and by him everyone that believes is freed from everything from which you could not be freed by the law of Moses" (vss. 38–39).

It remains to bring out the relations to 10:34–43. (*a*) We have already mentioned the correspondence of the formal address. (*b*) Paul must describe the earthly ministry (vss. 24–25) just as Peter did in 10:37*b*–38 and 11:16. (*c*) 10:36, $\tau\grave{o}\nu$ $\lambda\acute{o}\gamma o\nu$ [$\acute{o}$ $\theta\epsilon\grave{o}s$] $\mathring{a}\pi\acute{\epsilon}\sigma\tau a\lambda\kappa\epsilon\nu$ $\tau o\hat{i}s$ $\upsilon\acute{i}o\hat{i}s$ $'I\sigma\rho a\acute{\eta}\lambda$ corresponds closely without parallels elsewhere to 13:26 $\mathring{\eta}\mu\hat{i}\nu$ (as sons of Abraham) $\acute{o}$ $\lambda\acute{o}\gamma os$ $\tau\hat{\eta}s$ $\sigma\omega\tau\eta\rho\acute{i}as$ $\tau a\acute{\upsilon}\tau\eta s$ $\mathring{\epsilon}\xi a\pi\epsilon\sigma\tau\acute{a}\lambda\eta$. (*d*) in 13:31 Paul is made to state that "God raised Jesus from the dead; and for many days he appeared to those who came up with him from Galilee to Jerusalem, who are now his witnesses to the people." This corresponds closely to 10:40–41. (*e*) The Paulinism of 13:43 and its correspondence with 10:43 we have already noted. (*f*) While the introductory setting to the speech (vss. 14–16) is insignificant, the results of the speech are all the more significant. Since the Jews of the city determinately reject the Word of God (vss. 45–46*a*), Paul says, "we turn to the Gentiles. For so the Lord has commanded us, saying, 'I have set you to be a light for the Gentiles, that

you may bring salvation to the uttermost parts of the earth'"
(46b–47), quoting Isa. 49:6 (see also Acts 1:8 and 26:23b).
Here we have no doubt the most significant correspondence
to chapters 10 and 11. There Peter was convinced through
God's direct action; here Paul, finding Jewish opposition,
bases the necessity for mission to the Gentiles on Scripture
in truly Lucan fashion.

Now, after chapters 10 and 13, Paul's way is free for the
mission to the Gentiles (chaps. 14–28), and the next two
speeches of Paul are directed to Gentiles, at Lystra (14:15–
17) and at Athens (17:22–31).

8) The scene at Lystra (14:8–19) shows paganism at its
most superstitious. The speech itself (vss. 15–17), in spite
of its brevity, poses a number of problems – its seemingly
fragmentary character, the "enlightening" aspect of its content, and its relations to the preceding and subsequent
speeches. Here it suffices to say that it has at least two specific functions, first to offer at least one pure speech to Gentiles before the Apostolic Council (chap. 15) and second to
serve as a prelude to the Areopagus speech (chap. 17).

9) The speeches at the Apostolic Council, 15:7–11 by
Peter, and verses 13–21 by James. Peter begins (vss. 7–8)
with the simple, direct and impressive statement that the
question of the mission to the Gentiles had long been answered by God himself at the simultaneous visions granted
to Cornelius and to himself. The consequences which Peter
draws from this event (vss. 9–11) are so radical that we
must consider them as the strongest case of a Paulinism in
Acts. With a few slight changes it could be made into a
genuine Pauline speech to satisfy the heart of any modern
Paulinist. It is the counterpart of Paul's speech at Pisidian
Antioch (chaps. 13) where Paul is made to adapt himself
to Peter; here Peter is made to adapt himself to Paul, to
the best of Luke's ability. It is easier for Luke to make Peter
talk like Paul than Paul himself, although Paul's farewell
speech to the elders of Ephesus (20:18–35) abounds in more
or less general Pauline phrases.

James, in his seconding speech, begins by agreeing with

Peter's position (vs. 14) and then bases his agreement in the best Lucan manner (vss. 15–18) on a new scriptural text, a composite of Amos 9:11–12, Jer. 12:15, and Isa. 45:21: "After this I will return, and I will rebuild its ruins, and I will set it up, that the rest of men will seek the Lord, and all the Gentiles who are called by my name, says the Lord, who made these things from the very beginning (ἀπ' αἰῶνος)."

Thus we see that even the speeches at the Apostolic Council form an integral part of what we have come to know as the heart of Lucan theology.

### III. The Analysis of the Areopagus Speech (17:22–31)

Dibelius' studies on Acts in general and on the Areopagus speech in particular are very much responsible for the progress of research that has been made since. Dibelius' final conclusion is, that "for literary reasons the Areopagus speech must be regarded as a composition of the author of Acts. . . . Our analysis . . . has . . . shown that the theology of the Areopagus speech is absolutely foreign to Paul's own theology, that it is, in fact, foreign to the entire New Testament."[13] "Luke wrote this speech as an example of a typical sermon to Gentiles and put it in the setting of Athens . . . and for him Athens was obviously still the symbol of Greek culture."[14]

Thus Dibelius was the first to ask energetically the question of the place of the Areopagus speech in the composition of Acts. In his analysis of the speech he uses elements from the preceding speeches only in order to show that it is even within the speeches of Acts a "foreign body" (a *Fremdkörper*). He has not seen that these speeches (chaps. 2, 3, 7, 10, and 13) were all pointing to the Areopagus speech, each in its own way. To be sure, Dibelius' analysis, as far as it goes, is in almost all details breaking new ground and is correct. It would indeed be fair to say that in the rest of this paper one more step is taken beyond him. Doubtless we have in the Areopagus speech a thoroughly hellenized theology.

[13] Dibelius, *Studies*, p. 71.
[14] *Ibid.*, pp. 73, 75.

But it is the theology of Luke for which Luke here finds the universally valid, climactic formulation. To put it more concretely, the Septuaginta-biblical influence on the Areopagus speech is at least as strong as is the Hellenistic influence. The speech is a synthesis of both. These theses the following analysis will try to demonstrate.

The brevity of the Areopagus speech is matched only by the fine balance of its literary structure and the compactness of its contents. Most interpreters follow Dibelius, who finds a structure of five parts. In fact the five parts are the five periods which constitute the speech. The train of thought moves smoothly and evenly. It is here suggested that the speech from beginning to end has only one specific, clearly articulated theme. The identification of this theme explains at once the outstanding singularity of the speech as well as its significant relations to the preceding and subsequent speeches.

More specifically, the speech has a well-formed introduction (vss. 22b–23), a main part (vss. 24–29) and a peroration (30–31); the latter is no more and no less than the final and climactic part of the development of the one theme that dominates all three parts.

The introduction (vss. 22b–23). "Men of Athens, I observe (θεωρῶ) that in every way you are very religious. For walking around, inspecting the objects (or places?) of your worship (διερχόμενος καὶ ἀναθεωρῶν τὰ σεβάσματα ὑμῶν; an unmistakable reference to vs. 15 of the setting) I found (εὗρον) also an altar with the inscription: 'To an unknown God' (ἀγνώστῳ θεῷ). Now, then, what you ignorantly worship, this I proclaim to you (ὃ οὖν ἀγνοοῦντες εὐσεβεῖτε, τοῦτο ἐγὼ καταγγέλλω ὑμῖν)." Three points of this introduction are worth noticing: (a) Its I-style; all main verb-forms (three of them) are in the first person singular plus two dependent participle forms. It is a singular rhetorical feature of this introduction. The only parallel is the beginning of Peter's speech to Cornelius, 10:34 (ἐπ' ἀληθείας καταλαμβάνομαι, ὅτι . . .); (b) the subtle and obvious reference to the setting, e.g., the contrast between "you are very religious" and Paul's seeing the city full of idols (vs.

16*b*); the contrast between καταγγέλλω ὑμῖν and the καταγγελεὺς Ξένων δαιμονίων (vs. 18), etc.; (*c*) most important: the formal statement of the theme of the speech — In place of the unknown god whom you ignorantly worship I proclaim to you the true God. The true God — this is the all-dominating theme spelled out in the speech itself.

The development of the theme in the main part (vss. 24–29) and peroration (vss. 30–31) can be stated briefly, without omitting a single word, phrase, or clause, because the speech is brief; it must be stated, because the speech is unusually compact and structured with great care.

The God who made the world and everything in it
— he is Lord of heaven and earth — ;
he does not dwell (principal verb of the period) in manmade shrines, nor is he taken care of by human hands, as though he needed anything since he himself gives to all (men) life and breath and all things.

(First period: vss. 24–25)

And he made (ἐποίησεν) from one every nation of men, that they should inhabit (telic infinitive κατοικεῖν dependent on ἐποίησεν) the whole face (surface NEB) of the earth,

because he had set (ὁρίσας; causal participial construction) allotted periods (seasons) (προστεταγμένους καιρούς) and boundaries of their habitation (ὁροθεσίας τῆς κατοικίας αὐτῶν),

that they should seek God (ζητεῖν; telic infinitive dependent on ὁρίσας) and, it might be, touch and find him (NEB),

and *indeed* (intensive καί γε) he is not far from each one of us.

(Second period: vss. 26–27)

For in him (ἐν αὐτῷ γὰρ) we live and move and are, as some of your own poets have said, we are also his offspring (Haenchen and NEB).

(Third period: vs. 28)

Being then God's offspring we ought not to suppose

that the deity (τὸ θεῖον; only occurrence as a substantive in the New Testament; for the adjectival form see II Peter 1:3–4) is "like an image in gold or silver or stone, shaped by human craftsmanship," (NEB) or imaginative design.

(Fourth period, vs. 29)

Having overlooked the times of ignorance (τοὺς μὲν οὖν χρόνους τῆς ἀγνοίας ὑπεριδὼν ὁ θεὸς),

as of now God commands that all men should everywhere repent (ὁ θεὸς τὰ νῦν ἀπαγγέλλει τοῖς ἀνθρώποις πάντας πανταχοῦ μετανοεῖν),

because he has set a day (καθότι ἔστησεν ἡμέραν) on which he will judge the world in righteousness,

by a man of his choosing (NEB; ἐν ἀνδρὶ ᾧ ὥρισεν),

having given assurance to all men (πίστιν παρασχὼν πᾶσιν) by having raised him from the dead.

(Peroration; fifth period: vss. 30–31)

A few specific conclusions from this breakdown of the Areopagus speech may be drawn. A first and sure indication of the theme is furnished by the subjects and verb-forms of the speech. God is predominantly the subject of action, of principal verb-forms as well as of participial clauses. The only principal verb-forms of which men are the subject occur, significantly, in the two quotations from the Greek poets in verse 28, and in verse 29, which states the conclusion drawn from these quotations in verse 28. But in the context of the whole speech the exception is only syntactical, not material, for verses 28–29 deal just as much (from the point of view of Luke) with the proper relationship between God and men as do the others.

The outline also helps us to grasp the train of thought and the argument of the speech.

The first period (vss. 24–25) affirms and argues that the true God does not dwell in man-made shrines, is not in need of human care, because he created the world, because he is (οὗτος . . . ὑπάρχων) the active Lord of heaven and earth, because he continues to give to all life, breath, and all things.

Here God is at once seen as *creator* and *gubernator* (not *preservator*) of the world, a view most typical of many Psalms and especially of Deutero-Isaiah.

The second period (vss. 26–27) further develops what God as *creator* and *gubernator* did and continues to do as Lord of heaven and earth, who keeps giving all things to all men. God created from one man all nations of men. He caused them to inhabit the whole earth; he provided for them, allotted periods and boundaries in the expectation that they should seek and find him, for he is not far from any of them.

This period bristles with exegetical difficulties. Dibelius was sure that allotted periods mean the fixed seasons of the year, and that the boundaries mean the habitable zones known to us from Hellenistic astronomy and geography. It is W. Eltester's great merit [15] to have shown not only that the "boundaries" are the sea and therefore the habitable world is all firm land "on the whole face of the earth" (vs. 26a), but also that the twin conception of the orderly course of the seasons and of the boundaries of human habitation was strongly developed in pre-Christian Hellenistic Judaism and has deep roots in the Old Testament. Nevertheless, Eltester follows Dibelius, and is followed by Haenchen, H. Hommel, Käsemann, and others, in denying that the προστεταγμένοι καιροί mean "epochs of history" (so NEB) and that the ὁροθεσίαι mean political, historical boundaries. As a consequence, all these scholars deny that in the Areopagus speech there is a substantial theology of history.

There is no denying that they have made a convincing case for verse 26! A mere glance at Paul's speech in Lystra (14:15–17) suffices to show its strength. We have here a case in which what is affirmed is true, but what is denied is wrong, as we shall try to show in the next section (IV).

The third period (vs. 28) illustrates the last statement of

[15] W. Eltester, "Gott und die Natur in der Areopagrede," in *Neutestamentliche Studien für Rudolf Bultmann,* pp. 202–27; see also his essay "Schöpfungsoffenbarung und natürliche Theologie im frühen Christentum," *New Testament Studies,* 3 (1956–57): 93–114.

verse 27 — "and indeed, he is not far from each one of us" —
by the line of Greek poetry as yet not clearly identified (see
Haenchen *ad loc.*; "Luke could not have created such an im-
manentist saying: 'in him we live and move and are'")[16]
and by the Aratus line "we are also his offspring" (τοῦ γὰρ
καὶ γένος ἐσμέν).

The basic affirmation of the nearness of God is well attested in popular Hellenistic philosophy as well as in the
Old Testament, though in the latter it is, in some of the
most characteristic instances, balanced by the thought of
his distance (see, e.g., the well-known example of Isa. 55:6–
11, much of which reappears in hellenized terminology
throughout the Areopagus speech as a whole.)

The fourth period (vs. 29) draws the conclusion from
the Aratus quotation that being God's offspring we should
not suppose that the deity is like an image shaped by human
craftsmanship. Thus vs. 29 aligns itself with the similar negative statements of vss. 24b (God does not dwell in man-made
shrines) and of 25a (God is not dependent on human care).
Thus the unity of the main part of the speech is established,
and the three negative statements show that it is not Greek
philosophy and poetry which are attacked, but only popular
polytheism.

The peroration (vss. 30–31), however, continues without
a break the one theme of the speech. While verses 24–29
spoke of God's actions from creation up to now, vss. 30–31
proclaim his action from the present (τὰ νῦν) to the final consummation. Here we find ourselves, coming from the analysis of the preceding speeches, on more familiar ground.
Verses 30–31 are basically a selection, with significant variations, from the examples of God's action through Jesus Christ
which the preceding speeches contained. These concluding
verses of the Areopagus speech are not, as Dibelius and
Hommel thought,[17] a timid, casual and expendable epilogue;

[16] Ernst Haenchen, *Die Apostelgeschichte* (Meyer's Kommentar;
Göttingen: Vandenhoeck & Ruprecht, 1956, rev. ed. 1961).

[17] For H. Hommel's view that the final verses (30 f.) of the Areopagus
speech are a dispensable, anticlimactic ἐπίλογος see his article "Neuere
Forschungen zur Areopagrede Acta 17," in *Zeitschrift für die Neutesta-*

they are an impressive and necessary climax. The Areopagus speech is unthinkable without them. Dibelius and others have done brilliant work and have achieved lasting results in their rigorous search for Hellenistic antecedents and parallels. If they neglected to look for both in Luke-Acts itself and particularly in its speeches, we must do so all the more, with due regard for their work.

## IV. Antecedents in the Preceding Speeches of Luke-Acts

1) God as creator. This theme is insisted upon on all sides as the basic affirmation of the Areopagus speech. Its special "forerunner," the Lystra speech, substantially confirms that judgment. But we have seen that within the first cycle of speeches, in the communal prayer of 4:24–30, God is also solemnly addressed as creator: σύ, ὁ ποιήσας τὸν οὐρανὸν καὶ τὴν γῆν καὶ τὴν θάλασσαν καὶ πάντα τὰ ἐν αὐτοῖς.

This is a literal and complete rendering of Ps. 145:6 (LXX). And nothing could be more remarkable and significant than that the rendering of 14:15 is literally and completely the same (except for the verb-form; it is in 14:15 ὃς ἐποίησεν, being adapted to the syntax of the period of which the relative clause is a part). And what could be more natural than that in 17:24 Luke should base his formulation on another LXX passage, namely, Isa. 42:5 which reads: κύριος ὁ θεὸς ὁ ποιήσας τὸν οὐρανὸν καὶ πήξας αὐτόν, ὁ στερεώσας τὴν γῆν καὶ τὰ ἐν αὐτῇ καὶ διδοὺς πνοὴν τῷ λαῷ ἐπ᾽ αὐτῆς καὶ πνεῦμα τοῖς πατοῦσιν αὐτήν. The changes which Luke made in 17:24–25 from Isa. 42:5 are instructive, because they are deliberate and show subtle judgment: ὁ θεὸς ὁ ποιήσας τὸν κόσμον καὶ πάντα τὰ ἐν αὐτῷ οὗτος οὐρανοῦ καὶ γῆς ὑπάρχων κύριος . . . (25) διδοὺς πᾶσιν ζωὴν καὶ πνοὴν καὶ τὰ πάντα.

---

*mentliche Wissenschaft*, 46 (1955): 145–78. Dibelius arrives at similar conclusions based on different observations; see in his *Studies* the essay "Paul on the Areopagus," pp. 26–77; esp. pp. 54–57. My view that verses 30 and 31 are an indispensable, climactic peroration is ably and independently argued by H. Conzelmann, *Die Apostelgeschichte* (Tübingen: Mohr, 1963), *ad loc*. Verses 30 and 31 must be regarded as a purely formal hellenizing and universalizing of Luke 24:46–47; the Jerusalem situation of Luke 24:46–47 is adapted to the Athens situation of Acts 17:16–31.

(a) τὸν κόσμον is a deliberate adaptation of τὸν οὐρανὸν καὶ τὴν γῆν to Greek terminology; (b) πάντα τὰ ἐν αὐτῷ is added by Luke, perhaps by remembering Ps. 145:6, or just because he wanted to put into the Areopagus speech as many forms derived from πᾶς as he safely could; (c) the phrase οὗτος οὐρανοῦ καὶ γῆς ὑπάρχων κύριος accomplished two desirable ends; by it the Greek term κόσμος and the Biblical terms (οὐρανὸς καὶ γῆ) are brought together, and it makes clearer, for Greek readers, the characteristic inseparability, in Deutero-Isaiah, of God's all-encompassing sovereignty and creative activity; (d) in verse 17:25 only three (out of 12) words of the LXX text remained. Instead of saying διδοὺς [ὁ θεὸς] τῷ λαῷ he said, consistently in line with his universalism in general and with that of the Areopagus speech in particular, διδοὺς πᾶσιν. The LXX wording διδοὺς [πᾶσιν] πνοὴν καὶ πνεῦμα would have suited the stoicizing hearers at Athens beautifully — and Luke knew it! — but it did not at all suit Luke's theology or that of his prospective Christian readers, for Luke took great pains to teach all his readers that the gift of the spirit was available to all men only on the condition of faith or repentance or baptism. Here is a striking example of Luke's reader-consciousness, at a centrally important point of the Areopagus speech, on an issue of great importance. This single example goes far toward showing that the Areopagus speech was written, like all the preceding speeches, with the reader in Luke's mind at every step.

2) God does not live in man-made shrines (vs. 24b). This, we have seen, is the principal clause of the first period. It is directed against Greek popular polytheism, but the same statement is made in the same basic words in Stephen's speech, where it is one of the few sentences in which this speech comes to grips with the accusations (6:11–14) raised against Stephen to the effect that he never ceased to speak against the Jerusalem temple (κατὰ τοῦ τόπου τούτου τοῦ ἁγίου). In 7:48 Stephen says ἀλλ' οὐχ ὁ ὕψιστος ἐν χειροποιήτοις κατοικεῖ. Acts 17:24b reads ὁ θεὸς ὁ ποιήσας τὸν κόσμον . . . οὐκ ἐν χειροποιήτοις ναοῖς κατοικεῖ. And Stephen immediately backs up his judgment by quoting scripture (Isa. 66:1):

254

## The Place of the Areopagus Speech

ὁ οὐρανός μοι θρόνος,

ἡ δὲ γῆ ὑποπόδιον τῶν ποδῶν μου.

ποῖον οἶκον οἰκοδομήσετέ μοι, λέγει κύριος,

ἢ τίς τόπος τῆς καταπαύσεώς μου;

οὐχὶ ἡ χείρ μου ἐποίησεν ταῦτα πάντα; (Acts 7:49 f.)

Thus the argument is the same in both speeches: God does not dwell in man-made houses or shrines, whether Jewish, or pagan (or Christian); because he is the creator of heaven and earth or of the world it is entirely proper to assign definitely causal meaning to the participle ποιήσας in 17:24.

3) God has set allotted seasons and boundaries of their habitation (vs. 26) (ὁρίσας [ὁ θεὸς] προστεταγμένους καιροὺς καὶ τὰς ὁροθεσίας τῆς κατοικίας αὐτῶν). The evidence for the view that Luke here refers to the seasons and boundaries of nature and not to "epochs of history" and political-historical borders of nations is overwhelming. (I must confess that I have long and faithfully held out against the evidence — alas, without success.) If there is any theology of *history* in the Areopagus speech, the evidence must be sought elsewhere, but not in verse 26.

In fact, it is impossible to find anywhere in Luke-Acts clear evidence on special epochs of history, still less on political border lines, except that there are two great historical epochs, the first from creation to John the Baptist, and the second from Jesus of Nazareth to the consummation of the plan of God (ἡ βουλὴ τοῦ θεοῦ).

To be sure, in Stephen's speech, reference is made *once* to a divinely foretold specific period of history — the four hundred years of Israel's oppression in Egypt and the promise of the liberation that should come and did come, on time and in time (Acts 7:6 and 36). But this is a single instance only. At best, one might wonder whether Luke intentionally went no further than he did in his attempts to write down God's dealings with Israel in its history (7:2–53; 13:16–25).

In fact, it can easily be shown that Luke is characteristically wary of periodizing specific epochs of history. Back of this caution is his consistently antiapocalyptical eschatology. It must suffice here to recall such characteristic and well-

255

known passages as Luke 17:20, "You cannot tell by observation *when* the Kingdom of God comes" (NEB), and Acts 1:7, "It is not for you to know times or seasons, which the Father has set within his own control" (NEB). Luke does indeed strongly believe in God's free and responsible action in history, but such "allotted times" are beyond even the knowledge of faith or better, perhaps, beneath it. Luke knows this too.

Thus, Luke 17:20 and Acts 1:6–8 do their part in supporting the interpretation of 17:26 primarily at least as seasons of the year and boundaries of nature.

4) The next parallel concerns the clause immediately following (27*a*): "God has fixed (ὁρίσας) (fruitful) natural seasons and natural boundaries safe for human habitation, so that they should seek God and . . . find him." Taking this affirmation together with the detail furnished by the Lystra speech (14:17) that even in past generations among the Gentiles "God did not leave himself without witness, for he did good (ἀγαθουργέω) and gave you from heaven rains and fruitful seasons (καρποὺς καρποφόρους), satisfying your hearts with food and gladness," we find expressed the common view, shared alike by Greeks and Israel, that the blessings of nature and nature in all its manifestations move man's heart to seek God.

In Acts 15:16–18 James, in his speech at the Apostolic Council, quoted Amos 9:11–12:

After this I will return
and rebuild the dwelling of David,

(which, according to an earlier speech, 13:22–23, is Jesus as Christ and Lord)

that the rest of men may seek the Lord,
and all the Gentiles who are called by my name,
says the Lord, who has made these things known
from the very beginning.

This is not a direct antecedent of 17:27*a*, but it is a complementary theologoumenon: to the seeking for God from the manifestations of nature (in 17:26) is joined the surer route (15:16 ff.), especially for the Gentiles, of seeking to find God in God's action through Jesus Christ.

It is not surprising that there are no antecedents or parallels for verses 28 and 29, for these verses and only these, with their quotations from Greek poets and the conclusion drawn from them, represent indeed the completely new and singular contribution of the Areopagus speech. Some interpreters (Dibelius and Haenchen, etc.) hold that these quotations "serve as documentation, in the same way, as in other speeches quotations from the Bible serve." How would one prove such a judgment? Is it not better to regard these quotations in the same way as the introduction (vss. 22b–23), i.e., as a *captatio benevolentiae*, as a point of contact rather than of equality? After all, it is still a long way, across several abysses, from Luke to Clement of Alexandria, before Greek philosophers can rank alongside the Old Testament.

5) The very first clause of the peroration states a characteristic, profusely documented theologoumenon of Luke-Acts. Verse 30a reads: τοὺς μὲν οὖν χρόνους τῆς ἀγνοίας ὑπεριδὼν ὁ θεὸς τὰ νῦν ἀπαγγέλλει . . . μετανοεῖν. The chief antecedent is in 3:17–19 in a similar function and context: καὶ νῦν, ἀδελφοί, οἶδα ὅτι κατ᾽ ἄγνοιαν ἐπράξατε, ὥσπερ καὶ οἱ ἄρχοντες ὑμῶν. How did Peter know that they acted in ignorance? He knows it in the same way the reader of Luke 23:24 does, i.e., on the authority of the dying Lord who prayed, "Father, forgive them, for they know not what they do" (οὐ γὰρ οἴδασιν τί ποιοῦσιν). Stephen, similarly inspired, prayed while being stoned κύριε, μὴ στήσῃς αὐτοῖς ταύτην τὴν ἁμαρτίαν (Lord, do not hold this sin against them). Also in 13:27 in Paul's speech at Pisidian Antioch, "the people of Jerusalem and their rulers did not recognize him (ἀγνοήσαντες αὐτόν) or understand the words of the prophets . . . which they fulfilled by condemning him." In the introduction of the Areopagus speech itself Paul says that what you ignorantly worship (ὃ οὖν ἀγνοοῦντες εὐσεβεῖτε) I proclaim to you. To be sure, the ignorance of the Gentiles and of the Jerusalem Jews have different objects, but we have here

PAUL SCHUBERT

throughout Luke-Acts a single theologoumenon: ἄγνοια in both cases is ignorance of the "plan of God," of the βουλὴ τοῦ θεοῦ.

6) The next case of equally massive antecedents follows in the principal clause of the same sentence (vs. 30b), τοὺς μὲν οὖν χρόνους τῆς ἀγνοίας ὑπεριδὼν ὁ θεός, τὰ νῦν ἀπαγγέλλει τοῖς ἀνθρώποις πάντας πανταχοῦ μετανοεῖν. Since we have thoroughly canvassed the numerous antecedents of the call to repentance, and have seen the central place which it occupies in Luke's understanding of the Word of God, it suffices here to recall the closest and most striking parallel, 11:18: ἄρα καὶ τοῖς ἔθνεσιν ὁ θεὸς τὴν μετάνοιαν εἰς ζωὴν ἔδωκεν. God gives, makes possible, and himself commands μετάνοιαν — the turning of mind and heart to the God of Jesus Christ. We should note too that the formulation of 17:30, brief though it is, is pregnant, stylistically recognizable in the happy coordination of πάντας πανταχοῦ, and theologically recognizable in its final universalism.

7) The day fixed for universal judgment (31a). "Because God has set a day on which he will judge the world in righteousness through a man of his choice," ἐν ἀνδρὶ ᾧ ὥρισεν. The "day of judgment" as the day of the Lord (Acts 2:20, 3:19 f.) has already been dealt with. It suffices to add, emphatically, that in its slightly hellenized terminology at the very climax of the Areopagus speech, it carries great weight for the theses and arguments set forth here.

As to the second part of this clause, — "God will judge the world through a man of his choice," we should recall that this too is no new thing, because Peter furnished the clear antecedent in 10:42. Here the risen Lord "commanded the twelve" (παρήγγειλεν) to proclaim to the people that he is the one chosen by God as judge of the living and the dead.

By raising this man (Jesus) from the dead, God has given assurance to all men (πίστιν παρασχὼν πᾶσιν, vs. 31b). This final clause of the peroration highlights the fact everywhere observable that for Luke the significance of the death of Christ is subordinate to his earthly ministry, and especially to his resurrection, which for Luke is a fact of history, authenticated by prophecy and by the special witness of the Twelve.

258

(We must, however, observe that Luke has a very different view of history from any that are easily available to a twentieth-century Christian theologian.) It is God's act of having raised Jesus from the dead which for Luke "offers assurance" that the present call to repentance is from God, and that the final consummation will take place in God's time and in God's plan.

### V. The Areopagus Speech in the Light of the Farewell Speech (20:18–35)

The first thing to note is that there *is* such a farewell speech given by Paul. There is none by Peter or by anyone else. Paul, however, here speaks for himself and to the elders at Ephesus; he also speaks for the Twelve; he also speaks for Luke (or Luke speaks for Paul and the Twelve); he speaks not only to the elders of Ephesus but also to every reader of Acts. This farewell speech is and was meant to be the testament of the apostolic age to Luke's readers.

It is a farewell speech, because Paul says a final farewell to the elders and the readers, verse 25: "And now, behold that you all among whom I have gone about proclaiming the kingdom (κηρύσσων τὴν βασιλείαν) will see my face no more."

It is the testament of the whole apostolic age, because "you know, that in my proclamation and teaching (ἀναγγεῖλαι καὶ διδάξαι) I kept back nothing . . . witnessing to both Jews and Greeks (!) of repentance to God and of faith in our Lord Jesus Christ" (vss. 20–21) . . . [witnessing] "to the gospel of the grace of God" (vs. 24). . . . And finally, "Therefore I give witness today, that I held back nothing in proclaiming to you *the whole plan of God*" (πᾶσαν τὴν βουλὴν τοῦ θεοῦ), verses 26–27.

Note that these verses extend over the whole first half of the farewell speech, that verses 20–21 recall the message of repentance and faith; verse 24 recalls the gospel of the grace of God (which was, in Acts formulated only by Peter — 15:11); verse 25 the proclamation of the kingdom, and finally, verse 27, the proclamation of the whole plan of God. We have seen that none of these terms is, in Acts, specifically, Pauline

or Petrine. All of them are Lucan, and Luke's most characteristic term is the thematic βουλὴ τοῦ θεοῦ (2:23; 4:28; 5:38 f.;
13:36; 20:27). Here we have the most thematic occurrence
of them all, since here only he speaks of πᾶσαν τὴν βουλὴν τοῦ
θεοῦ. Obviously, in the literary intention of Luke, the unfolding of the plan of God found its culmination in the preceding
speech, the Areopagus speech.

Thus it is ultimately Luke who tells us, his readers, that
together with Peter, Stephen, James, and Paul he has given
us, in the speeches of the first and second cycle (which are
here completed), the whole plan of God as far as Luke
understood it.[18]

Thus on the total evidence adduced from our analysis so
far of Luke-Acts we may conclude that Luke regarded the
Areopagus speech as the final climactic part of his exposition
of the whole plan of God. The term βουλή, used in Luke's
technical sense taken from the LXX, especially from
Deutero-Isaiah, did not fit the special stylistic task Luke had
set for himself in the Areopagus speech. But another term,
the verb ὁρίζω, always closely associated with the βουλὴ τοῦ
θεοῦ (see 2:23; 10:42 and Luke 22:22) occurs there twice in
centrally significant contexts, — ὁρίσας προστεταγμένους καιρούς
(vs. 26), and ἐν ἀνδρὶ ᾧ ὥρισεν (vs. 31).

That is to say, the Areopagus speech is not only a hellen-

[18] An analysis of the remainder of Acts (chaps. 21–28) similar to that
offered in this paper of chapters 1–20 would show that formal and
informal, long and short speeches continue to play the same formal
and functional role in the final section of Acts, and that these speeches
should be regarded as the third, consecutive, and final cycle. Although
Luke's first basic intention to set forth the main lines of the βουλὴ τοῦ
θεοῦ had been accomplished with the Areopagus speech, the βουλὴ
τοῦ θεοῦ remains the main concern in the third cycle. His second basic
intention, stated in section I and developed in sections II–V above,
namely, to secure a firm place in the church for Paul and his contribution to the proclamation of the Word of God is continued from the
second cycle where it became prominent. It is skillfully brought to a
persuasive and proportionate climax in the so-called trial speeches
of chapters 22, 24, and 26 and in the account of the shipwreck, with
the significant pronouncements of Paul in chapter 27. The final speech
of chapter 28, addressed by Paul to the authorities of the Jewish community in Rome, is more definitely aligned with the all-embracing
βουλὴ τοῦ θεοῦ.

ized but also a universalized version of Luke's βουλή-theology. The speech at Athens is, in fact, more universal than it is Hellenistic. The Hellenism of it helped to make it so.

An additional stylistic detail may be noted here which underlines this universal character. It is the use of eight adjectival and adverbial forms of πᾶς in the last eight verses of the Areopagus speech: God who made the world and *all things* in it (vs. 24) — God gives to *all* men life and breath and *all things* (vs. 25)— God made from one man *every* nation to live (vs. 26a) on the *whole* face of the earth — God commands *all* men *everywhere* to repent (vs. 30) — God offers assurances to *all* men by having raised Jesus from the dead.

Finally, the affirmation that the Areopagus speech is intended to be read as the climax or capstone of Luke's theology of history (his theology) should be summarized in these conclusions.

First, the total thrust of this speech, even the content covered by it, is more historical than that of any other speech of Acts. It covers (from vs. 24 to vs. 30), in good order and balance, everything from creation to consummation, via the resurrection of Christ.

Second, the Areopagus speech stresses (with great emphasis) the unity of a theology of nature and of history. Here too, as throughout the speeches, Luke shows a noticeable affinity to Deutero-Isaiah. The main differences between Luke and Deutero-Isaiah are no doubt due to the fact that six hundred critical years in the operation of the plan of God had taken place between them. As an interpreter of the Old Testament and the apostolic witness to Jesus Christ, Luke, a Hellenist, had to write his whole work τῇ ὡρισμένῃ βουλῇ τοῦ θεοῦ to Hellenists.

# 12

## Pauline Thought: Some Basic Issues
### WILLIAM R. SCHOEDEL

"Every writer," says Jorge Luis Borges, "creates his own pre-cursors." The paradox sums up the thought that a writer brings to expression things which in a sense are in the works of his predecessors but which could not have been seen had he not written. Something like that could be said of the reflections of the great theologians on the letters of Paul. Most students of the New Testament, however, are unable to take the hermeneutical leap required to dispense entirely with a more historically oriented approach; and although they are aware of the limitations of their methods, they believe that their work may serve to call a halt to develop-ments that have apparently run wild and to point out fresh lines of inquiry.

It is with this in mind that we venture a look at Paul which holds clearly before the reader the historical setting of the apostle's work in the early church, especially his very practical concern to keep Jews and Gentiles together. Nor must we overlook the point that the man who faced this problem is of such profound interest because, as Professor Robert Grant said in response to this paper, he was also "holding together various aspects of his own past and pres-ent." Such considerations, however obvious they may seem, are often neglected in contemporary studies of Paul despite general commitment to "the historical method."

Harnack[1] familiarized the Protestant world with a sort of intermittent spiritual succession of theological heroes which included particularly Paul, Marcion (in part), Augustine,

[1] *History of Dogma,* trans. Neil Buchanan (London: Williams & Norgate, 1894–1903).

and Luther. Many today see a new burst of the same spiritual temper in a Barth, Bonhoeffer, or Bultmann. Although contemporary Protestant theology, under the influence of precisely such figures, operates with different critical standards whereby the true theological succession is established, that of Harnack still controls much thinking and writing in the area. This has an indirect yet important influence on the interpretation of Paul, for such an orientation contributes to the virtual isolation of the apostle from his setting in the early church and an overly subtle "modernizing" of his thought.

By necessity this essay has in view primarily contemporary renewals of the Reformers' interpretation of Paul, sharpened by the application of existentialist insights to this tradition. It is not certain that Luther himself can be so simply lumped together with his modern followers — or at least three of this particular variety. He can if Luther was what someone like Gerhard Ebeling says he was.[2] But since Ebeling may be wrong in sharply distinguishing the revolutionary themes of Luther from other elements in his thought, such as his sacramental theology, the line between the reformer and these interpreters may well be more tenuous than the latter think. In spite of this, our feeling is that the theology of the Reformation did underscore elements in Paul (especially "justification by faith") in a way which has distorted the apostle's message and has led to some of the more "radical" Protestant positions of our day. Naturally, it is possible to argue endlessly about the interpretation of the figures involved in this debate. What we have said about them is intended only to recall that the questions one addresses to Paul are inevitably determined by the history of interpretation; and we wish to furnish at least a glance as to how we see the lines drawn. It is to be hoped that some light may be shed on issues in Pauline thought even if the understanding of the situation outlined above seems defective.[3]

[2] *Word and Faith* (London: SCM Press, 1963), pp. 32–37 (cf. pp. 56–57, 135, 138).
[3] The difficulty in posing the questions is well illustrated by the work of H. J. Schoeps, *Paul* (London: Lutterworth Press, 1961), who

Views like those adopted in this paper are not novel.[4] But neither are they universally accepted. To state the issue briefly: we find ourselves drawn to those who regard the theme of "imputed righteousness"[5] as a one-sided interpretation of Paul and who see the center of the apostle's thought

(a) appreciates Schweitzer's work on Paul and frequently criticizes "Lutheran" interpretations of the apostle but (b) ends by assuring us that Luther was the restorer of "the original Paul" (p. 274). There are qualifications, of course; but it is obvious that the problem of the true theological succession goes on at more than one level. In this connection I would assent to the words of Professor Robert Grant in his response to this paper: "We must admit . . . that in Lowell's words 'new occasions teach new duties,' and that in some measure the new duties are discovered in the ancient texts — in other words, *eisegesis* is not wholly a mistake if the eisegete knows what he is doing. In the Reformation situation it was probably the case that justification by faith and imputed righteousness had to be emphasized in order to break up the ice of an over-rigid tradition; and just so in our time we may need to lay emphasis on other aspects of New Testament theology. We do so partly because they have been neglected, in order to restore something of a balance, and partly because the ecumenical atmosphere really forces us to admit that just as 'in Christ there is neither Jew nor Greek,' so in Paul there is neither — precisely — Protestant nor Catholic, but the potentialities of both."

[4] We may note especially A. Schweitzer, *The Mysticism of Paul the Apostle*, trans. W. Montgomery (New York: H. Holt, 1931) and H. J. Schoeps in the work already cited. A. D. Nock's book on Paul presents related views in an introductory form; R. M. Grant in his *Historical Introduction to the New Testament* (London: Collins, 1963), pp. 378–95, has sketched for us a Paul which runs counter to emphases stemming from the Reformers; in a dissertation written here at Chicago I found myself driven to conclusions which are hardly in conflict with such views. An important article by K. Stendahl (*Harvard Theological Review*, 56 [1963]: 199–215) has brought to the attention of many American scholars fresh insights to the theology of Paul along these lines. I should also like to express my thanks to a former student, Miss Linda Bedrick, whose work with me provided much of the stimulation for this paper. A number of small changes in the text of this address have been made in response to questions raised by Professor Paul Schubert; but the wider implications of his inquiries have not been dealt with.

[5] For a modern restatement see R. Bultmann, *Theology of the New Testament*, trans. K. Grobel (New York: Scribner, 1951), 1:270–87. I have been able to express only somewhat indirectly in what follows my understanding of the language in Paul which has given rise to the term "imputed." For the general line of approach adopted see especially notes 39 and 42.

in his awareness that mankind has passed from one age into another.[6] We hope that this paper will succeed in getting at a few things that seem to us to require further clarification. The arguments are not intended to reduce Paul's stature nor to suggest that he was not misunderstood by the early church. But, then, he was not the only one to be misunderstood; and one suspects that the "falling away" from Pauline insights of which we still hear much presupposes a one-sided question and has in any event been exaggerated; it seems misleading to stress the "radical" nature of the apostle's understanding of Christian faith if that means, as it often seems to, that Paul's thought is virtually isolated from his background and, in particular, the Christianity of the early period.

*Faith and Boasting*

One way of underscoring the "radical" nature of Paul's conception of faith is to point to its opposite — "boasting" (cf. Rom. 2:17, 3:27). To boast means to find sufficiency in oneself rather than in God. On the other hand, to recognize that one is God's creature is to know that one must rely on him and his promises. This is the attitude of faith. So far, the analysis is justified and rests upon widely recognized biblical themes, especially as they were understood in Paul's day [7] — themes which stress the initiative of God and man's dependence on him. But another step is then taken by those who sense in Paul a more penetrating application of these ideas.

Since boasting is associated with doing works, we are assured that Paul radically revises the Jewish (and for that matter early Christian) understanding of obedience to God. To put it somewhat baldly, the very effort to obey God (and his law) is suspect; for this effort represents a subtle idolatry;

[6] For Paul's eschatology see especially Schoeps, *Paul*, pp. 88–125.

[7] The Old Testament's *emunah*, fidelity, is carried in the direction of *pistis*, faith, in postbiblical writers other than Paul (Schoeps, *Paul*, p. 202). The thinking about "righteousness" and "flesh" in the Dead Sea Scrolls also anticipates Paul (e.g., Manual, 11.2–17; Hodoyth, 4.29–33).

to attempt to stand before God on the basis of one's own righteousness or achievement is the essence of boasting. The attempt to do God's will, then, is itself misguided. Man seeks "life" in this way, and precisely in this way loses it. He fails to recognize the nothingness of the creature and his achievements before God.[8]

Fundamentally, then, sin is pride — that is, boasting. And passages like Rom. 4:2 and 10:3 seem to justify referring to it also as "self-righteousness."[9] Such an analysis allows us to see in Paul one who grasps the nature of man in categories beyond the range of Jewish ethics and even the ethics of Jesus — at least as these are presented in the Synoptic Gospels.

It is possible, I believe, to cast doubt on this way of approaching Paul. It must be noted that the problem of boasting in Romans 2–3 is a problem that Paul identifies as specifically Jewish. We must keep the historical situation in mind: Paul is seeking to show that Gentiles too — quite apart from adherence to the requirements of the Jewish law (especially circumcision) — may participate in the blessings of the messianic age which has dawned in Jesus Christ. It is the Jew (perhaps also the Jewish Christian) who is tempted to "boast" that he has everything on his side — he is a child of Abraham and has the law of Moses. Paul of course admits a certain priority to Jews in the history of salvation; but he also insists that idle boasting in their spiritual heritage is insufficient. They must actually *keep* the law. "Doers of the Law" are justified (cf. Rom. 2:13, I Cor. 7:19). But Jews do not in fact keep it. Paul lists in vivid colors the violations against the law committed by them (Rom. 2:17–24).

The contrast between faith and boast, then, is open to more than one understanding. To state it crudely, Paul's complaint about the boasting of the Jews does not have to do with their effort qua effort to keep the law, but with the

[8] For a full statement of this interpretation of Paul see Bultmann, *Theology*, 1:187–352.

[9] H. Schlier, *Der Brief an die Galater* (Göttingen, 1962), p. 184.

fact that they have a law which they do not actually keep. This means that if Paul is concerned about "self-righteousness," it is only in this latter sense: a man has spiritual pretensions which he betrays in practice.[10]

[10] The theme of "boasting" in Paul is very difficult. It is impossible here to bring together all the passages involved. I trust, however, that they in some sense rule out the possibility of a final boast "before God" and that the principle stands, "Let him who boasts, boast in the Lord" (I Cor. 1:29-31; cf. Jer. 9:22). For only God makes life "in Christ" possible — Christ who is our "wisdom, righteousness, sanctification, and redemption" (I Cor. 1:30). In any event we have a line of thought in the early part of Romans sufficiently distinct to stand on its own feet. Yet a word ought to be said concerning Galatians 6 since this letter is also of great importance to our argument. At first Paul's general attitude toward boasting seems contradicted: "Let each man test his own work and then he will have reason to *boast* only in himself and in no other" (vs. 4). This is preceded by the admonition to "bear one another's burden and so fulfill the law of love" and followed by the remark "each man will bear his own load!" We seem to have contradiction upon contradiction. But we must remember that Paul is speaking to a situation in which some, as he presently says, "want you to be circumcised so that they may *boast* in your flesh"; these people he identifies as being circumcised themselves, and yet they "do not keep the law" (vs. 13). Again he is attacking a boast made on the basis of the supposed superiority of the circumcised; again he indicates that the law is not in fact kept. Consequently, "each man will bear his own load" (vs. 5) and "he will have reason to boast only in himself" (vs. 4) become intelligible as the opposite of "boasting in another's flesh" (vs. 13). Clearly the term "boast" in verse 4 serves only a limited function in the context. In verse 13 its significance is wider: Actual deeds are required, not spiritual pretensions — or feeding on someone else's religiosity; the deeds required take the form of the law of love; for we are to "bear one another burdens and so fulfill the law of love" — a statement which is obviously something of a variant of Gal. 5:14 ("the whole law is fulfilled in the one statement, namely, 'You shall love your neighbor as yourself'"). Thus the contradictions disappear. That a man could "boast" in himself even within the limits the context prescribes (vs. 4) may seem surprising; but we must recall that love is a fruit of the Spirit (Gal. 5:22) and that the Spirit is God's gift (cf. Rom. 5:2). In II Cor. 10:13-18 Paul bases his own "boasting" on his own evangelizing work, not on another's (as he stresses), and yet he manages to conclude with the admonition, "Let him who boasts, boast in the Lord!" We see a similar movement of the author's mind in II Cor. 11:16-33. These passages, then, are in fundamental agreement with Paul's attitude toward boasting in Romans 2-3. Thus we do not claim that Paul's concern for "boasting" has everywhere only to do with Jews. But we observe that within their varied settings they represent

The sin of the Gentile in Romans 1:18 ff. has a different thrust — he worships the creature rather than the Creator. It is illegitimate to link this critique — for which there is a good Hellenistic-Jewish parallel (Wisdom 13:1) — with the criticism of Jewish boasting and thereby finding in Paul the teaching that recognition of man's creatureliness, his very humanity, is violated by attempts to keep the law, that is, to establish his own righteousness. Paul deals with Jew and Gentile separately and employs different tactics to convict each of his sin. The limited extent to which some relation between the two critiques is actually operative will become clear later.

### Doers of the Law

Paul, then, is very much interested in the actual performance of the law. On the last day a man — and that includes the Christian — will be judged according to his works, whether they have been good or evil (Rom. 2:6–8, II Cor. 5:10, 11:15; cf. I Thess. 3:13, I Cor. 1:8, 4:5).[11] The basic problem with trying to live according to the law is that the law is *ineffectual* (Rom. 8:3) — the righteous life is not in fact achieved. Only the man who walks by the Spirit, that is, is "in Christ," has entered into the promises given to Abraham — only he has the "requirement of the law fulfilled" in him (Rom. 8:4).[12] To be Christian is to be enabled through divine power to obey God.

---

basically an appeal to avoid false pretensions. Paul is not suggesting that a concern for "works" per se is an idolatrous human concern.

[11] See R. Schnackenburg, *The Moral Teaching of the New Testament*, trans. J. Holland-Smith and W. J. O'Hara (Freiburg: Herder, 1965), pp. 278–82. A corollary of this is that although in Adam all men die, death is also the "punishment of actual sins committed by the individual man" (Schoeps, *Paul*, p. 189).

[12] Cf. Hodoyoth 4.29–33: "It [*'flesh'* and 'that molded of clay'] is in sin from the womb and to old age in the guilt of *faithlessness*. And I knew that with men there is no *righteousness* and in the son of man no *perfection*. With God most high are all the *works of righteousness* but man's path does not stand firm unless *by the Spirit* God form him, *to perfect the way of the sons of men* that they may know all his works in the power of his strength and the fullness of his mercy upon all the sons of his good pleasure."

For the argument to hold, however, Paul is compelled to claim that what Scripture requires of the man who lives by the law is obedience in every detail; for "cursed is everyone who does not abide by all[13] the things written in the book of the law to do them" (Gal. 3:10, Deut. 27:26). It is with this in mind that he contrasts law and faith and quotes Lev. 18:5 to the effect that "he who does them [the works of the law] shall live by them" (Gal. 3:12). Paul seems to be opposing a Jewish conception of "righteousness" (his own pre-Christian view perhaps) which would settle for a more or less consistent behavior, possibly marred by moral and ritual lapses which God in his mercy — and in view of Israel's election and the sacrificial system — forgives.[14] Such is the attitude he appears to have in mind in Romans 2:1 ff. where he complains of what he regards it seems as Jewish tendencies to take advantage of God's "goodness" and "long-suffering" — precisely those divine qualities to which the Hellenistic Jew writing Wisdom 15:1 ff. appeals in his confidence that "even though we sin, we are yours, knowing your power." What to the Jewish writer is a humble[15] confession becomes for Paul a terrible admission.

Despite the fact that Paul thinks constantly of Israel and the Gentiles and their role in the divine plan, the demand for a perfect keeping of the law is one that applies not only to Israel as a whole, but to every Israelite individually. In Gal. 5:3 he "bears witness again to every man who is circumcised that he is a debtor to do the whole law." To be sure, he is now applying the principle to misguided Gentiles in Galatia, but he is clearly referring to Gal. 3:10 ff. (which, at least in part, has to do with Jews), and there can be no deep gulf between

[13] The word "all" is not in the Hebrew text but is in the LXX.
[14] See M. Goguel in *Journal of Biblical Literature*, 53 (1934): 261–63.
[15] And a guarded one; for he goes on: "But we shall not sin . . . ." That Paul turns to the Jew in Romans 2:1 ff. may be gathered from the following observations: There is a break here despite the *dio* (which may be proleptic referring to the clause beginning with *en hō*). Paul shifts from the third person plural to the second person singular at this point. The "you" of Rom. 2:1, moreover, appears to be the same as the "you" of Rom. 2:17 ff. (who is identified as a Jew), while the content of Rom. 2:21–24 explicates that of Rom. 2:1.

these passages. Nor are we convinced by Phil. 3:6 that Paul regarded himself, for example, as a strictly "blameless" individual in his pre-Christian state. The word is used; but the passage has a polemical orientation which calls for a strong statement, and it probably presupposes the Jewish conception of righteousness just discussed; in any event, Gal. 1:14 shows that this same state could be described by Paul in somewhat less absolute terms: "I advanced in Judaism beyond many of my own age . . . ." Paul now demands perfection in the performance of the law if a man intends to live by it.[16]

The same Paul tells us that the man who actually "keeps the requirements of the law" or "fulfills the law" is the true son of Abraham (Rom. 2:25–29). It is precisely this that marks the distinction between the unregenerate Jew and the Christian Gentile.[17] It is this that marks the distinction between one who lives by the letter of the law (and cannot fulfill it) and one who lives by the Spirit (whereby he is enabled to fulfill the law). In many ways Rom. 2:25–29 represents the culmination of a line of argument and will be regarded in this paper as more of a key to Paul's thought than it usually is.

### The Requirements of the Law

This brings us to a traditional difficulty: How can Paul be trying to free the Gentiles from the law and at the same time claim that they alone fulfill the requirements of the law? Especially if Paul is worried about how Gentiles may share the blessings of Abraham "apart from the law," how can he then claim that it is Gentiles who in the Spirit keep the law? Of what law is Paul speaking? Must we say that there

[16] For the currency of such a thought in primitive Christianity, Jas. 2:10 alone may be cited. Rabbinic parallels are also difficult to find — though Gamaliel II is reported (Makk. 24a) to have been overcome with grief at the thought of the necessity of following *all* the commandments of Psalm 15 (see Schoeps, *Paul*, pp. 177, 193).

[17] I assume that Paul has Christians, not noble pagans, in mind in Rom. 2:25–29. Only in reference to Christians could Paul speak of the "Spirit" as he does here (vs. 29; cf. Rom. 7:6; II Cor. 3:6). The passage has been too often misunderstood.

is a profound dialectic here which in some sense "establishes" the law precisely when it seems to be threatened (cf. Rom. 3:31)? Once again, I think not.

If such a dialectic had been operative, Paul would have been "establishing" circumcision just as surely as he would be "establishing," say, love of the neighbor as a "requirement" of the new covenant as well as of the old.

Let us begin with the observation that those who live by the Spirit are said to keep "the just requirement" or simply "requirement [*dikaiōma*] of the law" (Rom. 8:4). The term *dikaiōma* is used sparingly by Paul and always in Romans: 1:32, 2:26, 5:16, 5:18, 8:4. In 5:16 it means the same as *dikaiōsis* or *dikaiosynē* and is chosen for rhetorical reasons — to balance the other words in the passage ending in -*ma*.[18] In 5:18 it means "righteous deed" and stands in rhetorical opposition to *paraptōma*. The other three passages are more closely related: pagans know "the requirement of God" (1:32), uncircumcised Gentile Christians "keep the requirements of the law" (2:26), "the requirement of the law is fulfilled" in those who walk by the Spirit (8:4). The last two passages have played an important role in our discussion already, and the first might be taken to cast further light on them. Even pagans know "the requirement of God, that those who do such things are worthy of death" (1:32). The clause "that those who do such things are worthy of death" is more *explanatory* than *exhaustive* of the content of the term *dikaiōma*. Paul is referring here to "such things" as homosexuality and other vices which he regards as marks of pagan degeneracy and the outpouring of God's wrath. Homosexuality is clearly identified as a usage not "natural" but "contrary to nature" (1:26–27). The statement that God has "delivered" pagans to such practices gives the passage a color which would be strange to the Greek, but he would if he were, say, a Stoic assent to the proposition[19] and recognize a fragment of natural law thinking. Is it too much to claim that the term *dikaiōma* is used by Paul to refer particu-

[18] In Enoch 104.9 *dikaiōma* stands for *dikaiosynē*.
[19] Following a tradition as old as Plato *Laws* I, 636b–c.

larly to those requirements of God — and hence of God's law — which are recognized (if not kept) by the majority of men who "from the creation of the world" have perceived God's "eternal power and deity" through his works (Rom. 1:20)?[20] Paul, of course, rejects the law qua law in its totality; but that, as we shall see, is because he understands law before the time of Christ as incapable of being anything other than a mixture of ethical and ceremonial elements thoroughly fused. Yet if his language about Gentile Christians "keeping the requirements *of the law*" (Rom. 2:26) makes any sense at all,[21] he must see in this mixture traces of the eternal will of God which through the activity of the Spirit have now become clear.

The emphasis, to be sure, is probably on the work of the Spirit by which God's will is realized (that is, "fulfilled" as in Rom. 8:4); nevertheless, since the term "law" also occurs in this connection, it does not seem artificial to ask what elements in Moses may have been regarded by Paul as expressing the essence of the law's requirement. Philo, as we might expect, gives a special place to the Ten Commandments (cf. *De decal.* 24 ff., 81; *De congr.* 120). Paul goes a somewhat different way. The "fulfillment of the law is love" according to Romans 13:10 and the sentiment is repeated in Galatians 5:14 — "for the whole law is fulfilled in one proposition, namely: You shall love your neighbor as yourself [Lev. 19:18]." Here the term "fulfilled" probably has to do, as usual, simply with the doing of God's will (cf. Rom. 13:8).

[20] *Poiēmata* can hardly refer to the mighty "acts" of God in the Old Testament (despite the usage in I Kings 19:4 LXX). The context is too clearly marked with Hellenistic or Hellenistic-Jewish motifs for that. See A. Fridrichsen in *Zeitschrift für die Neutestamentliche Wissenschaft*, 17 (1916): 159–68. At the same time it is not impossible that echoes of the Jewish doctrine of the Noachian covenant are to be found behind Paul's words (W. D. Davies, *Paul and Rabbinic Judaism* [London: S.P.C.K., 1948], pp. 115–17); they could easily be assimilated to the apostle's "natural theology."

[21] That the "requirements of the law "in this case turns out paradoxically to be "faith" (e.g., C. K. Barrett, *A Commentary on the Epistle to the Romans* [New York: Harper, 1957], p. 58) is too subtle to be convincing.

But in Rom. 13:9 all that is recommended in the law is said to be "summed up" in Lev. 19:18. Clearly Paul is exercising discrimination in his treatment of the legal requirements of Scripture, and such discrimination is a corollary of the present possibility of the "fulfillment" of the law. Jewish sages — for example, Akiba — also knew that the Law could be summed up in one or two pregnant statements (Gen. R. 24.7, where Akiba quotes Lev. 19:18). But it in no way hindered them from *also* affirming the full validity of Jewish ceremonies. Even Philo defends the literal observance of the ceremonial law in a famous passage, though he compares it to that which is required *thesei* rather than *physei* (*Migr. Abr.* 86–94). Paul, I should guess, is here reflecting tradition rooted in words of Jesus (cf. Mark 12:28–34) which affirm the law of love to the exclusion of any vital concern for, and often with profound criticism of, the ceremonial side of Jewish piety. But this does not exclude the possibility that he saw in popular natural-law thinking a helpful analogy to the reformulation of Jewish ethics preserved in the traditions about Jesus.[22] In Romans 13:9 he elaborates briefly on

[22] Paul elsewhere shows an appreciation for the appeal to nature: I Cor. 11:14; Rom. 2:14. Some deny that the latter passage has to do with the law of nature (cf. Augustine, *De Spiritu et Littera*, 43–47; F. Flückiger, in *Theologische Zeitschrift*, 8 [1952]: 17–42; and in a more modest form B. Reicke in *Svensk Exegetisk Årsbok*, 22/23 [1957/58], 154–67) and claim that Paul is speaking of Gentile *Christians*. The argument seems forced to me ("by nature" in any sense is hardly a suitable substitute for "by the Spirit" in Paul). In terms of our problem it is of course something of an embarrassment that Paul seems to suggest that *pagan* Gentiles actually "do the things of the law by nature." But I think this presses Paul's words too closely. He is trying to show how Jew and Gentile are basically on a similar footing before God. Both are responsible for the essentials of the law — the Jews because of the Old Testament, the Gentiles because of nature's law (known to them only in a diluted and distorted form? [See pp. 271–73.]). The inadequacy of Gentile behavior is shown by the fact that they accuse as well as excuse on the basis of their conscience. The point, then, is not that pagans "do the things of the law by nature," but that the fact that they do so indicates their responsibility for their rather less than perfect behavior. This puts a clear limit, of course, to the extent of Paul's indebtedness to natural-law thinking which presupposes the essential viability of nature's will (though the Stoics were remarkably clear as to how "rare a bird" the "wise man" in fact was).

the content of the law of love, and he does so in terms of the Ten Commandments (adultery, murder, theft, covetousness, "and if there be any other commandment") — about what we could expect from a Hellenistic Jew who had concerned himself with the problem of the law and who had been carried further than most under the influence of traditions stemming from Jesus. Paul, of course, is not interested in setting up a new code of laws; he recognizes as fundamental "an impulse towards the good coming from the Holy Spirit"; yet he is hardly speaking of "a purely inward inspiration of the Holy Spirit."[23]

The problem remains, however, why Paul so often seems to speak of the law as a whole in his critique of those who want to live by it. Two things must be remembered: (*a*) Paul is basically trying to show how Gentiles need not become Jews — that is, be circumcised — before they become Christians; (*b*) Paul is also trying to show that the law cannot "give life" (Gal. 3:21). His solution, then, involves some theory about the status of the law in the unfolding of God's plan for mankind and at the same time involves some general ideas about the nature of law itself in light of this plan. It is important not to take what Paul seems to say about the nature of law itself out of the context of the situation he faced.

I think it is clear especially from Gal. 4:1 ff. that the law qua law — that mixture of ethical and ceremonial matters which so concerned the Judaism of Paul's day — is regarded as obsolete. With the advent of Christ, this law has come to an end — at least for those who believe (Rom. 10:4).[24] Paul must regard it as more or less parallel to the laws and customs which characterized Gentile communities.[25] For there can be little doubt that the Gentile Galatians by seeking to obey the law — observing days, months, seasons, and years (Gal. 4:10) — are thought of as *slipping back* into some-

[23] Schnackenburg, *Moral Teaching*, p. 202.
[24] The law, according to some rabbis, ceases in the Messianic era (W. D. Davies, *Torah in the Messianic Age* [Philadelphia: Society of Biblical Literature, 1952]).
[25] See Schlier, *An die Galater*, pp. 193–94; B. Reicke in *Journal of Biblical Literature*, 70 (1951): 259–76.

thing — something pagan — out of which they had been called. The "elemental principles of the world" or "those that are by nature no gods" (Gal. 4:3, 8–9)[26] function in paganism much as do the "angels" who gave Israel the law (Gal. 3:19).[27] That pre-Christian law should contain (more or less in unrecognized form) elements of the eternal will of God ought to come as no surprise. The angels remain in some sense the executors of God's will (the law is "spiritual," Romans 7:14). On one side of the New Testament we may recall the figure of Satan in Job and the angelic hosts of Jewish apocalyptic; on the other side of the New Testament we may recall the Hellenistic doctrine of daemons (cf. Origen *Cels.* 8.24–34) which may have been a factor in Paul's angelology.[28] Deut. 32:8 LXX (cf. Deut. 4:19) may already have provided the exegetical basis for seeing a host of angels and demons, inferior, if not hostile, to God, as lords of the earth. In any case the law that characterizes the world before Christ's advent reflects the ambiguity of the status of the more immediate rulers of the earth. To live by such a law in the fullness of time is an anachronism. Even in the old era it served only to awaken in a sinful race a consciousness of guilt (Rom. 3:20, 7:13) and (probably) in this sense to "increase" sin (Rom. 5:12–14, 20). The suggestion is that generally speaking a righteous life was an impossibility in the old era. The law worked "wrath" (cf. Rom. 4:15). It may be that such "wrath" is thought of as fully manifesting itself only eschatologically since in Romans 1:17–18 God's "wrath" is apparently thought of as "being revealed" with the advent

[26] Another tag of natural theology? "Antisthenes, whose influence upon the Stoic philosophy was profound, had distinguished *physei theos* from the many *thesei theoi*" (W. Jaeger, *The Theology of the Early Greek Philosophers* [Oxford: Clarendon Press, 1947], p. 3; cf. Cicero *De natura deorum* 1.13.32). For *stoicheia* as a reference to astral deities or angels see M. Dibelius, *An die Kolosser, Epheser, an Philemon* (Tübingen, 1953), pp. 27–29; Schlier, *An die Galater*, pp. 190–93.

[27] Even in Rom. 5:20 the law is said to have "slipped in" — like the "false brethren" of Gal. 2:4.

[28] R. Liechtenhan, *Die göttliche Vorherbestimmung bei Paulus und in der Posidonionischen Philosophie* (Göttingen: Vandenhoeck & Ruprecht, 1922), pp. 14–16.

of Christ as is his "righteousness" — though here a distinction between God's dealing with Jews (Rom. 4:15) and with Gentiles (Rom. 1:18) may prevent us from connecting these texts. In any event, from the perspective of the new era the inadequacy of the old becomes clear, and any who heedlessly go on living by the standards of the old bring down on themselves God's wrath in a decisive way.[29]

Abraham, however, is father of all believers, and this may suggest that something is wrong with an understanding of Paul which stresses his two-age thinking and the unfolding of a plan in history rather than in some dialectic of the spiritual life which holds for all time.[30] Faithful Jews, however, are the exception even in the old era (cf. Rom. 11:1–6); and in Paul's sketch of Israel's spiritual history in Rom. 5:12–14, Abraham is ignored. It is a story of sin and law. The chronological argument in Galatians 3 concerning Abraham may be regarded as tailored to the particular requirements of the debate there. In any event, Abraham represents "promise" and not "fulfillment." This means, I would suggest, that Abraham is an archetypal figure belonging as much (or more) to Scripture as to history in Paul's mind and having eschatological relevance. At the end of his account of Abraham in Romans 4 Paul remarks that "it was not written *for his sake alone* that 'it was accounted to him,' but *also for our sakes*" (vs. 24). A similar formula recurs in I Cor. 9:9–10 where we have a clear trace of allegorical exegesis: "Muzzle not the ox that treads out the corn" was written "for our sakes" — to teach us that preachers of the gospel may receive physical sustenance from their flocks. For, as Paul explains, "Surely God is not concerned about oxen!" The writer of Pseudo-Aristeas (144) was also convinced that it was a "degrading" idea to think that God was concerned about, say, mice and weasels. The latter are disapproved of because they

[29] A further refinement is, of course, involved in what Schweitzer, *Mysticism*, pp. 193–96, has called Paul's doctrine of the *status quo.* "In the state in which each was called, therein shall he continue" (I Cor. 7:20).

[30] With, say, Old Testament man looking forward, New Testament man looking back, to the coming of Messiah.

symbolize vices to be avoided by the good Jew (the weasel, for example, conceives through the ear and brings through the mouth [165]).[31] For Paul even the experiences of the Jewish nation in the desert have relevance for Christians "typologically" (I Cor. 9:11) — Christians "upon whom the ends of the ages have come."[32] The Old Testament for Paul is not the "book of the acts of God" but "the oracles of God" (Rom. 3:2) — an inspired document having relevance primarily in the new era. The history of God's people which it presupposes is primarily a history of disobedience.

With this in mind, we may return for a moment to Rom. 2:29 — the famous distinction between living "by the Spirit, not the letter." It seems certain that Paul is here contrasting two modes of existence as we have indicated. But the patristic suggestion that Paul is also contrasting a spiritual and literal sense of the law (e.g. Origen De principiis 4.2.4–6, 4.3.6) has been brushed too lightly aside. The latter contrast after all may *complement* the former. In this connection Paul in fact mentions a "circumcision of the heart," and although this may simply echo the language of Deut. 10:16 or Jer. 4:4, there is probably more to it (cf. Philo Spec. Leg. 1.304); for here we have the same atmosphere as in Romans 12:1 where Paul speaks of Christians presenting their bodies as a "living

[31] Paul, then, "establishes" the law (Rom. 3:31) quite specifically in the sense that he shows how the scriptural account of Abraham, which immediately follows, teaches the priority of faith. Since this "faith" is not bound up with the Mosaic law, it may be significant for our understanding of Paul that Philo saw Abraham as a "living law" — a sort of incarnation of the law of nature (cf. De Abr. 5–6, 60–61, 275–76; Quod Omnis Probus 62).

[32] I have not hesitated to alternate between the word "allegory" and "typology" above. I grant that the "predictive" (or historical) element in the New Testament's view of the Old justifies a special use of the term "typological" and that in some contexts the distinction is significant. But (a) Paul himself uses the term "allegory" (Gal. 4:24), (b) I do not see that the exegetical method in either case is significantly different, and (c) the technical terms used suggest no sharp break between Paul's "predictive allegory" (H. A. Wolfson, The Philosophy of the Church Fathers, 1 [Cambridge: Harvard University Press, 1956]: pp. 24–43) and other nonliteral exegesis: thus in the case of both allegory and typology the events of the past are only a "shadow" (cf. Col. 2:17; Philo Conf. 190, Migr. Abr. 12).

sacrifice" and identifies this as "rational service" (cf. *Poimandres* 31).[33] The theory is more clearly enunciated in Col. 2:17 — Old Testament ceremonial represents "a shadow of things to come" (cf. Heb. 10:1). Thus from another angle we see the possibility that Paul finds the "spiritualizing" tendencies of Hellenistic Judaism a suitable vehicle to express one aspect of what it means to have entered the new age. The positive significance of the ceremonial obligations of the law — never stressed by Paul — is allegorical and eschatological.

This, however, is only one aspect of what it means to have entered the new era; for the new covenant is characterized by "freedom," the old by "slavery" (cf. Gal. 4:21–31). Seen within the framework we have uncovered, we can perhaps understand what this may mean. Living under a law which is a mixture of ethical and ceremonial norms is slavery. Precisely the mixed character of such a law points to the enslavement of man by powers less than God. The law qua law is incapable of any other expression and hence cannot give life (Gal. 3:21). The new covenant brings a new power which enables a man to keep that which is basically required by God in the law (Rom. 8:4).[34] It is this power that is the

[33] Professor Robert Grant has made further suggestions along these lines which I am happy to support: "To me it looks as if the problem [of the law] was not fully solved in Paul's time because he was unable or unwilling to deny the fact that in many regards the law was really the law of God. In so far, however, as it was a universal law it could not contain commandments about literal circumcision or other literal ceremonies. Paul knew this not only from the Old Testament passages he cites but also, I suspect, from those he did not cite. I find it hard to believe that he quoted Isa. 1:9 in Rom. 9:29 without reading the subsequent verses directed against sacrifices and other ceremonies, or Hos. 1:10 and 2:23 (Rom. 9:25–26) without at least glancing at the verses between. Perhaps he sometimes used a book of testimonies for ready reference; I believe that he also read much of the Old Testament."

[34] Paul's expectations of Christian behavior are high. Sin is virtually eliminated as a possibility in many passages (e.g., Rom. 6:6, 8:5–9). The "normal" Christian is a blameless one (H. Windisch, *Taufe und Sünde im ältesten Christentum* [Tübingen: Mohr, 1908], pp. 98–225). Many current estimates of Paul's teaching which emphasize the eschatological nature of "righteousness" and "holiness" with a view to defending a less rigorous or more dialectical view (e.g., A. Richardson, *An*

essence of Christian freedom. A spontaneous fulfillment of God's will becomes possible. This gives to life in the new era a new quality. The old era lacks this quality; but if we can trust Paul's own biographical statements (Phil. 3:4–7; Gal. 2:13–14), and if our general understanding of Gal. 4:1 ff. is correct, "slavery" is bound up in Paul's mind not with a feeling of *anxiety*, or with an awareness (even by hindsight) of the *inauthenticity* which comes from trying to justify oneself before God, but primarily with the idea of *obsoleteness*. It is interesting to note that the two main divisions of Galatians 3 — Gal. 3:16–18 (on Abraham) and Gal. 3:19–29 ("why then the law") — end with statements that are designed to show why Gentiles can side-step the requirements of the law, that is, circumcision. Such an *obsolete* law, of course, is also thought of as "shutting up" men under sin (Gal. 3:22–23; Rom. 3:9–19); but this is viewed as God's act "that the promise might be given to those who believe" — that is, it had a limited function in the history of salvation (to show the *powerlessness* of men in the old era) just as the present disobedience of Jews in general has a function in ringing down the curtain on the eschatological drama (God has "shut all men [including Jews] up" in disobedience "that he might have mercy on all" [Rom. 11:32]). It is this that interests Paul, not some dialectic between the function of the law and preaching about Christ in the life of Christians; nor does he give his understanding of history an autobiographical ex-

Introduction to the Theology of the New Testament [London: SCM Press, 1958], p. 237) are misleading. The imperative, to be sure, follows upon the indicative; and a certain futurity often attaches to Paul's discussion of man's justification and sanctification. But more often than not, it is asumed that this state of perfection *will speedily be achieved in practice that a man may stand before the judge on the last day* (for "sanctification" see II Cor. 1:12, 7:1, Rom. 6:19, 22, I Thess. 3:12–13, 4:3–8; for "righteousness" see especially Phil. 1:9–11, 3:9, 12–14). In Gal. 5:5 "the hope of righteousness" which we "await" (*apekdechometha*) is eschatologically oriented; yet Gal. 5:6 explains this in terms of the abolition of the distinction between circumcision and uncircumcision and, more generally, "faith active in love"; our "waiting," then, for the fulfillment of the hope of being regarded righteous or acquitted is in no way separable from our behavior here and now.

pression — not even in Romans 7.[35] The law was and is slavery because it cannot effect righteousness; the gospel is freedom because the requirements of God can be fulfilled in Christ through the Spirit. Paul's ethic culminates in an emphasis upon the concrete deed of love; and this emphasis is hardly qualified by introspective categories which focus on the struggle of the soul or by existentialist categories which lend to terms like "slavery" and "freedom" a color that goes beyond (or falls short of) the boundaries of Paul's thought.

## God's Righteousness and One's Own Righteousness

If the general line of our argument has been correct, Pauline thinking concerning the righteousness of God has as its background a concern for the unfolding of God's plan in history, and particularly the overwhelming significance of the dawn of the new era. The term righteousness, then, may be regarded as an abbreviated form of a longer formula, central to which is an awareness of what it means to be in Christ, to be buried with Christ by baptism (cf. Gal. 3:27), to be a member of the body of Christ, to walk by the Spirit. Albert Schweitzer, I think, was right about this.[36] If it is asked: "Why, then, did Paul bother with this misleading vocabulary about righteousness?" the answer is that he was meeting his opponents on their own ground as much as possible. That

[35] See W. G. Kümmel, *Römer 7 und die Bekehrung des Paulus* (1929). This insight, however, can be variously used. Thus Bultmann employs it to strip Paul's theology of a subjectivistic or introspective character ("Romans 7 and the Anthropology of Paul," in *Existence and Faith*, ed. and trans. S. Ogden [New York: Meridian Books, 1960]): Paul is looking back on unredeemed mankind from the point of view of the converted Christian. Only from this vantage point can Paul know what he perceives in Romans 7 about pre-Christian man; hence Paul's own lack of anxiety in the pre-Christian state (Phil. 3:4–6). But Bultmann also talks of unredeemed mankind in this connection as though Paul were speaking simply of Everyman. The historical and eschatological framework of the apostle's thought is ignored or, better, "internalized." It is obvious that our arguments take this framework more at face value. Certainly what Paul says in Romans 7 would apply to those in his day who sought (anachronistically) to live by the law; but the analysis of their condition must be determined by Paul's understanding of the function of the law from Moses to Christ.

[36] Schweitzer, *Mysticism*, pp. 205–26.

meant Scripture, and especially the figure of Abraham; and here Paul looks for whatever may help him establish the priority of God's grace. He found "it was accounted to him for righteousness" (along with Hab. 2:4 "the righteous by faith shall live" [Gal. 3:11, Rom. 1:17]) the most reliable peg on which to hang his interpretation.[37] It is significant that the term "righteousness" occurs primarily in Galatians and Romans and that in other letters — where he faced problems of another kind — it occurs infrequently, and usually[38] in a sense which hardly suggests the special overtones that have been read into it in Galatians and Romans.[39]

There are, however, passages in Paul in which God's righteousness and one's own righteousness are contrasted in a way that our analysis may not fully explain. Do we not have in this juxtaposition that more penetrating analysis attributed to Paul which sees in man's very effort to keep the law or to stand before God on the basis of his "works" a subtle idolatry? We cannot deal with all the passages which may be found to support such a view, but we shall try to indicate how at least one key text fits in with our line of argument: Rom. 10:1 ff., especially verse 3 — "for not knowing the righteousness of God and seeking to establish their own, they did not submit

[37] Abraham "is the great exemplar of faith" also in Judaism (G. F. Moore, *Judaism* [Cambridge: Harvard University Press, 1927], 2:237). Hab. 2:4 is the one commandment to which the prophet is said to have reduced the law (Makk. 24a). C. G. Montefiore and H. Loewe, *A Rabbinic Anthology* (London: Macmillan, 1938), pp. 336–37, show that (in addition to Exod. 14:31) Gen. 15:6 and Hab. 2:4 "are also frequently quoted" by the rabbis.

[38] With the notable exception of Phil. 3:6, 9 (for which see note 42 below).

[39] I Cor. 1:30 and 6:11 are especially noteworthy. Paul identifies Christ as our "wisdom, righteousness, sanctification, and redemption" and links being "washed" (baptized), being "sanctified," and being "justified." This suggests that righteousness is one of many terms which have to do with the transformed existence of the man "in Christ." Even where the forensic sense is to the fore, "acquittal" or "anticipation of acquittal" before God's tribunal on the last day presuppose the sanctity of the man to be acquitted. (*Dikaiosynē* occurs 52 times in Paul: 33 times in Romans, 4 times in Galatians, 4 times in Philippians, once in I Corinthians, 7 times in II Corinthians. *Dikaioun* occurs 25 times in Paul: 15 times in Romans, 8 times in Galatians, twice in I Corinthians.)

to the righteousness of God." It seems clear. Do we not have juxtaposed two fundamental orientations — one which seeks to win its own way before God (by works), the other which submits to God? A number of things, however, are to be noted. First, Paul again is speaking of Jews (vss. 1–2). Second, he is thinking of their unwillingness to submit to the revelation of God's will in Christ — "for Christ is the end of the law to everyone who believes" (vs. 4). In other words, Paul has in mind a particular point in the history of salvation; the categories are not timeless. Third, and most important, "for Moses writes that as to the righteousness from the law, 'the man who does it shall live by' it" (vs. 5). Again we have the quotation of Lev. 18:5 as in Gal. 3:12. This, then, is the meaning of righteousness from the law properly understood — the actual doing of the law. Surely, as in Galatians, Paul is suggesting that such doing is out of the question. The content of God's righteousness, on the other hand, is the gracious words which Paul finds in Deut. 30:12 ff. (for which interpretation the Targums provide a model),[40] and the section again ends with a statement nullifying the distinction between Jew and Greek (vss. 11–13)!

The juxtaposition, then, remains within the limits of our analysis: righteousness by works is an impossibility; a man is pronounced "righteous" by God only by virtue of the power to fulfill God's will which God himself gives. The emphasis, to be sure, is on "faith" as the presupposition of righteousness or justification; and faith is simply the recognition that we must rely on God and his promises. Paul's remarks, however, are intended to show how the invidious distinction between Jew and Gentile is obliterated. We may summarize our understanding of this emphasis simply by quoting I Cor. 7:19 — "For neither circumcision counts for anything nor uncircumcision, but *keeping the commandments of God*" (cf. Gal. 5:6, 6:15). Consequently there is no need to read into such passages the further idea that the very effort to keep the law is a subtle idolatry which leads to death.

[40] D. Macho, "Targum y Nuevo Testamento," in *Mélanges E. Tisserant* (Vatican, 1964), 1:155.

"Death" is the "wages of sin" (Rom. 6:23), and "sin" is understood very concretely as "uncleanness" and "lawlessness" (vs. 19) such as would be imagined by an antinomian who misunderstood Paul (vs. 1). The Jew "did not attain to" or "succeed in fulfilling the law" (Rom. 9:31) because he did not acknowledge the need of faith and stumbled over the "stumbling stone" (vs. 32).

Two orientations are contrasted; but the emphasis is on the ineffectuality of righteousness by the law to accomplish its purpose. Faith is that which acknowledges God's grace and initiative in salvation; but it is not simply a renewed understanding of what it means to be a creature of God; it is not simply that which frees us for good works;[41] as Paul uses it, it is unintelligible apart from a transforming power which brings with it obedience to God's will and, in one important text, the performance of miracles (cf. Gal. 3:5 — "does he, then, who supplies you the Spirit and works miracles among you do it on the basis of works of the law or on the basis of hearing with faith?"). This feature of Paul's thought can only be eliminated by a violent demythologizing of his remarks about baptism, the Spirit, being in Christ, and so forth. Faith indeed is the acknowledgment of God's authority in human life and, consequently, of the sovereignty of his grace; but in Paul it is an acknowledgment of that sovereignty precisely as it manifests itself in baptism and the common life in Christ's body. The term "faith" like the term "righteousness" tends to be used as an abbreviation for a more complex formula. Again the statistics are relevant; for of the 109 uses of the term faith in Paul (excluding the Pastorals) 40 are found in Romans, 22 in Galatians. In the other letters this element in the description of man's salvation — important as it is — plays a lesser role. Again the language of the LXX about which the debate centers controls Paul's usage to an extent. Faith and law in

[41] On a related issue R. Luecke, summarizing G. Ebeling, says: "The Word gives not 'power' for good works, but simply 'freedom' for them" (*Dialog*, 4 [1965]: 290). Such a view seems to me to lie at the heart of much contemporary interpretation of Paul.

Paul, then, do have to do with contrasting orientations as well as with contrasting periods in the history of salvation; but the significance of the first contrast is misconstrued if the second is ignored. When their interconnection is observed, the fact that a Gentile Christian who "fulfills the law" receives "praise . . . from God" (Rom. 2:25–29; cf. I Cor. 4:5) becomes intelligible in a way that it does not when all the emphasis is on the nothingness of man and his achievements before God.[42]

[42](*a*) The same striking contrast between "my righteousness based on the law" and "the righteousness of [or from] God" occurs in Phil. 3:2–11. Here the choice of interpretation is not as clear as I find it in Rom. 10:1 ff. But certainly I see nothing that rules out the possibility of reading it along the lines suggested. And if this is done, the concluding clauses, "that I may know him and the power of his resurrection and the sharing in his sufferings, being conformed to his death that if possible I may attain the resurrection from the dead," are more to the point. God's righteousness, the verdict of acquital, presupposes a transformed existence. (*b*) The difficult passage in Rom. 4:2 may also be read in these terms: "For if Abraham was justified by works, he has something to boast about; but not before God." Paul then goes on to show that according to Gen. 15:6 Abraham's faith was the presupposition of the (true) righteousness accounted to him. Surely it is not artificial to suggest that Abraham's righteousness by works which makes possible a certain boast (see I Macc. 2:51–52 where Gen. 15:6 is also referred to) is that righteousness of the Jew — imperfect and constrained (according to Arakhin 17*a* not even the patriarchs could stand before strict justice) — which (as Paul sees it) makes no approach to God possible; whereas the righteousness "accounted" him is that which involves reliance on God's grace and promise as it manifests itself in Christ and transforms his members. The apparent artificiality of the latter equation is to be traced solely to the necessity Paul feels here to stick close to the language of the LXX. The "praise" which a man receives "from God" in Rom. 2:29 is that which comes when Abraham's "secret" descendents — faithful Gentiles — actually "fulfill the law" (vss. 25–29). Is not that the basis of Abraham's own worth in God's eyes? (*c*) Concerning Gal. 2:15–21, the key verses are 17–18, and I think that this is what they mean: "If we, Peter and Paul, who are Jews, while seeking to be justified in Christ are found ourselves to be 'sinners' — that is, living like the Gentiles without paying attention to Jewish ceremonial law (for note that in vs. 15 "sinners" seems to mean little more than non-Jews — that is, those who are not "by nature Jews"), has Christ become the servant of 'sin'?" Paul is here playing on words: "sinners" implies "sin" — but he wants to make it clear that living without the law on its ceremonial side, that is, eating with Gen-

Few, I think, would doubt that Paul stresses the importance of the concrete deed of love as surely as does Jesus in the tradition preserved by the Synoptics. This paper, however, has sought to show that the dialectic which today is often invoked to lead up to this insight, and almost inevitably overshadows it, is not to be found in Paul. The focus of Paul's concern is not that the striving for righteousness per se is a subtle idolatry; his problem is more immediate, as I hope we have shown. He goes beyond Jesus and the Synoptic Gospels in seeing the new obedience grounded in a new creation (whereas Jesus takes for granted the created potentialities of men as he addresses them and appeals for "repentance"); but Paul no more calls into question the concern for the righteous act as the presupposition of blamelessness in the day of judgment than Jesus' awareness of the existence of hypocrisy calls into question the need to do God's will in order to inherent the Kingdom of God.

tiles — does not in fact involve "sin" in the true sense of that term. Hence his answer: "Surely not!" What makes a person a "transgressor" — and here he must have in mind Peter (and Barnabas) — is to "build up" what one has "broken down" — that is, out of fear of the visitors from Jerusalem to leave off eating with the Gentiles and submit again to the law's (ceremonial) requirements.

# 13

---

## Church History in the Early Church
### ROBERT M. GRANT

Maurice Nadeau began his *History of Surrealism* with the
words "A history of surrealism — then surrealism must be
dead!" and answered the charge by claiming both that "the
surrealist state of mind, or, better still surrealist behavior, is
eternal" and that the movement did belong precisely to the
period between the wars; its history, therefore, could be
written. Something similar, we may suppose, was in the
minds of those ancient Christians who at various times
investigated the history of the Christian movement and set
forth their conclusions in order to influence others. Like sur-
realists, Christians believed that their states of mind and
forms of behavior were eternal, for they were based on divine
revelation; like the historian of surrealism, Christians concerned with church history recognized that there were relatively clear stages in the life of the communities and that it
was necessary to interpret the meaning of these stages so
that past solutions could be imitated or avoided. The theory
we shall try to demonstrate in the following pages is that the
creation of historical interpretations is especially characteristic of times of crisis and rapid transition, and that these
interpretations can be either conservative with emphasis on
continuity or radical with emphasis on change. Neither the
conservative nor the radical historian is concerned primarily
with the past as such. Both derive examples from it in order
to illustrate the necessity for maintaining continuity in the
face of change or for making a more radical break.

## The Apostolic Age

It is fairly clear that the problem of continuity was acute within the apostolic age. What was one to make of the relationship between Israel and the church, between the Old Testament and the gospel, between the prophets and Christ? What was one to decide about the relationship of the apostle Paul not only to the Judaism out of which he came, but also to the church in Jerusalem, to those who had been apostles before him? If the New Testament consisted only of the Gospels and of the certainly authentic Pauline epistles, we should find it difficult to discover what connection there was between Paul and his contemporaries. But in the New Testament there is the book of Acts, at least in part composed in order to emphasize the connecting links — on one hand between the earliest apostles and their successors, on the other between Paul and Jerusalem. Similar concerns are prominent in the Pastoral Epistles, written in Paul's name to show that he was concerned with continuity and with the kinds of ministries current in the latter half of the first century.

We should not suppose that Acts and the Pastorals are the only representatives of this kind of historical concern. It is evidenced in the Four Gospels, in which traditions (themselves subject to gradual modification) about the life and work of Jesus are presented with varying emphases to meet various kinds of situations. It remains true, however, that Acts represents the most significant presentation, if not re-presentation, of the life and work of the early Christian communities. Its author was concerned with the unity of the early communities — an urgent problem, as the New Testament epistles show — and therefore wrote his history in such a way as to minimize the extent of disagreements and to dramatize the unity of the apostolic age. At the very beginning of the book this unity is emphasized by the apostles' remaining together in Jerusalem, by their agreement upon the choice of Matthias to replace Judas Iscariot among the Twelve, and by their common experience of the gift of the Spirit at Pentecost. The author makes his point especially clear by the use of summaries to show the unity of the apostolic community in teaching and in action (2:42, 44–45; 4:32). This unity was not only human but divine, for like the work of Moses (7:36) and Jesus (2:22) and as predicted in the book of Joel (2:19) it was accompanied by "signs and wonders" — characteristic of the apostles at Jerusalem (2:43, 4:30, 5:12), of the martyr Stephen (6:8), and of Paul and Barnabas (14:3, 15:12).

In the course of his two volumes (Luke-Acts) the author clearly indicates that there was a definite succession from the twelve apostles, appointed by Jesus himself (Luke 6:13–16), and Matthias, whom they appointed to succeed Judas Iscariot (Acts 1:13–26), to other leaders of the church. In nearly every instance where significant persons are mentioned, their relation to the continuity of order is emphasized. Barnabas recognized the primacy of the apostles (4:36–37); it was he who introduced Saul to the apostles (9:27) and later was sent to Antioch (11:22), where he was recognized by the church and sent on a mission with Saul (13:1–3). The martyr Stephen was commissioned by the apostles, as was the evangelist Philip (6:5–6), whose mission made it clear to Simon Magus that the Spirit was imparted only through the apostles (8:16–18, an emphatic statement). Philip later baptized an Ethiopian eunuch who had already read the Old Testament (8:27–38), but the mission to Gentiles really got under way only under the guidance of the apostle Peter (9–11). The convert Saul was given the Holy Spirit only when Ananias of Damascus laid his hands on him and he was baptized (9:17–18). Later at Jerusalem he was taken to the apostles by Barnabas (9:27), and his absence from the city was due to a plot against him (9:29–30). Later on his relations with Jerusalem, like those of Barnabas, were close (11:30, 12:25). Barnabas and Saul were officially commissioned by the church at Antioch (13:2–3); they could be called apostles (14:4, 14); in turn they appointed presbyters (14:23).

The crucial council in Jerusalem is described as necessitated by the teaching of "some persons" at Antioch, and although there was a dispute the council ended amicably;

Paul and Barnabas were to be accompanied by two prophets from Jerusalem, even though they themselves soon parted company. The reason for the break was "merely personal" — Barnabas wanted to take Mark along, while Paul did not (chap. 15). Thereafter, even so, Paul remained on good terms with the Jerusalem church.

A few items in this account are not fully explained, and perhaps are due to Luke's lack of information about them. More probably, it would appear, he simply did not wish to enter into the rather complicated details. For instance, he does not explain how Christianity arose at Damascus. We learn only that the high priest had given Saul instructions to make prisoners of Christians there (9:2). Presumably the author intended to say that Christianity reached Damascus after the persecution consequent upon Stephen's death (8:1). Again, he does not say how there happened to be presbyters in the church of Jerusalem; they simply appear in Acts 11:30 and are occasionally mentioned thereafter. The case of James, "bishop" of Jerusalem, also presents problems. He is not mentioned in the lists of the apostles; he is not James the son of Zebedee, whose death is explicitly noted (12:2). Instead, as Peter leaves the Jerusalem scene (reappearing briefly for the apostolic council), he sends a message to "James and the brothers" (12:17), and when we next hear of James he is rather clearly the leader of the Jerusalem church (15:13–30), as he definitely is at the end of Paul's missionary travels (21:18–26).

The problem of the presbyters can probably be solved by analogy. If Barnabas and Paul could appoint presbyters, presumably the apostles in Jerusalem could do likewise, especially since they could make new apostles. The problem of James is more difficult. Paul's own letters are quite clear on the subject. In Jerusalem he had once visited the apostles Cephas and James "the Lord's brother" (Gal. 1:18–19); later he had dealt with the "pillar" apostles there, James, Cephas, and John (2:9). In I Corinthians he correlates his own apostolate with his having seen the (risen) Lord (9:1) and speaks of "the rest of the apostles" with special emphasis on "the Lord's brothers" and Cephas (9:5). In a list of witnesses to the risen Lord he begins with Cephas and the Twelve, evidently including the former among the latter, and continues with James and all the apostles; only then does he mention himself as an apostolic witness (15:5–11). This evidence clearly suggests that like Paul himself James became an apostle by virtue of a vision of the risen Jesus, by what is called a "resurrection appearance." But Luke was unwilling so to describe it. Just as in Paul's case he treats the vision of the risen Lord not as a resurrection appearance but as a vision — or rather an audition of a heavenly voice, according to all three accounts — thus making the epiphany no more significant than the one given Stephen (7:55), so in the case of James he could not enter into the question of vision and apostolate without raising again the thorny problems related to the apostolate.

These points, not to mention all the difficulties raised by the comparison of Acts with the Pauline epistles, clearly show that Luke's history is somewhat schematic and that he is writing it in a time when the communities need to look back to their common origins, forget the leaders' controversies, and hold together in a critical situation. The overall picture of Lucan ideas provided by H. Conzelmann, for example, suggests that there has been a waning of primitive expectations and that there is an occasion for the churches to find a place for themselves in the world.

Certainly Luke was concerned with locating the beginning of the church's mission in world history. This point is especially clear from the elaborate synchronism he provides, for the coming of the word of God to John the Baptist (Luke 3:1–2). Not content with mentioning the fifteenth year of Tiberius Caesar, he names the procurator of Judaea, the tetrarchs of nearby territories, and two high priests at Jerusalem. He is even more definitely concerned, however, with the past as foundation of the present. He alone among the evangelists depicts Jesus as bequeathing his kingdom to the apostles (Luke 22:29; cf. 12:32); and this concern for order is carried through to the end. At the close of Paul's ministry in Asia Minor he calls together "the elders of the church" of Ephesus (Acts 20:17–38). Like Jesus at the Last Supper, he reminds them of their common experiences and tribulations and warns of impending troubles. In the middle of the farewell discourse, Paul refers to the elders as having been set over the sheepfold as "overseers" (*episkopoi*, 20:28). Much earlier in the book of Acts (1:20) Luke had quoted Psalm 109:8 in order to refer its mention of *episkopē* to the apostolic office which Matthias was about to assume. In conjunction with the evidence we have already mentioned, this point shows that among Luke's historical concerns one of the most important was that of insisting upon the organizational continuity of the Christian church.

It will be obvious that our picture of Luke's ideas is not altogether in agreement with that presented by Conzelmann in his valuable commentary on Acts.[1] Conzelmann insists that there is "no programmatic presentation of continuity." There is no "apostolic succession"; instead, the most important factor in continuity is the unaltered teaching of the church and the Spirit as the church's possession. The continuity of church history is not one of institutions, for the position of Paul is not defined "officially" but purely soteriologically. Much of what Conzelmann says is undeniably true. For example, on Acts 1:20 he comments that "not every apostle will be replaced but only one lost one, so that the necessary number of twelve can be reestablished." But this is to say no more than that for Luke (as for Paul, I Cor. 15:5) there was no Twelve after the Twelve. Acts 14:4 and 14 are from a "source" — but Luke used it. The appointment of presbyters in Acts 14:23 is "unpaulinische" — but it does occur in Acts. Conzelmann rightly states that in Acts 20:28 "bishops" of the Pauline type (Phil. 1:1) are combined with presbyters, and he adds that "institution and Spirit are bound together." But then he argues that "this synthesis is still not to be understood as catholic, for it is not made secure through an idea of succession, and the office does not yet bestow any 'character' (indelibilis) on its bearer." As we have argued, the

[1] *Die Apostelgeschichte* (Tübingen: Mohr, 1963).

idea of some kind of succession is present in Acts, even though it is not fully worked out; and the question of indelibility is one which was not to be raised until a much later date. Certainly it had not arisen in the time of Polycarp, who expressed regret that the presbyter Valens "is ignorant of the place which was given him," spoke of God's future judgment, and urged the community to recall Valens and his wife "as fallible and straying members, so that you may save your whole body" (Phil. 11).

Certainly the continuity reflected in Acts is not simply ministerial, but ministerial continuity is depicted in the book, with the exceptions we have already noted.

## The Period of the Apostolic Fathers

Within the New Testament itself there are a few passages which reflect the passage of time from one generation to another, from the age of the apostles to the age of the apostolici. These include the preface to Luke, with its reference to the eyewitnesses who transmitted the traditions (Luke 1:2), a verse at the end of John attesting the authenticity of the Gospel as a whole (John 21:24), and a mention of those in the past who heard the Lord (Heb. 2:3). The backward look is more in evidence, naturally enough, among the Apostolic Fathers. Clement of Rome insists upon the historical existence of a succession from the apostles (chaps. 42–44) and recognizes that the martyred Peter and Paul, although put to death in his own "generation," are heroes who belong to the past (chap. 5). Ignatius refers to his own inferiority to both Peter and Paul, who unlike him were apostles.[2] Polycarp insists upon his own lack of wisdom as compared with Paul's understanding (Phil. 3:2). While the doctrine of Hermas is rather vague, on this subject as on others, it is clear that for him the apostles belonged to a previous generation (Sim. 9.16.5).

Somewhere around the beginning of the second century Papias of Hierapolis stated his preference for oral traditions as contrasted with evidence to be derived from books. In pur-

---

[2] Ignatius Eph. 12.2; cf. Rom. 4.3.

suit of these traditions, he was accustomed to ask followers of the "elders" what these elders had reported about the teaching of the Lord's disciples — if this is what his sentence means.[3] If, as is possible, the elders are to be identified with the disciples, Papias got his information from second-generation witnesses; if they are not so identified, it came from the third generation. More probably the second generation was involved, for we know that he obtained traditional information from the daughters of the evangelist Philip (Acts 21:8).[4] It is probably significant that when he lists the ultimate sources of his information he begins with Andrew, Peter, and Philip — the first to be called as disciples of Jesus, according to the Gospel of John (1:40–43). When he explains that the Gospel of Mark was written accurately but not "in order," he is probably relying on a tradition of the Johannine school, which must have held that the order of John was the correct one.

What we find in Papias is a concern for historical tradition, some recognition of the difficulties involved in establishing it, and an attempt at a historical solution of the differences among some of the gospels. The combination of rather rhetorical Greek and Jewish concern for tradition which we encounter in his fragments shows that he stands on the border line not only between the apostolic age and the later life of the church but also between the two cultures whose interweaving resulted in the culture of Christianity. He is not writing in a vacuum, however. His preface shows that he is deeply concerned with the reliability of the true traditions. Unlike "the many," he is delighted not with those who say the most but with those who teach the truth and do not make mention of "alien commandments."[5] This polemical concern has driven him to his search for the commandments really derived from the Lord.

[3] Eusebius *H. E.* 3.39.3–4.
[4] *Ibid.*, 3.39.9.
[5] "Alien" means "false"; cf. Ignatius *Philad.* 3.3, and F. Wotke in Pauly-Wissowa, *Realencyclopädie der classischen Altertumswissenschaft.* 28:3, 970. "The many" does not necessarily refer to a majority.

Perhaps around the same time as Papias a Christian apologist named Quadratus referred to men healed by the Savior who had survived "even to our own day."[6] Once more we find a clear recognition of the distance between apostolic times and the later age.

As far as we can tell, however, the Christian writers of this period did not undertake the compilation of anything like the "church history" provided by Luke-Acts. They were chiefly concerned with severely practical problems and left history — and, to a considerable extent, theology — to one side. Perhaps it could be claimed that the *Didache*, set forth in the name of the twelve apostles, reflects historical concern, but pseudepigraphy is not quite the same thing as historical investigation. In fact, the only writers we know from the early second century who were interested in describing Christian beginnings were the Roman historians Tacitus and Suetonius.[7]

## Heresy, Orthodoxy, and the State

One might expect that when Christian writers self-consciously began to confront the world outside their communities concern for their own history might arise. Such was, in fact, the case. At the same time, however, it was necessary for most of them to conduct a two-front war. Their enemies were inside as well as outside, and the churches were faced with a double crisis. History was involved on both sides, especially at Rome.

Between 137 and 144 the Roman church was strongly influenced by Marcion, who presented it with a rigorous alternative to its traditional ideas closely related to Hellenistic Judaism. In Marcion's view the original gospel had been corrupted by Jesus' earliest disciples, who after his resurrection tried to win converts by modifying it for Jewish hearers. Only the apostle Paul recovered the true gospel. His letters reflect his controversies with the Jerusalem pseudo-Christians, even though these letters, as well as the written gos-

---

[6] Eusebius *H. E.* 4.3.2.
[7] Tacitus *Ann.* 15.44; Suetonius *Claudius* 25.4, *Nero* 16:2.

pels, were interpolated by those who sympathized with Judaism.[8]

Other groups within the communities provided more modest revisions of traditional views. The followers of Basilides, for example, claimed that he had received the true teaching of Jesus from an "interpreter" of Peter (Papias said that Mark was Peter's interpreter) named Glaukias. The followers of Valentinus said that he had been taught by Paul's disciple Theodas; and the Valentinian teacher Ptolemaeus insisted that Valentinian doctrine was derived from "apostolic tradition."[9] As far as we know, in these instances there was no attempt to explain how the true teaching had been corrupted. It was enough to know that true disciples were spiritual, and could understand traditions spiritually, while ordinary Christians were not.

Some heretics seem to have ventured into the turbulent seas of archeology, for at Rome Justin was told that a statue on the Tiber Island had been dedicated to Simon Magus by the Roman Senate in the reign of Claudius. The inscription on the statue's base actually read SEMONI SANCO DEO — to the old Latin deity Semo Sancus — but the Simonians read it as SIMONI SANTCO DEO. Since Justin explicitly requested the destruction of the statue, it is evident that he was convinced by the Simonian interpretation.[10]

Justin himself shows us that Christian concern with historical matters was increasing, for he is able to say that Christ was born not only under Quirinius, "first procurator in Judaea" (an error based on Luke 2:2),[11] but indeed, a hundred and fifty years before the *First Apology*.[12] In relation to the heresies he argues that all of them arose "after the ascension of Christ." The statue of Simon was erected under Claudius; Menander was Simon's disciple; Marcion is still

[8] Cf. R. Grant, *The Letter and the Spirit* (London: S.P.C.K. 1957), p. 64.
[9] *Ibid.*, p. 69.
[10] *Apol.* 1.26, 56.
[11] *Ibid.*, 34.
[12] *Ibid.*, 46.

teaching.[13] Presumably Justin developed his chronological critique more fully in his lost work *Against all heresies*, to which he refers; if, as is probable, it underlies Irenaeus' account of early heresies, it must have been arranged in order to trace heretical successions.

It is conceivable that Justin was more interested in such successions than in those of more orthodox Christians, to which he does not refer, for he knew a good deal about the history of philosophy and the divisions which had arisen after ambitious successors took over schools from their founders. His ideas about the history of philosophy, presumably acquired before his conversion to Christianity, must have influenced his picture of the rise and spread of heretical teaching.[14] On the continuity of ordinary church life he seems to say nothing but that the divine gift of prophecy has continued "until now."[15]

During the reign of Marcus Aurelius, as heresy and persecution continued to present problems and, especially in Asia Minor and at Alexandria, Christian leaders continued to seek a *modus vivendi* with the state, there was a sharp rise (according to the evidence we have) in Christian concern for Christian history.

We begin at Rome. During the decade between 160 and 170 the famous aedicula under the Vatican was erected, either to contain the bones of Peter or to mark the spot of his martyrdom.[16] This event clearly marks the historical concern which Roman Christians felt for their past. For them the Christian movement deserved to have memorials equal in significance, if not in magnificence, to those provided for leaders of the Roman state. Around the same time Dionysius, bishop of Corinth, wrote a letter to Soter, bishop of Rome. On Sunday, Dionysius stated, the Corinthian church read

[13] *Ibid.*, 26.
[14] Cf. Grant in *Wolfson Jubilee Volume* (Jerusalem: American Academy for Jewish Research, 1965) 1:365–68.
[15] *Dial.* 82.1.
[16] Cf. J. Toynbee and J. W. Perkins, *The Shrine of St. Peter* (New York: Longmans, 1957); H. Chadwick in *Journal of Theological Studies*, 8 (1957): 31–52.

not only Soter's letter but also the one written from Rome
through Clement (I Clement). He added that such letters
have united the Roman and the Corinthian churches — both
founded by Peter and Paul, who taught together in Italy and
were martyred on the same occasion.[17] This picture of the
apostles' labors looks like a synthesis of I Clement 5 with
I Cor. (1:12, 22, and 9:5) and reflects the concern of both
Romans and Corinthians with the apostolic age.

The same concern is to be found in a letter from Dionysius
to the church at Athens. He traced its ancestry back to Paul
and to the first bishop, Dionysius the Areopagite (Acts
17:34). More recently, after the death of the martyr-bishop
Publius, the church had "nearly abandoned the word of
God"; the present bishop, Quadratus, had to be supported in
his drive to restore unity.[18] Dionysius is evidently setting
forth a theory according to which there was no heresy or
schism in the apostolic age. Such a theory may have corresponded to the actual facts, but theories about golden ages
are often subject to correction by evidence. This one does
not fit well with what we know about Corinth from Paul's
letters.

Corinth itself was discussed by Hegesippus, a Christian
from the East who wrote at Rome during the episcopate of
Eleutherus, Soter's successor. He stated that he had visited
Corinth and found the church still reading I Clement; he
learned that it "continued in the true faith until Primus was
bishop."[19] If we knew the date of Primus we should be in a
better position to evaluate this statement. If Primus was
bishop when Hegesippus paid his visit, the church apparently never experienced a decline; on the other hand, if
Primus was bishop earlier, the Corinthian situation probably
resembled that of Jerusalem (which we shall presently discuss).

For Hegesippus as for other Christians of his time, Rome
was the bulwark of orthodoxy, and he made a list of Roman

[17] Eusebius *H. E.* 2.25.8; 4.23.10–11.
[18] *Ibid.*, 4.23.2–3; cf. P. Nautin, *Lettres et écrivains chrétiens des ii^e et iii^e siecles* (Paris: Les Éditions du Cerf, 1961), pp. 18–19.
[19] *Ibid.*, 4.22.1.

bishops which ended with Anicetus, Soter, and Eleutherus.[20] Presumably he relied on Roman sources. Given the Roman concern for tradition, it is hard to imagine that the Romans waited for a visitor to provide them with a list.

It is possible that Hegesippus viewed the Roman church as analogous to the church of Jerusalem, as various scholars (including A. A. T. Ehrhardt[21]) have suggested. It may be, however, that he took Rome as his model and then rightly or wrongly arranged his Jerusalem traditions in relation to it. What he says about Jerusalem is this. James the Just was the first bishop, and in his day the church was still a "pure virgin," i.e., not corrupted by heresy. After the death of James, Symeon (son of Clopas and nephew of Joseph) was appointed bishop; Thebuthis, the unsuccessful candidate, began to corrupt the church with doctrines derived from sectarian Judaism. During the reign of Trajan, when Symeon was one hundred and twenty years old, the heretics informed against him and he was crucified by the Roman authorities. According to Hegesippus, up to this time "every church" (in Palestine?) was ruled by members of the Lord's family. Afterward came the rise of heresy and the development of other forms of government.[22]

Hegesippus thus sets forth the theory already indicated in Justin's writings and made explicit by Dionysius of Corinth: heresy is a postapostolic phenomenon. The apostolic age was a golden age and in later times heresy could be prevented only by adherence to legitimate authority.

We shall later return to Rome in order to consider some of the ideas of Irenaeus of Lyons, since his relations with Rome were close. Before dealing with him, however, we must examine the rise of historical concern in Asia Minor.

In Asia tradition was personified in the living witness of Polycarp of Smyrna; he had known John the Lord's disciple and had encountered Ignatius bound for martyrdom at Rome. He had outlived most of his contemporaries; according to the acts of his martyrdom, he was the twelfth martyr

[20] *Ibid.*, 4.22.2–3.
[21] *The Apostolic Succession* (London: Lutterworth, 1953), pp. 62–66.
[22] Eusebius, *H. E.* 4.22.4–5; 3.32.6.

at Smyrna.[23] When he died, at the age of eighty-six, it must have been evident that an era had come to an end. Asian Christians obtained his relics and treasured them.[24]

Among other Asians concern for history was due to the problem of good relations with the state. In about 175 Apollinaris, bishop of Hierapolis in Phrygia, claimed that a Roman victory over barbarians, assisted by a miraculous storm, was due to the prayers of Christian soldiers.[25] Soon afterwards, Melito of Sardis pointed out that Christianity arose along with the Roman empire, in the reign of Augustus, and should therefore be encouraged by the state. Only the emperors Nero and Domitian, misled by bad advisers, persecuted Christians, while the ancestors of Marcus Aurelius favored them. In proof of this favor Melito mentioned the letter of Hadrian to a proconsul of Asia and the letters of Antoninus Pius to various cities and to "all the Greeks."[26] He was thus invoking historical and legal precedent in favor of a reconciliation between church and state. Both empire and church would benefit if the church were to be recognized as the bearer of the official "philosophy." We do not know what Melito thought of heresy, but no doubt he contrasted authentic, original Christianity with sectarian innovations. Both he and Apollinaris must have regarded history as the story of the providentially governed accord between church and empire.

At Ephesus, at least as a conflict arose with Rome over the traditional date of Easter, history was more specifically local, and indeed archeological. Romans might point to the tombs of Peter and Paul; Polycrates of Ephesus claimed that the validity of Asian custom was guaranteed by the resting spots of the "apostle" Philip, the priest-apostle John, and the bishops Polycarp, Thraseas, Sagaris, Papirius, and Melito.[27]

[23] *Mart. Polyc.* 19.1.
[24] *Ibid.*, 18.1–2; possibly an addition: cf. H. v. Campenhausen, *Sitzungsberichte der Heidelberger Akademie der Wissenschaften*, 1957, *Philosophisch-historische Klasse*, no. 3, 28–31 (cf. 47).
[25] Eusebius *H. E.* 5.5.4.
[26] *Ibid.*, 4.26.7–10.
[27] *Ibid.*, 5.24.2–5.

Irenaeus, as we have said, represents the confluence of Roman and Asian traditional points of view. Indeed, his writings reflect the combination of all sorts of earlier traditions, as Loofs showed.[28] More than that, he treats the Christian revelation from a philosophical-historical standpoint, showing that there has been a progressive revelation of God first to the Jews and later to the Christians. Before his time anticipations of such a theory, chiefly in relation to Greek philosophy, occur in Justin; and Theophilus of Antioch worked out a chronological scheme of world history from Adam to Marcus Aurelius;[29] but Irenaeus owes little to them, and more to his own study of the Bible from a traditionalist point of view.

His standpoint is clearly set forth by the nature of his major work, explicitly directed against heresies. In it he apparently relies on Justin's treatise *Against all heresies* in order to trace the genealogy of heresy. More important, he relies on Roman and Asian tradition to show that orthodox communities in which the succession of apostolic teaching and ministry were preserved were free of heresy. The cardinal instance was provided by the church of Rome, for which Irenaeus possessed an official list of the twelve successors of Peter and Paul, from Linus to Eleutherus.[30] He was also aware of the antiquity of the Asian church, for Polycarp, appointed bishop of Smyrna by apostles, was militantly opposed to Marcion and Cerinthus, who were both later than, or opposed by, the apostles themselves.[31] Isolated items of information reveal that Irenaeus also knew a good deal about the history of the relations between Rome and other churches in the second century.

Essentially the same basic viewpoint is presented by Clement of Alexandria in his criticism of "human conventicles"

[27] F. Loofs, *Theophilus von Antiochien und die anderen theologischen Quellen bei Irenäus* Texte und Untersuchungen, 46:2 (Leipzig, 1930).

[29] *Ad Autolycum* 3.16–28.

[30] *Adv. haer.* 3.3.1 (in the ed. of W. Wigan Harvey [Cambridge, 1857], vol. 2:9).

[31] *Ibid.*, 3.3.4 (in Harvey, 2:12–14).

as novel, compared with the Catholic church. The argument is chronological. The teaching of the Lord was given during the reigns of Augustus and Tiberius; that of the apostles was set forth until, for example, the death of Paul in the reign of Nero. (Clement's "for example" [ge] avoids the problem presented by the tradition about John's longevity.) The founders of heresies, on the other hand, began their work about the time of Hadrian and continued, in some instances, into the reign of Antoninus Pius. In this connection Clement mentions Basilides, Valentinus, and Marcion.[32]

Naturally not everyone agreed with these defenders of conservative tradition. Certain teachers at Rome who maintained that Jesus was a man "adopted" by God held that their view was the authentic Christian and Roman position. It had been "maintained by all the men of former days and by the apostles themselves." It had been preserved "until the times of Victor, who was the thirteenth bishop of Rome from Peter," but "the truth was falsified from the days of his successor Zephyrinus." An orthodox opponent of these teachers inevitably took up the historical question and argued that the tradition was against them.[33]

In large measure, we see, the origins of historical study within the Christian movement were due to the necessity for justifying theological and political positions in relation to the past history of the movement. It may be added that apparently the more concern there was for history the more conservative the position taken was. The heretics who appealed to history were usually hanged, so to speak, on the gallows they had erected.

### Montanists and Anti-Montanists

Early in the last quarter of the second century the movement known as Montanism came to the fore. This movement, which arose in Phrygia, was immediately attacked by Apollinaris of Hierapolis, whom we have already met as a student of Roman history. This was no coincidence, for the views of

[32] *Strom.* 7.106.3–107.1.
[33] Eusebius, *H. E.* 5.28.3–4.

the Montanists were essentially radical and their emphasis on apocalyptic eschatology was opposed to the attempts of other Christians to make the church at home in the world. The Montanists themselves referred to their movement as "prophecy" or "the new prophecy" — but because of the general Christian attitude in this period they could not avoid claiming that they too had predecessors. They too appealed to history. The third-century Montanist Proclus was probably not the first to argue that there had been a prophetic gift in the church from the earliest times. It had passed from the evangelist Philip to his four daughters, and he was buried with them at Hierapolis.[34] Other Montanists referred to a certain Quadratus (presumably not the bishop of Athens), to Ammia of Philadelphia, and to their group in general.[35]

Most of the discussion about Montanism, naturally enough, was not related to the historical question. A "very learned" Roman presbyter named Gaius, however, shows us how literary and historical criticism was sometimes used in opposition to novelty. In the first place, Gaius tried to cut some theological ground out from under the Montanists by denying the authenticity of the Gospel and Revelation ascribed to John — since they relied on both books.[36] In the second place, he insisted on the archeological evidence.

> But I can point to the trophies of the apostles. For if you are willing to go to the Vatican or to the Ostian Way, you will find the trophies of those who founded the church.[37]

This fragment needs a good deal of exegesis. First, what does "but" mean? Presumably, since Gaius was arguing against Proclus, the Montanist had claimed to be in some sort of possession of the tomb of Philip and his daughters. Gaius is replying that Rome has the "trophies" (which in

[34] *Ibid.*, 3.31.4.
[35] *Ibid.*, 5.17.3–4.
[36] Cf. e.g., P. de Labriolle, *Les sources de l'histoire du Montanisme* (Fribourg: Gschwend, 1913), p. lxx–lxxiv.
[37] Eusebius, *H. E.* 2.25.7.

the context must be tombs) of the apostolic founders of orthodox Christianity. Second, the whole tendency of Gaius' argument suggests that Proclus accepted, and proves that he himself accepted, the belief which may be summed up as *cuius tumulus eius religio*.

It is interesting to observe that neither Proclus nor Gaius seems to have referred to the tomb of John at Ephesus. We know that it was carefully maintained there; Justinian I later built a great basilica over it. Perhaps a clue to their silence is given by Dionysius of Alexandria, who states that there are two tombs of John at Ephesus.[38] Could it be that one was the "orthodox" tomb, the other a Montanist shrine? We know that in the third century at Rome there was also a private, and perhaps not altogether orthodox, cult of Peter and Paul on the Appian Way under Saint Sebastian.

*Archeology and History*

Our consideration of Montanists and anti-Montanists had led us to consider the conservative influence of the possession of tombs; we may add that John of Ephesus, bishop in 550, took a decisive anti-Montanist step when he was able to dig up the bones of Montanus and the prophetesses and burn them.[39] In general the conservative tendency became progressively stronger during the third century, and it reached a momentary climax in the *Church History* produced by Eusebius of Caesarea early in the fourth. Eusebius clearly had in mind the points we have already discussed. He was militantly opposed to heresy, always a late corruption of earlier orthodoxy, and he was determined to support the Constantinian reconciliation of church and state. It is no accident that he preserved most of the passages to which we have appealed.

If we now look back to the book of Acts with which we began, we can see that Luke's work was genuinely programmatic. Luke reinterpreted the early Christian eschatology or, at any rate, emphasized that aspect of it according to

[38] *Ibid.*, 7.25.16.
[39] Labriolle, *Sources*, p. 238.

which the Kingdom of God was not to appear immediately (Luke 19:11; cf. 17:20–21; 24:21; Acts 1:6–8). Similarly Eusebius viewed the life of the church under Constantine as practically equivalent to life in the kingdom. Luke was concerned with showing that in principle the church had no quarrel with the Roman state and that Roman authorities protected Christians; Eusebius' outlook was much the same. Luke, like Eusebius, endeavored to trace the legitimate succession of offices in the church and to contrast heresy (cf. Acts 20:30) with orthodoxy. Indeed, one might even regard the three major works of Eusebius as extensions of Luke's principal themes: the *Church History* continues Luke's history, while the *Demonstratio Evangelica* develops Luke's proof-from-prophecy and the *Praeparatio Evangelica* deepens the semiphilosophical ideas found in Paul's Areopagus address.

Even the later concern for relics is anticipated in Acts, where we read that "devout men buried Stephen and made lamentation over him" (8:2). In Eusebius' time and afterward there was a tremendous increase of interest in relics of the apostolic age. Precedents already existed in Jewish circles, where the tombs of kings and prophets were carefully preserved.[40] But under Constantine and his successors archeology came into its own. Not to mention the "true cross," perhaps discovered in 326, there were also the relics of Timothy, Andrew, and Luke, taken to Constantinople in 356–57. Among these Timothy and Luke are especially important, for both were regarded as Paul's lieutenants and they symbolized the continuity of Christian history. Still later, further bodies or bones were found — including those of Stephen himself, discovered in 415. These discoveries were related to the continuing development of the Christian historical self-consciousness. They mark the end of an old period and the beginning of a new one, as had been the case in earlier times of crisis and transition.

Church history, then, arose in the early church in response

[40] Cf. J. Jeremias, *Heiligengräber in Jesu Umwelt* (Göttingen: Vandenhoeck & Ruprecht, 1958).

to crises both internal and external. It provided a means of determining and setting forth the nature of Christianity and of supporting views related both to society and to church life. It always had both social and theological implications. The history of the early church cannot be understood without consideration of why its historians wrote as they did, and in turn their writings cannot be understood without reference to their historical circumstances. The book of Acts marks an early stage in the process, and some of its author's purposes are very similar to those reflected in the work of Eusebius.[41]

This is not to say either that Luke was a fourth-century bishop "born out of due time" or that Eusebius' interests were not his own. Eusebius wanted to describe (1) "the successions from the holy apostles," along with chronology, (2) important affairs and leaders, (3) teachers by word or writing, (4) heretics, (5) "the disasters that fell upon the whole Jewish nation," (6) persecutions, (7) martyrdoms, and (8) the peace of the church.[42] Nevertheless, as we have argued, in his own way Luke was concerned with all these matters, from some sort of successions on to the peace of the church, proleptically implied in Paul's preaching and teaching at Rome "without hindrance" (Acts 28:31). The Eusebian church was much more rigidly organized than that of Luke's day, but its unity and continuity had been worked out in two and a half centuries of conflict.

[41] On Eusebius' ideas see especially W. Völker, *Vigiliae Christianae* 4 (1950): 157–80, and J. Sirinelli, *Les vues historiques d'Eusèbe de Césarée durant la période prénicéenne* (Dakar, 1961).
[42] Eusebius, *H. E.* 1. praef.

# Biographical Notes

JERALD C. BRAUER was born in Wisconsin in 1921, graduated from Carthage College and Northwestern Lutheran Theological Seminary, and received his Ph.D. from the University of Chicago in 1948. He taught at Union Theological Seminary, 1948–50. He is professor of the history of Christianity and dean of the University of Chicago's Divinity School. His publications are in the area of English Puritanism, Reformation, and religion in America.

GÖSTA W. AHLSTRÖM is associate professor of Old Testament at the Divinity School, where he joined the faculty in 1963. He received the degree of Doctor of Theology in 1959 from the University of Uppsala and became assistant professor of Old Testament there. He has studied also at the Universities of Basel and Heidelberg. Besides contributions to *Svenskt Bibliskt Uppslagsverk*, his writings include *Psalm 89: Eine Liturgie aus dem Ritual des leidenden Königs* and *Aspects of Syncretism in Israelite Religion*.

WILLIAM ARMITAGE BEARDSLEE is professor of religion, vice-chairman of the Executive Committee and chairman of the Department of Biblical Studies at Emory University. His theological training was at New Brunswick Theological Seminary. He holds an A.M. from Columbia University (1948) and a Ph.D. from the University of Chicago (1951). Since 1961 he has been associate editor of the *Journal of Bible and Religion*. His publications include *Human Achievement and Divine Vocation in the Message of Paul* (London, 1961) and *Reading the Bible: A Guide* (2d ed., 1964).

307

KENNETH WILLIS CLARK studied at Yale and at Colgate-Rochester Divinity School. He received his Ph.D. from Chicago's Divinity School in 1931. He is professor of New Testament at Duke University, and has been visiting lecturer at the Universities of Manchester and Athens. In the Society of Biblical Literature he has served as secretary (1946–50) and as vice-president (1964). His specialty of textual criticism is evidenced by his having been director of manuscript microfilming in Jerusalem and at Sinai and by his publications: *Descriptive Catalogue of Greek New Testament Manuscripts in America* and *Eight American Praxapostoloi.*

ERNEST CADMAN COLWELL had his theological training at Candler School of Theology. He received his Ph.D. in 1930 and joined the faculty of the Divinity School, later becoming its dean (1939–45). In 1951 he became dean of faculties and vice-president of Emory University. In 1957 he assumed the presidency of Southern California School of Theology. He serves as chairman of the executive committee of the International Greek New Testament Project. His publications include *John Defends the Gospel* (1936), *What is the Best New Testament?* (1952) and *A Beginner's Reader-Grammar for New Testament Greek* (1963).

DONALD E. GOWAN studied at the University of South Dakota and Dubuque Theological Seminary. The University of Chicago granted him a Ph.D. in 1964. He began as a teacher of Bible at North Texas State University. At present, he is assistant professor of Old Testament at Pittsburgh Theological Seminary. In the summer of 1965 he participated in the excavation of Ashdod.

ROBERT MCQUEEN GRANT received his Th.D. from Harvard University in 1944. From that time until 1953 he was on the faculty of the School of Theology of the University of the South. Since then, he has taught at the Divinity School in New Testament and Church History. He served as president of the Society of Biblical Literature in 1959. His biblical publications include *The Bible and the Church* (1948) and

# Biographical Notes

*A Historical Introduction to the New Testament* (1963), plus numerous articles in books and journals.

NORMAN PERRIN is associate professor of New Testament at the Divinity School. Previously he served on the faculty of Candler School of Theology. He received his doctorate in Theology from the University of Göttingen, and holds degrees also from Manchester University and the University of London. His publications, among which are *The Kingdom of God in the Teaching of Jesus* (1964) and *Rediscovering the Teaching of Jesus* (1967), manifest his interest in *Leben-Jesu-Forschung* and redaction criticism.

FREDERICK CARL PRUSSNER is professor of Old Testament at Candler School of Theology. After attending Garrett Biblical Institute, he received an M.A. from Northwestern University. He was an instructor at the Divinity School (1944–46) and received his Ph.D. from the Divinity School in 1952.

MARTIN RIST holds his Th.D. from Iliff School of Theology (1929) and his Ph.D. from Chicago (1934). He is professor of New Testament and Christian history at Iliff. He has written the commentary on Revelation in the *Interpreter's Bible* and *Modern Reader's Guide to Revelation*, plus articles and chapters in other books.

JOHN COERT RYLAARSDAM is professor of Old Testament Theology and chairman of the Biblical Field of the Divinity School. His theological education was at New Brunswick Theological Seminary. He received his Ph.D. from Chicago in 1944 and joined the faculty in 1945. He has been co-editor of the *Journal of Religion* since 1953. He has written the introduction and exegesis of Exodus in the *Interpreter's Bible* and *Revelation in Jewish Wisdom Literature*.

WILLIAM RICHARD SCHOEDEL received his Ph.D. from the Divinity School in 1963, after having studied at the University of Western Ontario and Concordia Theological Seminary. At present he is associate professor of Religious Studies at Brown University. He translated "The Gospel of Thomas" in *The Secret Sayings of Jesus.* His publications include *The Apostolic Fathers, Vol. 5: Polycarp, Martyrdom of Polycarp, Fragments of Papias* (1967) and articles in books and journals.

PAUL SCHUBERT studied in Germany at the Universities of Munich, Bonn (Ph.D., 1925), and Heidelberg. He received his Ph.D. from Chicago in 1935. He was visiting associate professor of New Testament at Chicago's Divinity School in the Spring of 1946 and professor of Early Christian Literature, 1947–49. He is now a professor of New Testament at Yale Divinity School. His interest in Paul is shown by his publication, *Form and Function of the Pauline Thanksgivings* (Berlin, 1939).

JAY A. WILCOXEN received his B.D. from Chicago Theological Seminary and the Divinity School of the University of Chicago. He has been teaching at the Divinity School since 1961 in the Biblical Field, and presently holds an assistant professorship. The title of his doctoral dissertation was *The Israelite Passover: Its Context and Function in the Late Old Testament Period.*

WALTER GEORGE WILLIAMS received his Ph.D. from the Divinity School in 1934. He is professor of Old Testament Literature at Iliff School of Theology. He has written *Prophets, Pioneers to Christianity* and *Books of the Law.* His latest book is *Archaeology in Biblical Research* (1965).

# Acknowledgments


Grateful acknowledgment is hereby made to the publishers for permission to quote from the following works:

To Harper & Row, Publishers, Inc., New York, for permission to quote from Edmond Jacob, *Theology of the Old Testament* © 1958 Hodder & Stoughton, Ltd., London; and from Gerhard Von Rad, *Old Testament Theology*, Volume 1 © 1962 Oliver & Boyd, Ltd., Edinburgh.

To The Macmillan Company, New York, to quote from Albert Schweitzer, *The Quest of the Historical Jesus*, 1964 ©.

To Charles Scribner's Sons, New York, for permission to quote from R. H. Fuller, *The Foundations of New Testament Christology*, 1965.

To H. Veenman & Zonen N. V., Wageningen, for permission to quote from T. C. Vriezen, *An Outline of Old Testament Theology*, translated by S. Neuijen, 1958.

A special word of thanks is due to Mr. John J. Schmitt, who served as Editorial Secretary in the preparation of this book. Mr. Schmitt, a graduate student in Old Testament, now spending a year in Sweden, gave many hours to correspondence, to prepare the essays for publication. Subsequently, he did most of the hard work incident to seeing the volume through the Press. It owes much to his valuable suggestions and painstaking efforts.

# Index

313

# Index

# Index

Stendahl, K., 265 n
Steuernagel, C., 48 n, 66 n
Streeter, 146, 150, 151
Strobel, A., 103 n, 105 n
Suetonius, 295
Systematic theology, 8, 9, 10, 25–26

Tacitus, 295
Talmon, S., 124 n
Tasker edition, 159
*Theologia gloriae*, 187
Thiele, E. R., 62 n
Thiele, W., 153
Thomas, gospel of, 201
Thompson, H., 164
Thompson, R. J., 93 n
Tischendorf, 141, 144
Tithing, 90
Tödt, H. E., 174 n, 175, 177 n, 178, 186, 187, 219, 231
Tradition criticism, 12, 195
Treaty; *See* Covenant

Ugarit, 35, 75, 115

Vatke, 17
Völker, W., 306 n
Von Rad, 23, 26–29, 33 n, 77, 79, 89, 113, 120 n, 122 n

Voss, D., 142 n, 152 n
Vriezen, T. C., 23–24

Weiser, A., 95 n
Welch, A. C., 120 n
Wellhausen, J., 17, 48 n, 49, 93, 103 n, 105 n
Westcott-Hort edition, 131 n, 137, 139, 143, 158–67 *passim*
Whitehead, 188, 189, 190
Whitley, C. F., 93 n, 94
Widengren, G., 126 n
Wieman, 189
Wikgren, A. P., 2
Wilder, A., 194
Wilderberger, H., 55, 93, 108 n
Williams, C. S. C., 134
Williams, D. L., 118 n
Windisch, H., 279 n
Wisdom element in "Q," 177
Wisdom literature, 28, 40
Wolf, C. U., 47 n
Wolff, H. W., 94 n, 100 n, 106 n, 111 n
Wolfson, H. A., 278 n
Wotke, F., 294 n
Wright, G. E., 29, 30, 83
Würthwein, E., 94 n, 110 n, 115 n, 120 n

Zoroastrianism, 202